*MainStays*

*Some of the women for whom this book was written — MAINSTAYS in their own right. Clockwise from top: Joan, Jennifer, Nicole, Donna, Kristy, Anke.*
(COURTESY ROLF HICKER, RAINBOW PRODUCTIONS)

December 1999

Merry Christmas to the absolutely
Most Wonderful Woman in
our World !!

With more love than you can possibly
imagine....

Your girls... Cath, Laura, Sheeba & Fye

Mimi
&

# MAINSTAYS

## *Women Who Shaped BC*

Cathy Converse

Horsdal & Schubart

Horsdal & Schubart Publishers Ltd.
Victoria, BC, Canada.

Cover by Pat McCallum, Victoria, BC.

Front-cover photographs, clockwise from top left: Helen MacInnis, courtesy of BC Archives; Alexandra Morton, courtesy of Chris Bennett; Agnes Deans Cameron, courtesy of BC Archives; Sister Frances Redmond, courtesy of City of Vancouver Archives; Pauline Johnson, courtesy of BC Archives; Phyllis Munday, courtesy of BC Archives. Back-cover photographs, clockwise from top left: Mary Ellen Smith, courtesy of BC Archives; Agnes Deans Cameron, courtesy of BC Archives; Rosemary Brown, courtesy of BC Archives; Gloria Cranmer Webster and her mother Agnes Cranmer, courtesy of Vickie Jensen, Vancouver; Helen Gregory MacGill, from *My Mother The Judge*, by Elsie Gregory MacGill.

This book is set in Classical Garamond Book Text.

We acknowledge the support of the Canada Council for the Arts for our publishing program. Also, we acknowledge the assistance of the Province of British Columbia, through the British Columbia Arts Council.

Printed and bound in Canada by Kromar Printing Ltd., Winnipeg, Manitoba.

Canadian Cataloguing in Publication Data

Converse, Cathy, 1944-
  Mainstays

Includes bibliographical references.
ISBN 0-920663-62-1

  1. Women—British Columbia—Biography.  2. British Columbia—Biography.  I. Title.
FC3805.C66 1998    971.1009'9    C98-910703-5
F1086.8.C66 1998

Printed and bound in Canada.

DEDICATION

For my grandmother, my mother, my daughter and my grand-daughter.

# Contents

## Acknowledgments

W RITERS, WHEN WORKING, tend to be somewhat reclusive, ignoring the comings and goings of life swirling around them. But no book is written in exclusion, and there are many people in my life who have been important in helping with this manuscript. There is first of all my family, who supported, encouraged and sheltered me from unnecessary interference. My mother, a writer in her own right, spent hours editing this manuscript. Brian and Dori, my taskmasters, kept me supplied with enough coffee to write several books. Whenever I felt my spirits flagging, Christina was always there to get me back on track. Thanks go to Bill, Donna, Jim and Mrs. P. for providing me with dock space and electricity during my summers at Telegraph Cove. Kathryn Bridge, from the British Columbia Archives, was an invaluable source of information as was Ann Doyle from the Xwi7xwa Library at the University of British Columbia, Carol Haber from the City of Vancouver Archives and Lyn Gough. Special thanks go to Vickie Jensen for her support in and of this project.

## INTRODUCTION

THIS BOOK GREW out of the work that was initially done for *In Her Own Right* which I co-edited with Barbara Latham in 1980. *In Her Own Right* was an exploratory book examining the lives of women in British Columbia with a view to moving women to the forefront of contemporary scholarship. Since that time, many books on women's biography have helped to increase our awareness of women's past and present, but for all that, there remains a dearth of understanding about the importance of women's contribution to the province's history.

Frequently, in writing, surnames are used for men, implying formality and power, but first names for women, suggesting a more familiar, perhaps less assertive, image. I have chosen to identify the women in these biographies by their surnames, and their husbands, when applicable, by their first names. This can become a little awkward, but it is merely an attempt to minimize complications; most of these women will be known best by their surnames. In cases where a woman has had more than one name at different times, I have used her most recent surname.

Little of women's history, and contributions to society, have appeared in our children's texts. When women are included in schoolbooks they are treated as a separate entity, as if somehow women's lives are completely divorced from the political, economic and cultural spheres involved in nation building.

This separateness has done a great disservice to the understanding of our history. The message it sends is that while some women may be interesting and have noteworthy biographies, they were the exception. And yet the study of women's lives tells another story: women have always been in the forefront of shaping the direction, community and history of the province. Hence, the theme that frames this book is one not of partition but of inclusion. The women who are described here should be written into our history, for they helped forge the direction of British Columbia and in many cases were the architects of the knowledge and policies that have become the defining characteristics of the province.

The really remarkable part of women's achievements is that they were able to fashion new directions despite living in a society that valued women mainly as homemakers. Throughout history, gender has always played an important role in defining women's lives and yet women have had the courage and strength to transcend prevailing notions of "place." For many, this set them unexpectedly along the path of activism. Many of these women didn't set out to be activists but they were adaptable and flexible, and when they saw a need to improve something, they took action. In reconstructing the experiences and insights of the lives of the women in this book, it is obvious that people can change things in society around them, and they can change the course of their own lives.

As in any collection of biographies, whom to include is a problem, and somewhat arbitrary. Gaps occur in the discussion of East Asian and early First Nations women. In part, this is a result of a lack of written records; not all cultures document their history in writing. Also, British Columbia's periodic bouts of racism have caused some biographies to remain inaccessible. Racism and discrimination, for example, played a part in the lack of individual biographies of East Asian women. The early histories of First Nations people were often collected by male anthropologists and Christian missionaries, all of whom talked little about women and if they did, interpreted their lives through a haze of paternal attitudes. East Asian and First Nations women's histories are rich and varied, and it remains to the children of those women to gather their stories so that they can be told.

Women's stories are vital to the understanding of British Columbia as a province, for its growth and direction have been made up of the combined efforts of numerous cultures. The women profiled in this book all represent the hope and courage of hundreds of women just like them, who have been the mainstays of their communities and have helped to shape the province of British Columbia.

# CHAPTER ONE

# WOMEN IN EDUCATION

DURING THE EARLY 19th century, economic growth created a great deal of social and economic instability. One response of British Columbians was to turn to education as a means of achieving success and economic security. The concept of mass education spread widely and an organization of school systems was set up throughout BC to meet the demand for schooling. Differing perceptions on curriculum content, educational structure and bureaucracy quickly surfaced. The ideas promoted by the social leaders and school advocates in the community sometimes conflicted with the needs and desires of parents.

The primary concern of the school promoters was to have an effective system for instilling appropriate modes of thought and behaviour in children. Schooling, they maintained, was not for the purpose of acquiring academic knowledge but was intended, instead, to solve social problems associated with poverty and crime. Also, as immigrants continued to come to BC, schooling was seen as a way to instill British cultural values. Parents cared little for these assimilative notions. Instead, spurred by their fear of poverty, they were anxious for their children to receive both knowledge and the skills that would enable them to succeed in the new economy.

Teachers often found themselves caught between the contrasting needs of the two groups. Conflict was a natural reality of their lives. Unfriendly trustees and hostile parents sometimes both demanded that the teachers be responsive to their differing perceptions of education. Teachers in rural areas faced additional hardships such as isolation, loneliness, poor housing, inappropriate curriculum, inadequate classrooms and insufficient teaching materials. For a few teachers this pressure was more than they could endure.

Twenty-year-old Mabel Jones, a teacher in the remote community of Cowichan Lake, had difficulty with constant criticism and committed suicide in 1928. A note left at the scene of her death read, "There are a few people who would like to see me out of the way, so I am trying to please them. I know this is a coward's way of doing things. Forgive me, please. Say it was an accident."[1] Her jurors talked of the isolation and stresses for rural teachers and made a statement about it in a legal testimony. "Mabel Estelle Jones," they wrote, "came to her death whilst temporarily insane." They went on to say, "We are further of the opinion that the mental state was the result of unjustifiable, unfeeling and underhanded criticisms of her work on the part of two members of the school board."[2]

By the mid-19th century women began to be employed as teachers and in 1900 most of the elementary school teaching was done by women. As the increasing expansion of schools weighed heavily on the taxpayers it was thought that women could be paid less than men. The rationale for women's lower wages was often wrapped in platitudes about notions of women as primary bearers of the emotional, physical and spiritual nurturing of children. As early as 1872 the BC superintendent of education declared that a woman's mission was "predominantly that of an educator," specifically of infants and young children.[3]

Such views served to reinforce the idea that women were not as valuable as men. They were paid less than male teachers, kept in the lower ranks and supervised by male administrators who felt that they were the real teachers. The annual salaries for women elementary-school teachers working in an urban area in 1910 were in the range of $300 to $1,000 and for men from $600 to $1,400, and as teachers had neither job security nor bargaining rights it was relatively easy to maintain such wage disparities.

Teachers responded in a number of ways; some negotiated, some worked at downplaying the problems, some questioned themselves, some quit and some fought. But fighting back and standing up for their rights could be costly, as Agnes Deans Cameron discovered when she went against the wishes of school trustees. Yet despite the hardships, many women found that teaching provided challenges and gave them a sense of accomplishment and satisfaction. The teaching profession offered women a position in the community independent of their family status, an important element in the drive to achieve control over their personal lives.

Agnes Deans Cameron
1863 - 1912

When Agnes Deans Cameron died in 1912, at the still-youthful age of 49, British Columbia lost one of the most remarkable women to grace this province. Her funeral cortege was the largest Victoria had witnessed. The Victoria City Council met and voted a message of sympathy to her family, the mayor presented a striking tribute and newspapers recounted her life and contributions, noting that she was an outstanding woman who brought much to the city. *The Victoria Times* devoted three and a half columns to discussing her life and impact on the city. Victoria's *Daily Colonist* said of her, "It is possible that when the history of British Columbia comes to be written, the name of Agnes Deans Cameron will be inscribed therein as the most remarkable woman citizen of the province."[4]

Perhaps the most thorough description of Cameron came from a local newspaper which wrote, "She combined high intellectual culture with the romantic temperament and humour of the Celt and the pride of the Highlander, the daring and dash of the British Columbia prospector and the winning sympathy of a woman of much strength and character, added to which she was a laborious and detailed worker. This rare personality has passed from our midst and her loss will be felt far and wide as a personal one."[5]

Agnes Deans Cameron was among the first generation of Canadian feminists to be called an "equal rights feminist." Above all else, she believed in the natural equality of all human beings. Cameron was an educator, journalist, explorer and orator of extra-ordinary ability. She devoted her energies to two causes: the reform of education and the promotion of immigration to western and northern Canada. During her teaching career she attained a number of firsts. In 1890 she became the first female high school teacher in British Columbia and in 1894 she was appointed the first female principal in the province.

Cameron's constant challenge to what she saw as a rigid curriculum, devoid of academic content, resulted in the Victoria school trustees suspending her first-class teaching certificate for a period of three years. Forced to contend with the loss of her job, she turned to journalism and public speaking, and became a woman of national and international acclaim. She never returned to teaching.

Cameron was a dynamic woman with a quick wit and a sense of humour. All those who knew her said she was sophisticated and yet determined in character. When newspapers wrote about Cameron they sprinkled their writings with favourable passages, referring to her as "a sweet faced lady, possessed of lucid polished diction and a delightful sense of humour,"[6] or "A gallant comrade filled with the joy of living."[7] *The Toronto News* described her as "brave, brainy, and brilliant."[8] What goes into making such a woman, particularly when the dictates of the 19th century defined a woman's realm as belonging to hearth and home? There were few female role models for Cameron but then, women like her do not need to look to others for examples or approval. Then too, changes for and about women were in the offing.

As early as 1848 two American women, Lucretia Mott and Elizabeth Stanton, were making headlines by demanding full legal and educational equality for women at a women's convention in New York. By the 1870s and 1880s, women's missionary societies were beginning to push at the confines of the notions of women's place. Organizations such as the Young Women's Christian Association, the Women's Christian Temperance Union, the Dominion Order of King's Daughters and the National Council of Women of Canada sought to improve society for families by demanding legislation for female suffrage, mothers' allowances and prohibition. Increasingly, women felt responsible for reforming society. By 1912, one out of every eight women belonged to a women's group.

Agnes Deans Cameron herself was a member of several clubs, including the BC Women's Council, the Canadian Women's Press Club, the Ladies of the Maccabees and the YWCA. She may also have been influenced by the dynamism and challenge brought by new technologies. Cameron grew up in an era of firsts in Canada. She witnessed the first street lighting, the first electric streetcar, the first gasoline car, the first trans-Atlantic wireless, the first university degree granted to a woman, the first free provincial schools, the first bill for women's suffrage and the entrance of British Columbia into the Dominion of Canada. The atmosphere was rife with enthusiasm and conviction.

Cameron's upbringing instilled in her a sense of independence. Her parents operated from the belief that all of their children should earn their own way in life, as they had done. Both were hardy individualists. Her mother, Jessie Anderson, was a teacher, as was her mother before her. Jessie was born in Scotland and emigrated to California with her brother during the gold rush. While there she met and married Duncan Cameron, a restless, adventure-seeking Scot who had been lured to North America by tales of gold. Unfortunately, not much is known of their lives. In the winter of 1860 they moved to Victoria, seeking their fortunes in the goldfields of British Columbia.

Duncan was apparently quite successful in his mining and contracting ventures, so the family settled comfortably in the city. They had six children: William George, Charles Napier, Margaret Helen, Barbara, Jessie Clara and Agnes Deans. Of Cameron's three sisters, only Barbara married. Her brother William served as an alderman for the city of Victoria and was elected as a member of the BC legislature in 1903. Their father died tragically in 1884 when Cameron was 21 years of age. He was returning from a shooting excursion when he was thrown from a spring-cart on the Gorge Road, only a few miles from his home.

Cameron was a member of the first student body to attend Victoria High School when it opened its doors in 1876. She received her teaching certificate when she was a mere 13 but continued with her education until she was 18; then she took a teaching position at Angela College in Victoria, a private school run by the Church of England. Of all her accomplishments, her career as an educator was probably the most significant.

The public school system of the 19th century was concerned primarily with the standardization of curriculum, tests, classroom organization and textbooks, and demanded strict adherence to the prescribed methods of instruction. Educational planning and policy were determined by the clergy and influential laymen, and were designed more for the shaping of values, social and political attitudes and proper behaviour than for the acquisition of academic knowledge. This gave rise to narrowness of purpose and rigidity in the classroom.

Cameron, however, felt that schooling was much more than this. Education to her was the soul of society. It was through education

*Agnes Deans Cameron.* (Courtesy BC Archives, G-03578)

that children would be better prepared to analyze, evaluate and knit ideas together in order to contribute to their world in a meaningful way. Around the turn of the century, the economic climate of British Columbia was changing and with it, parents' expectations of education. Land ownership no longer ensured a family's status so education was seen as the way to continued success in the eyes of

the community. Parents sent their children to school to learn mathematics, reading and writing, and to obtain the skills to cope in the
new merchant and industrial society.

Cameron was an immensely popular teacher. She made school
interesting for her pupils and created a learning environment that
encouraged them not only to hone their scholarship skills but to
pursue knowledge for the enrichment of their minds. Ada McGeer,
one of her students, wrote, "There are many of her former pupils
who remember her for her criticism of outmoded ideas and her
untiring work for school reform. It is the fortunate pupil who in the
course of school days encounters a teacher who kindles a spark of
learning. Agnes Deans Cameron did this for many of her pupils.
Thankfully, I was one of them."[9]

This is not to say that Cameron was indulgent with her students;
she was a strict disciplinarian and intolerant of slovenly work. The
very same student who praised her teaching skills was not easily let off
the hook when she presented careless work. It seems that Ada
McGeer sent an essay to one of Victoria's newspapers in response to a
contest for the best paper on the current play in town: *The Merchant
of Venice*. A delighted Miss McGeer won the prize. The newspaper
printed her essay, spelling mistakes and all. Cameron, rather than
congratulating McGeer, castigated her in front of the class for failing
to correct her spelling before entering her composition.

Another time, Cameron whipped Herbert Burkholder, one of her
students, and dismissed him from class for insubordinate behaviour.
The boy had already repeated the same grade four times and was
obstreperous and unco-operative. His father was enraged and went
to the school board to see why his son had been dismissed. The case
created such a stir that it was reported in *The Daily Colonist*. The
board sided with Cameron and Herbert apologized to her for his
unruly behaviour, promising it would not happen again. Only then
did she allow him back in the classroom.

Over time, educators recognized the force of the new industri-
alism and revised the curriculum to offer relevant courses for their
students. Home economics programs were developed to teach the
girls cooking and cleaning skills, and shop courses to teach the boys
manual trades. This was a move wholly supported by the Local
Council of Women, of which Agnes Deans Cameron was a member.
In fact, they arranged to provide the necessary equipment for the
schools. Although for the most part women accepted their role in
the domestic sphere and sought to enhance their knowledge of

household skills, to Cameron, domestic science and shop had no place in the curriculum. She was completely against this move, feeling that school should teach children citizenship and how to live, not how to make a living.

In an article Cameron wrote in 1900, "Parent and Teacher," focussing on the co-operation between parents and children in the education system, she stated her opinion of domestic science: "Last year this Local Council of Women were all agog for domestic science. When I, opening my eastern windows which look towards the sun, saw the procession of cooking stoves and stew pans, carpenters' benches and jack planes heading for the schoolroom door, I lifted up a feeble wail for mercy. In this whole Council of Women I found no friend. I was anathema and ultra-conservative. I was unprogressive and lazy. Did[n't] I know that cooking was a good thing, a most necessary thing?"[10] She defined herself as obstructionist in this matter and felt such programs would "teach every boy to be a carpenter and every girl to cook."[11] Her attitude put her at odds with the Local Council of Women which would later deny her support when she ran for the position of school trustee.

By 1887 Cameron was teaching at Victoria High School. She was the first female teacher the school hired and her contribution was noted on the occasion of its 75th anniversary: "[The] 75th anniversary of Vic High brings memories of outstanding women who worked tirelessly for the public good before the turn of the century. None were more brilliant than Miss Agnes Deans Cameron, first woman teacher in Victoria High ...."[12] She taught there for seven years and then her career took another turn.

A new school in Victoria was about to be opened and a principal was needed. Agnes Deans Cameron was selected for the position. It must have been an exciting time for her because she would be the first woman in the province to become a school principal. South Park School boasted the very latest in architectural features and technology. A newspaper report proudly described the opening of the school: "The handsome gabled red brick building at the northwest corner of Douglas and Michigan streets is South Park School. It was opened for the fall classes of 1894, and William Ridgeway Wilson, the architect, based his design on the Queen Anne style."[13]

The school began with 343 students and eight classrooms. There was a large assembly hall that could hold 580, there were automatic flushing toilets and heating was supplied by the latest hot-air systems. South Park School was situated in a beautiful, semi-rural area, near the sea and adjacent to Beacon Hill Park. Cameron loved her school and the surrounding environment. She could regularly be seen taking walks or riding her bicycle in the park, enjoying the trees and the wildlife.

Cameron was a progressive school principal, well regarded by both students and parents, but her constant striving toward educational reform and equality began to annoy the school trustees who were, after all, the arbiters of the education system. Paternalism may have been the accepted norm of the time but not for Cameron. She and the school board came to verbal blows when, in 1901, a decision was made to increase the wages of male teachers only. This infuriated Cameron. Her deliberations on the subject were duly reported and had the backing of the newspapers. Flashing her feminist temperament she lashed out and said, "Women teachers are one in the opinion that it is a vicious principle to establish any such basis of payment or salary as that of sex."[14] The school trustees winced at her audacity but maintained their stance. The male teachers got their raise.

It is possible to get the impression that Cameron was hot-headed and aggressive but nothing could be further from the truth. Her modus operandi was one of kindness. In fact, the inscription she chose to put in her book, *The New North*, was, "Do your work well and be kind." It is true that her actions were often reported by the newspapers but she was a popular figure. While it may have seemed that she was contentious by nature it is more likely that circumstances kept conspiring to put her in adversarial positions. She simply could not and would not subject her intellectual beliefs to those who were contemptuous of equality. Cameron was good-hearted and compassionate but tenacious when her ire was roused.

Cameron was living in an age of conquest and intolerance, and relations went smoothly as long as people knew their place. She chose not to be bound by the parameters of discrimination and racism. Willing to see cultural systems as relative to time and place, Cameron exhibited a breadth of vision and tolerance far beyond her time. During her journey to the Arctic Circle, for example, Cameron described the aboriginal people she met with a dignity that flew in the face of the commonly held belief that they were heathens.

In *The New North* she wrote, "It is an age of classification .... What then must we call these splendid fellows so full of integrity and honour, whose every impulse is a generous one? Heathens? The question sets us thinking. The Century Dictionary defines heathen as 'any irreligious rude, barbarous or unthinking class of person.' This Eskimo is not 'irreligious,' for he has a well formed conception of a Great Spirit and an Evil one, he looks to a place of reward or punishment after life. He is not 'rude,' but exceedingly courteous, with a delicacy of feeling that is rare in any latitude."[15]

In the meantime, the school trustees were still smarting from the attention Cameron had drawn to the issue of salaries. They drummed their fingers and bided their time, hoping for an opportunity to rid themselves of this pesky woman. That opportunity came in June 1901. The school board decided to replace written exams with oral ones. According to the board, Cameron ignored that directive. Behind closed doors and without being given a hearing, she was charged with disobeying the ruling, and the board abruptly removed her from her principalship. She was dismayed by the injustice of the procedure and wrote to the board, denying the charge and requesting an investigation. Her request was summarily dismissed. However, the board could not be freed of her so easily. The newspapers, students and parents rose to her defence. The superintendent of education had travelled this road before and probably did not want to risk angering the public, so the case was dismissed and Cameron was reinstated.

Agnes Deans Cameron settled back into doing what she most enjoyed, teaching and managing South Park School. She also embarked on a journalistic career at this time, writing for American as well as Canadian magazines and newspapers. Among her topics were travelogues about British Columbia, the latest bicycle craze, the first Pacific steamer, Vancouver Island, and the Royal Canadian Mounted Police. She also ventured into fiction with the publication of "The Avatar of Jack Pemberton" in a Canadian magazine, *The Pacific Monthly*.

Cameron's next challenge was an incident involving the administration of high school entrance examinations. The examinations were held in June 1905 and Cameron and her art teacher, Miss Fraser, were charged with allowing South Park students to use rulers for their tests. In the drawing portion of the examination the students were to sketch a number of objects freehand: a bowl, a design within a rhombus, a bottle, chalk boxes, cubes, cylinders, two shallow square boxes and some scale drawings. When the test was completed the examiners had to certify that the students had not used rulers; this she did. While correcting the students' booklets, the graders felt that Cameron's students had used rulers for some of the drawings.

Could it be that Miss Cameron and her art teacher "falsely" certified the exam booklets? If she did, she was not the only one, for three male school principals were equally accused. However, the outcome for the two women was quite different than for the men. The school trustees convened and discussed the matter, eventually deciding to dismiss both women. Miss Fraser quietly accepted the decision and resigned. The three male school principals were reprimanded and went back to teaching. Cameron, on the other hand, rolled up her sleeves and prepared for a fight. She was not going to give up her teaching certificate or her livelihood so easily.

The trustees ruled that Cameron was to leave her post by December 15, 1905. Again, the newspapers rallied to her support and a petition was signed by notables of the community, seeking the reinstatement of Cameron as principal of South Park School. The Right Reverend Bishop Cridge, Charles E. Redfern, F. B. Pemberton, Lindley Crease, the Archbishop of Victoria and the Honourable H. S. Helmcken were among the signers. Because of her earlier criticism of the Local Council of Women for their participation in and support of cooking classes for girls in the curriculum, it was not surprising that they declined to help her. Also, Margaret Jenkins, the only female school trustee and one who was in a position to assist Cameron, turned her back on her because as a member of the Local Council of Women, Jenkins felt she too had been publicly disparaged.

The school trustees were wary of more controversy surrounding Cameron so they sent the case to a judicial inquiry. This was a smart move by the board, for the records of the school trustees showed that they had planned to move or dismiss Cameron, along with two other teachers from South Park School, before the drawing incident. This clearly gave them a way to avoid the public debate such an unsolicited move would have created.

The commission convened on December 15, 1905, under the chairmanship of Judge Peter Secord Lampman, a justice of the County Court of Victoria. The inquiry took two months, during which time Cameron was never allowed to defend herself to the board, despite repeated requests to do so. But events were to take a strange twist for both the school trustees and Cameron. While the judicial proceedings were going on there was great excitement over an election for school board members, and to the chagrin of the school trustees, Cameron was encouraged by a strong group of supporters to stand for election.

The day of the election, January 19, 1906, was an ideal one. The sun had burst forth and the air was crisp and frosty; people cast their votes and waited. The following day the front page of *The Daily Colonist* carried the results. "Agnes Deans Cameron Heads the Poll in School Trustee Election," the newspaper declared. "Outside the Mayoralty contest perhaps the most exciting feature of this campaign was the contest for seats at the school board. The South Park School controversy and Agnes Deans dismissal being made an issue which engendered the keenest public interest. Miss Cameron was aptly and successfully supported by her friends, heading the poll when the ballots were counted."[16] She won the election with 1,291 votes, securing a position with the very board that had been trying to rid itself of her.

The irony did not escape Cameron for she later wrote, "The little scene in the committee room where, after seventeen hours of unremitting work the last ballot was counted at 2 o'clock in the morning, was not without its features of humor. I was half amused I confess, when the 'congratulations' were offered and I said, 'Well, I can scarcely understand your position, Mrs. Jenkins. I can't see how you can consider me worthy to fill the one position and unfit to hold the other.' I have been consistently fighting for six months for the sacred rights of truth and justice, I cherish no personal animus toward Mrs. Jenkins, or any other member of the board and trust that I can work with them all for the general good. There is much to do. May I take this opportunity of thanking the many citizens who have reposed their trust in me."[17] Margaret Jenkins was also elected to the board but with 204 votes fewer than Agnes Deans Cameron.

Shortly after Cameron took up her position as a school trustee the BC Commission handed down their decision. After all the students were interviewed and the case thoroughly considered, Justice Lampman ruled against Cameron. In his summarizing statement he said, "It appears that there was a great deal of ruling and I think there was ample to justify the Examiners and the Department in the course they took. I think when the Examiners receive drawing books certified by the teachers they should be able to rely on the certificate as indicating that the work has been done according to the regulation."[18] Cameron's first-class teaching certificate was rescinded for a period of three years, effective June 1, 1906.

The drawing book incident, while a contentious issue, appeared trifling next to the general stuff of commissions which up to then had dealt with more serious issues such as an explosion in a coal mine, the provincial jail, and the Canadian Northern Railway. Was this a case of unfair extremism? The question is difficult to answer. The three male principals, who were also found to be at fault, were allowed to continue teaching with their certificates firmly in hand. It was only Cameron and her art teacher who were stripped of their certificates. There was certainly one trustee who was opposed to a woman being a school principal, but on the other hand three women had previously been on the board: Helen Grant, Margaret Jenkins and Maria Grant.

What Agnes Deans Cameron did was confront her foes by rattling the cages of the authority structure. The three male school principals did not do this; they quietly went about their business and did as they were told. She was also constantly pushing at the parameters of educational theory and practice, thereby threatening established notions. Since Cameron was never allowed to defend herself, the truth of the accusation remains unknown. In the end, the school trustees had won the day, except that this issue continued to resurface in the media and in government discussions for several years thereafter.

Was Cameron daunted by all that had happened to her? The thing she loved most, teaching, had been taken from her; she was jobless, $800 in debt from her fight to retain her teaching certificate, and her mother, with whom she had always lived, had just died. No one would have blamed her if she had become introspective and reclusive but that was not in her nature. She firmly believed that she was mistress of her own fate. Cameron did, however, want to get out of Victoria. She moved to Chicago to work for the Western Canada Immigration Association. The only regret she had was that her move meant she had to give up her seat as a school trustee. As a non-resident of Victoria she could not hold office.

A smiling fate must have been waiting in the wings for her because she came by her new job in an interesting way. During the years that she had been teaching, Cameron was also writing for magazines throughout Canada. Her excursion into journalism had attracted the attention of the Canadian Press Association and they asked her to be a speaker at their 1906 convention in Winnipeg. After the convention she was invited to spend the next two weeks travelling the northwest as a guest of the Western Canada Immigration Association. The adventure was made to order. She loved travelling and said as much: "Can anything compare with the dear delights of travelling when you do not know and nobody knows just what lies around the next corner?"[19]

During the next few years Cameron became an active promoter of immigration to the Canadian West. She travelled, wrote articles and gave talks on topics as diverse as buying buffalo on the hoof, fruit growing for women, growing wheat, the fur market, homesteading and ranching. Her articles were well researched, filled with information and energetic in style. In an article on the glories and benefits of British Columbia, she wrote, "And to-day in Victoria harbor sail the fleets of all the world. ... The pheasants are rolling in the long grass, a homing sea-gull flies overhead, a near-by meadow lark announces to all and sundry, 'God's in His heaven, all's right with the world.'... Fifty miles north is the town of Duncan, a ranching community of English younger sons, where *Punch* and *The London Times* are read and British Politics discussed and where the small landed proprietor in immaculate Bond Street clothing peddles his own wares and pours out Browning with the morning milk."[20]

The distinctive feature of the Canadian West was its large tracts of unoccupied land. In 1897 Clifford Sifton became Minister of the Interior in Sir Wilfrid Laurier's cabinet. He pursued a vigorous immigration plan to settle the prairies. The idea was for the region to become an agricultural resource populated by immigrants who would develop family farms. It was to this exciting venture that Cameron applied her literary talents. She wrote prolifically and with conviction. She was thrilled by the immigrants coming to the west. Cameron saw this new melange of people as an important resource for Canada, giving strength and character to the nation. "Greater Canada must have an analysis of destiny," she wrote, "for a country depends not upon its material resources, but upon the character of its people."[21]

While on her writing tours Cameron began preparing for an adventure that would be the experience of a lifetime and make her an international celebrity. Her plan was to spend six months wending her way some 15,000 kilometres along the Athabasca, Peace and Mackenzie rivers to the Arctic Circle and back. Her main reason for taking the trip, she said, was "to call attention to the great unoccupied lands of Canada, to induce people from the crowded centres of the Old World to use the fresh air of the New."[22] But it was also something she just wanted to do. She had always promised to take her niece travelling and this was her chance. Accommodations for herself and Jessie Cameron Brown were often of their own making. For this they were well prepared; they had packed a tent and bedding, cameras, film and a typewriter to capture images and expressions on the trip. Cameron and her niece started from Chicago on a rather gloomy day.

Beginning her journal on the day she left, Cameron recounted the uninspiring conditions of their departure: "At seven in the morning the stage pulls up for us, and it rains, no gentle sizzle-sozzle, but a sod-soaker, yea a gully-washer."[23] They spent months in open scows, sleeping on the ground and stretched out on blankets on the decks of small boats. Cameron talked not of fear but of wonder and described her encounters with exuberance. Of their first rendezvous with rapids she wrote, "Now begin the rapids, ninety miles of which we are to run. This rough water on the Athabaska is one of the only two impediments to navigation on the long course between Athabasca Landing and the Polar ocean. These first rapids, frankly, are a disappointment."[24] The next set of rapids was more challenging. "The next morning we are all keyed-up for the rapids. The great rapid stretches from shore to shore and the drop is sheer. Much excitement. No one speaks, and the big awkward craft is brought up for a jump. It is an elephant drawing his feet together to take a water-fence. For all we own in the world we wouldn't be anywhere but just where we set. If it is going to be our last minute, well Kismet! Let it come."[25]

She wrote much about the Eskimo she encountered and her belief in equality comes through in her reflections. "We are better able to understand, to appreciate, to help, and be helped by our brothers, red, brown, and parti-colored, when we begin to recognize the truth that basically and in the last analysis, we are all very much alike."[26] She was game to try everything, including moose hunting. In her account of the hunt she was quick to chide those who would find such behaviour offensive. "I have killed my premier moose. 'Cruel!' you say? Well, just you live from mid-May to mid-September without fresh meat, as, flesh-pots, we have done, and then find out if you would fly in the face of Providence when the Red Gods send you a young moose."[27]

She was even plucky about the food she was offered. "We tasted many new Eskimo dishes. When, on our return, we confessed that the brain of the seal served here is a delicious dish, we ran against the sensibilities of refined natures. But why is it cruder to enjoy seal's brains a la vinaigrette, than to tickle our taste with brains of the frolicking calf?"[28] Cameron did, however, balk at the notion of eating muskrat. "There is a limit to everyone's scientific research, and, personally until insistent hunger gnaws at my vitals and starvation

*Agnes Deans Cameron.* (Courtesy BC Archives, G-04056)

looms round the edge of the next iceberg, I draw the line at muskrat and am not ashamed to say so."[29]

People were eager for accounts of the far north. Excursions were being made to the North and South Poles, and exploration of the Arctic was whetting the public appetite for armchair adventure. Consequently, Cameron became a favourite on the lecture circuit.

She was an eloquent and entrancing speaker. "A gallant comrade filled with the joy of living," said one news account.[30] She gave talks to the Royal Geographical Society in England and travelled all over Canada with her epic tales of the Arctic. At the Walker Theatre in Winnipeg she spoke to an audience of over 2,500; 1,500 others had also hoped to hear her but were turned away due to lack of seating. *The Toronto Globe* reported that "A Canadian woman, Agnes Deans Cameron, has just completed what is without doubt the most remarkable journey ever accomplished by a woman of this country. We know of no one, man or woman, who in one season between ice and ice had been able to follow the Mackenzie to the sea, and to return against current by the Peace, and so out to civilization to the Lesser Slave."[31]

*The Rockford Republic* of Illinois compared her to Kipling: "What Kipling has done for India, Agnes Deans Cameron is doing for Canada."[32] At the Imperial Institute in England she was enthusiastically greeted by a crowd of over 1,000 people. The Duke of Argyle stated what many in the audience were thinking. "Miss Cameron," he said, "the feeling left in my mind after listening to your travels is one of unadulterated envy."[33]

These were very busy years for Cameron with more on the horizon. Sadly, not long after she published her account of her voyage in *The New North*, she underwent emergency surgery for appendicitis. The operation was successful but she could not fight off the ensuing pneumonia, and died just eight days later, on May 9, 1912.

What can be said of such a remarkable life? Agnes Deans Cameron lived her life with a sense of purpose, integrity and adventure which is instructive to this day about the virtues of dignity, determination, self-confidence and fairness. She seized every opportunity with energy and enthusiasm. An article in *The Toronto Globe* summarized the distinctions she had achieved and defined just what Agnes Deans Cameron meant to Canada. "In the list of women of Canada who have achieved distinction, Agnes Deans Cameron must be given high place. As a writer, storyteller, platform speaker, the daughter of Vancouver Island excels. There is character in everything she does. Her contributions to periodical literature have virility and vision."[34]

\*\*\*

By the late 19th century, the idealization of women as wives and mothers left little room for them to advance their education. Even those women who managed to obtain a higher level of education were not expected to put their learning to use. Women's destiny lay in marriage and once married, they were expected to focus on their family and home. These notions changed, however, beginning with the work of the University Women's Club and the dedication of its members like Evlyn Farris, Rosalind Watson, Madge Robertson, Helen Gregory MacGill, Laura Jamieson, Mary Ellen Smith and Kate McQueen. The credit for founding the University Women's Club belongs to Evlyn Farris. The club proved to be a strong advocate in the fight for women's equality in education and for legislation to improve conditions for women.

To be considered eligible for membership, an applicant to the University Women's Club had to have a four-year degree from a college or university. The initial purpose of the club was to stimulate intellectual activities in college-bred women in the arts, science, literature and civic reform, and to promote the social welfare of their members. At first, the goals of the University Women's Club were modest but, as the club developed, the members directed their energies toward creating educational opportunities for all women. One of the early projects the club undertook was a provincial university for British Columbia.

Until 1876, education beyond elementary school was available only for that small minority of students who were able to travel out of the province to study in Europe or eastern Canada. British Columbia had neither high schools nor a university. It was not until the late 1870s that Victoria built the first high school in the province, and shortly thereafter, high schools were built in Nanaimo, New Westminster and Vancouver. In 1894, an amendment to the Public School Act permitted McGill University to affiliate with any of the four existing high schools in the province. By 1899 Vancouver High School, renamed Vancouver College, began offering courses in first-year Arts with a McGill-controlled curriculum. Unfortunately, students needed to go to McGill to complete their education. This arrangement proved to be quite unsatisfactory and subsequently an act to allow McGill University to establish a University College in BC was passed in the provincial legislature.

In 1906 McGill University College of British Columbia offered first- and second-year programs in Arts and Applied Sciences at

Vancouver College. The time seemed right for the University Women's Club to fulfil their dream of a provincial university. Together with other supporters, the club lobbied the government for a provincial university and success was realized when, in 1908, the Legislative Assembly passed The University Act establishing the University of British Columbia.

When the University of British Columbia opened its doors in 1915, the University Women's Club was there to ensure equity within the university for women. When the university prevented women from taking classes in the Faculty of Science, the club, insistent upon change, castigated the Conservative government for their apathetic regard of women.

Evlyn Farris, speaking for the University Women's Club and individually as a member of the university senate, voiced her displeasure at the government when she said, "What annoys the women of the University Women's Club particularly is to find that the government has drawn up the curriculum dealing with the education of women (which is power expressly given to the Senate) without giving us a chance to be heard in the matter. For instance, the calendar says that women may attend the classes in Arts, but does not say that they may attend the classes in the Faculty of Science, the omission being equivalent to a prohibition. I am quite sure that this would never have occurred if the calendar had passed through the hands of the Senate, for if nobody else had drawn attention to it, I should have done so myself."[35] The University Women's Club went on to work on other agendas for improving social conditions for women, but they were truly indebted to Evlyn Farris for the advances she made toward the development of higher learning in the province.

## Evlyn Farris
### 1878 - 1971

Evlyn Farris was an academic, feminist and activist. She was one of the most renowned women in her time for advancing the cause of university education for women in British Columbia. She pushed for the development of the University of British Columbia and was one of two women appointed to its first Senate. Farris founded the University Women's Club of Vancouver and helped to start the Women's Liberal Association in Vancouver. For her outstanding work in the field of education Farris was given two honorary LL.D. degrees.

Evlyn Fenwick Kierstead was born in 1878 in Windsor, Nova Scotia. She was raised by her widowed father who was a professor at Acadia University. Farris' early life was steeped in the world of academia and it is not surprising that she grew up believing in the merits of a university education. She held that knowledge was power and wealth, and looked to education as a means by which women could break the bounds of conventionality and submission, and reveal their natural abilities. For her, education and equality were intertwined and she never lost a chance to tutor people on the value of these twin assets.

Farris believed that educated women would produce a fresh and desirable way of thinking for Canada. For a speech at Horton Collegiate Academy in Nova Scotia, She talked about the importance of higher education for women. Her topic, "Wux Femina Facto," meaning "A Woman Leads the Way," explored the influence of educated women upon society, emphasizing the point that women were a very necessary part of the political, social and economic decision-making process.

"The desire for education is becoming almost a passion in all enlightened nations," she said. "That knowledge is power and wealth has long been regarded as axiomatic and now the people generally are seeking to obtain knowledge for the sake of power and wealth, and in this work women will certainly have a grand opportunity for displaying their natural and acquired abilities."[36] Her speech was enjoyed by the young women in the crowd but some thought her topic too free thinking. The Attorney General of Nova Scotia, who was present at the ceremony, strongly criticized the content of her speech, saying that the subject was inappropriate. Not one to be dissuaded, Farris ignored her critics and gave other talks with a similar message.

Her penchant for discussing the benefits of post-secondary education for women became quickly known and while she was delivering a speech on women's influence in 1899 she was asked by her host not to mention higher education but to focus instead on dress and etiquette. Such a request only served to raise her ire so Farris included her ideas from "Wux Femina Facto" in her talk. Not much is known of the outcome of this talk but it did prove, once again, that Farris was adamant in her beliefs about education and equality. It also indicated that she was persistent and strong-willed.

Farris began her own advanced scholastic training at Acadia University in 1894. She completed her Bachelor of Arts degree in

1898, attaining first-class honours, and went on to gain a Master of Arts degree in Philosophy and German from Acadia one year later. From 1899 to 1905 she taught at a high school in Connecticut where she was the Chair of the History and Political Science Department. It was while she was in Connecticut that Farris learned about the intellectual and social benefits of women's clubs, through her membership in the University Club.

In 1905 she married Wallace de Beque Farris, a lawyer from Vancouver. After their marriage, the Farrises made their home in Vancouver and over time, became a powerful couple. (In 1916 Wallace, an MLA, was appointed Attorney General and Minister of Labour of British Columbia by the Liberal government.) Initially, however, Farris felt the loss of the academic stimulation that she had experienced in Connecticut. Her remedy was to start a women's club in Vancouver, modelled after the University Club in Connecticut. In 1907, only two years after her arrival, Farris organized the University Women's Club, which went on to become one of the driving forces for the promotion of women's issues in the province.

Farris' original intent was to use the University Women's Club to advance science, literature and art, but once organized, the club became very active in civic and educational reform and worked to improve social conditions for women in the city. A partial list of their endeavours includes buying a building in Vancouver to house women's societies; promoting employment for women physicians; ensuring women physicians were appointed as the medical officers for girls attending public schools; improving working conditions for women by securing legislation that limited the number of work hours per day; changing unjust social legislation affecting both women and children; successfully lobbying for pensions for widows. The club by its very nature had a great deal of expertise within its membership. The study of law for the club was initiated by Helen Gregory MacGill while Farris headed the Education Committee.

When Mabel French, a lawyer from New Brunswick, was refused admission to the British Columbia Bar in 1912, both MacGill and Farris worked toward amending the Legal Profession Act to allow women lawyers admission to the Bar of BC. It seems that the Law Society ruled that Mabel French had been disallowed on the grounds that only "persons" who were British subjects were eligible to practise law. As a woman, Mabel French was not a "person." This decision was confirmed by the Court of Appeal of British Columbia.

*Evlyn Farris, with her husband, children and in-laws, in Victoria, CA. 1920.*
(Courtesy BC Archives, G-06274)

Farris used her considerable influence to gain the attention of
William Bowser, the Attorney General of the province. As he knew
her quite well and was all too familiar with her tenacity, he could
hardly deny her an appointment. She told him that the women of
the province would not tolerate such a decision and that it was time
the Legal Profession Act was amended. Knowing the power of
women that Farris would bring to bear on the situation, Bowser
agreed to bring a bill before the legislature, and on February 27,
1912, the Legal Profession Act was amended.

Recounting the incident in a personal letter in 1979, Farris' son
John wrote, "Saturday, she went down to the Vancouver office of
W.J. Bowser, K.C., the Attorney-General for British Columbia.

Notwithstanding that they were on opposite sides in politics, Bowser consented to see her. Knowing mother, he didn't have a choice .... After some pussyfooting, Mr. Bowser said, as the House was going to be prorogued on Tuesday there was not time to do anything about it. Mother said there was time and he was going to do something about it. Finally, he agreed and the Bill was introduced on the Monday and passed on the Tuesday, after which the House was prorogued."[37]

Though Farris was involved with social reform she also worked diligently at promoting education in the province, giving talks to other women's clubs in the city on the importance of a provincial university and the benefits of a university education for women. She promoted women's accomplishments and delivered speeches on Canadian women in literature, the arts and science. Hoping to get parents involved with their children's education, Farris formed the Parent-Teacher Associations in Vancouver. She was also very much involved in the establishment of the University of British Columbia. She sat on boards to establish a university in the first place and then she attended endless meetings detailing the plans for the new university, eventually being appointed to a committee to choose a site for it.

It was a heady time for Farris. All of her efforts were about to come to fruition with the building of the University of British Columbia. In the early stages, when it looked as though the Conservative government was about to renege on the promise they had made to fund the university, Farris was outraged. She badgered the government, accusing them of being apathetic when it came to post-secondary education in the province, and telling them they would be the laughing-stock of the nation. She threw as many public punches at the government as she could. Public pressure mounted and the money came through; the university would be built.

As Farris was well respected by her academic colleagues and esteemed as a woman of learning it was not surprising that she was appointed to the first UBC Senate, and went on to other positions of prominence in the university. In 1917 Farris was appointed to the Board of Governors at UBC, which made her the first woman in Canada to participate as a member of a governing body of a university. In 1923 she was awarded an honorary Doctor of Laws by Acadia University for her service to education and as a promoter of social change. This was the first time that Acadia University had invested a woman with an honorary degree, and Farris was the third woman ever in Canada to be so honoured. Farris received a second

LL.D. in 1942 from the University of British Columbia, the institution she had worked so hard to establish. Evlyn Farris died in 1971 at the age of 93 and is well remembered as a woman who was a pioneer in educational reform and in advancing equality for women in British Columbia.

\*\*\*

In 1965 two new provincial universities were opened, the University of Victoria and Simon Fraser University. Technical training was offered by the establishment of the BC Institute of Technology. Two church-affiliated institutions, Notre Dame University in Nelson and Trinity Western College in the Fraser Valley, were added to the growing post-secondary sector. Perhaps the most significant contribution to educational accessibility during the 1960s and 1970s was the gradual introduction of a number of community colleges around the province.

At the same time as British Columbia was moving to meet the demand for technical training and student spaces, curriculum content was being debated. A number of studies documented the absence in the curriculum of Canadian studies and the history of the province. Margaret Ormsby, a professor in the University of British Columbia's Department of History, was commissioned to write a provincial history to commemorate the 1958 centennial of the colony. Her resulting book, *British Columbia: A History*, became the starting point for thinking about the province.

Dr. Margaret Ormsby
1909 - 1996

Every school child from the late 1950s on, who studied the history of British Columbia, has been affected by Dr. Margaret Anchoretta Ormsby. Ormsby was a professor of history and wrote the primer on British Columbia history that serves as the base for textbooks from elementary school through to university. Ormsby, referred to as the doyenne of BC history and one of the most distinguished members of the University of British Columbia, is remembered for her pioneering work in the field of BC history. She was a social historian, author, teacher, professor and head of the Department of History at UBC for ten years. Perhaps no other scholar has been so identified with the history of a province as has Ormsby.

Ormsby was born in Quesnel to parents of Canadian-Scottish and Anglo-Irish descent but spent her childhood in the Okanagan. She loved her home and wrote numerous articles on the history, geography and people of the Okanagan. She edited nine annual reports for the Okanagan Historical Society, which became the leading anthology of the life and times of the Okanagan, and throughout her life she continued to chronicle the history of her home.

During the late 1920s women were entering university as never before. They represented 23% of all undergraduates and 35% of graduate students. As a girl recently out of high school, Ormsby followed that trend. Encouraged by her parents to advance her studies at the University of British Columbia, she enrolled in 1925, the year the university moved to its permanent site on Point Grey, and received her Bachelor of Arts degree four years later. At that time, women were expected to engage in work that was non-threatening to their womanhood and to the position of male workers. That meant that professional women could be employed mainly as teachers, secretaries or nurses. Ormsby quickly learned that a BA in history did not allow her many opportunities for work, so to increase her employability, she took a year of teacher training at UBC and proceeded to teach high school.

After a relatively short time Ormsby went back to UBC to complete a Master's degree in history. University funding for graduate work and research was generally not provided so most students had to have some other means of financing their education. Fortunately for Ormsby, she was awarded a scholarship by the Canadian Pioneer Problems Committee. When she graduated in 1931, Ormsby had the distinction of receiving one of the first graduate degrees conferred by the Department of History at UBC.

Wanting to continue her studies, she went to the United States to take a doctoral program in Medieval and American History at the prestigious eastern college of Bryn Mawr. She was awarded a Bryn Mawr Fellowship in History, accompanied by a scholarship the following year. Ormsby's studies were temporarily interrupted as the 1930s Depression swept across both Canada and the United States, when to make ends meet she took a job as an assistant in the Department of History at UBC for one year. She was then able to go back to Bryn Mawr to complete her studies. In 1937 Ormsby was granted her Ph.D.

With her new degree, Dr. Ormsby joined the academic élite of Canada. However, for a scholar with a degree in history, there were no academic positions available in Canada. Many universities, UBC included, were at a standstill during the 1930s, so Ormsby went back to the United States and took a teaching post in San Francisco. She taught at a private high school until a faculty position became available at McMaster University in Hamilton, Ontario, in 1940.

Despite her Ph.D., Ormsby was not readily accepted into the prevailing male university culture. Women who took up a male profession were seen as challenging the clearly defined border between women's and men's spheres, and suffered the consequences accordingly. Women academics had to contend with the constant questioning of their credibility and the merit of their work. They were often isolated and ignored, even within their own departments. Ormsby's office at McMaster, for example, was a table in the women's washroom. When she was first assigned this "office" the chairman of the History Department explained that there were no faculty offices for females.

Ormsby stayed three years at McMaster and then returned to the University of British Columbia to teach in the Department of History. Although women scholars had to work harder and stay the grade longer before they got a promotion, she attained the status of Full Professor by 1955; she was the first woman to become the Acting Head of the Department of History in 1963 and Chairperson in 1964. She held the position of Chairperson until her retirement in 1974.

Ormsby was a friendly and compassionate person with a sense of jollity about her. She was popular with her students and had a gift for energizing and motivating them. She wrote extensively and her publications investigated such topics as pioneer women, Okanagan history, the fur trade, colonial and provincial politics, and agriculture. Her writings gave shape to British Columbia and placed the province within the larger history of Canada. In 1957, Ormsby was commissioned to write the history of British Columbia. It was a massive undertaking, as no such work existed in Canadian literature. To accomplish the task she had to study archival material, read the personal diaries of the early settlers, and search through decades worth of newspapers.

Her book, *British Columbia: A History,* was published in 1958 and sold for $4.75. It was a bestseller, establishing the tone and study of history in the province for years to come. Her writing was not the stuff of fusty old curmudgeons whose manuscripts about antiquaria were produced in an obtruse and detached manner. Ormsby's approach was fresh and relaxed, providing a highly readable and lively insight into the life and times of British Columbians. Ormsby forged her own path and her book remained free of the 1950s historical analysis which attempted to explain development in terms of regional tensions. Ormsby believed that the writing of history should be like art, whose substance was moulded in the past and liberally infused with the personalities and impressions of the citizenry.

Writing about the discovery of British Columbia by Europeans in *British Columbia: A History*, Ormsby paints a sublime picture of the coast: "Had the facts been known, there would have been little to encourage a voyage of discovery to the remote region off the coast of British Columbia. The Pacific ocean completely belies the name given to it by Magellan. Whipped by cruel winds, the waters of the sea strike islands that rise as the peaks of a submerged mountain chain, or attack an indented mainland shoreline, swirling at the base of cliffs and dashing into narrow inlets and straits ...."[38]

The wide acclaim she received for this monumental work was only the beginning of a succession of honours. In 1959 Margaret Ormsby was elected a Freeman of the City of Vernon. In 1965, in recognition of her contribution to Canadian history, she became only the second woman president of the Canadian Historical Association. In 1967 she was elected a Fellow of the Royal Society of Canada. She felt deeply appreciative, for to be elected a Fellow is a coveted professional accolade. Ormsby also received five honorary doctoral degrees from Canadian universities and in 1990 was invested into the Order of British Columbia; in May 1996 she received the highest honour for a Canadian citizen, the Order of Canada.

Ormsby also served on a number of important boards. Between 1960 and 1967 she chaired the Historical Sites and Monuments Board of Canada and the BC Heritage Advisory Board, and she was a member of the Board of Governors of Okanagan College from 1980 to 1985. Perhaps the paramount tribute accorded to her was the founding, in 1993, of the Margaret Ormsby Scholarship Program by a group of devoted graduate students. The scholarship continues to be awarded annually to a promising student beginning a doctorate in British Columbia history. One other lasting endowment, for the many students who attend one of the university-oriented programs in colleges in BC, is the Margaret Ormsby Prize for the Best Essay on British Columbia History.

Dr. Margaret Ormsby left a legacy that will affect generations of historical scholarship to come. As a teacher she was respected, and

*Dr. Margaret Ormsby, 1964.* (Courtesy Special Collections and University Archives Division, UBC Library, Negative #5.1/2330)

served as a role model for many a young student. As an academic administrator Ormsby bore the primary responsibility for the growth of the Department of History at UBC and the development of its post-graduate programs. As a woman she led the way toward a climate of acceptance for other women in the history profession. Through her writings, Ormsby interpreted British Columbia eloquently, as a province within the Canadian nation and also as part of the larger international community. She died in her home at Coldstream, near Vernon, BC, on November 2, 1996. She was 87 years of age.

* * *

Since the 1970s there have been dramatic increases in the numbers of women entering post-secondary education and earning degrees, and most educational institutions are committed to educational equality. Women equal men in diplomas granted in community colleges and universities; nonetheless, there are still problems. There is an obvious difference in the courses of study that young men and women choose. At the community college level women make up 90% of the students in nursing, rehabilitative medicine and secretarial science, 80% in social work and library science and more than 50% in education and liberal and applied arts. In universities, women are underrepresented in engineering, forestry, dentistry, architecture, computing science, law, business, and science. In terms of employment, the women who work as academics in colleges and universities are a privileged élite but positions of power and senior academic appointments remain elusive.

There is increasing skepticism about women's ability to break through the "glass ceiling." Recent reports from campuses across Canada are beginning to detail patterns of stereotyping, overt harassment, and isolation experienced by female students and faculty. The President's Advisory Committee on the Status of Women at the University of Saskatchewan noted that "For these women, the temperature is always minus 40 with a high wind-chill factor."[39]

It is of great concern to women that our work is often devalued and considered unimportant, particularly if the subject is women's lives and women's history. Women in academia say that they are treated, sometimes, as though they are invisible and that their ideas, suggestions and contributions or scope of authority are ignored.

The overall picture for employment equity in the post-secondary sector remains very patchy, with some institutions and departments making considerable progress in recruiting and retaining a more diverse faculty, and others seeming to have done very little. What is important, however, is that women like Agnes Deans Cameron, Evlyn Farris and Margaret Ormsby looked beyond the constraints of conventionality and worked to change perceptions and behaviour.

# CHAPTER TWO

# WOMEN IN COMMUNITY BUILDING

BECAUSE OF THE lack of women's stories in literature and history books, the impact of women on British Columbia's communities may be thought to be indirect — influence, perhaps, rather than substantive power — but the accomplishments of many ordinary women show that these notions need to be challenged. Women working at the grass roots of society have continually asserted their power to change their communities, and throughout the history of BC, women have been highly visible in addressing the social issues of their surroundings. The women in this chapter have all shown concern, commitment and leadership in improving the well-being of the citizens within their communities. They stand as examples for the thousands of other women who, through their work, have been catalysts for social change.

Today, women continue to work for their communities, tending to the needy, valuing the environment, working for justice and economic improvement, and searching for solutions. Women like Elaine Holmes who, seeing the need for a program for youth at risk in Victoria, developed GOALS to help young people recover from substance abuse, or Dr. Norma Mickelson, chancellor of the University of Victoria, who has devoted her career to improving both literacy among Canadians and equity within universities. Dr. Elinor Powell, a physician of internal medicine, is an advocate and spokesperson for peace and serves as a councillor with the Nobel Prize-winning International Physicians for the Prevention of Nuclear War and as president of the Canadian affiliate, Physicians for Global Survival. Whether they know it or not, their efforts link them together as they bring health, well-being and enjoyment into their communities. Perhaps most importantly, these women act as reminders to all citizens that, individually or in groups, people *can* make a difference.

*** 

By the end of the 19th century many women were questioning the restrictions of their rights. Women gathered together and formed organizations like the Women's Christian Temperance Union, the Young Women's Christian Association and the National Council of Women. The women who joined these organizations were not necessarily feminists. Many accepted women's domestic role but were of the opinion that their feminine temperament could help bring about needed social reform. Increasingly, 19th-century society intruded on family life. Alcoholism, prostitution, crime and disease were common, particularly in growing urban areas.

These early women's groups proved to be a significant sorority in women's struggle for equality, for they built the substructure for political action. The women learned how to be administrators and fund raisers; they honed their political skills and became competent at lobbying. Most importantly they came to know that unless they had the right to vote, politicians would not listen to them nor respond to their requests. Cecilia Spofford, as a founding member of the Victoria Women's Christian Temperance Union, exemplifies the dedication and fervour of these women.

## Cecilia Spofford
### 1859 - 1938

Cecilia Spofford was a teacher, politician and social reformer. She was a founding member of the Victoria Women's Christian Temperance movement and the Victoria Local Council of Women. Born Cecilia Anne MacNaughton in Sydney, Nova Scotia, in 1859, she moved west to Victoria with her parents in 1877. Shortly after

her arrival Spofford launched her lifelong career in women's organi-
zations by becoming the secretary-treasurer of the women's
Missionary Circle of the First Baptist Church. Wanting a profession,
Spofford worked toward her teaching certificate and after passing
her examinations taught in a variety of schools in Sooke, on Salt
Spring Island and in Saanich. In 1883 she married William Henry
Spofford, a carpenter by trade; the couple remained childless.

In the late 1800s urbanization, with its raw values of individu-
alism, supplanted the community energy of the smaller rural towns.
For a time it seemed that these new cities were morally bereft. Social
aid was negligible and cities appeared to be given over to saloons
and street drunkenness. All of the unpleasantness of urban life, such
as poverty, disease, immorality and unemployment, were thought to
be caused by alcohol. The temperance movement was an attempt to
moderate the use of alcohol and improve public morals. Out of that
movement grew the Women's Christian Temperance Union. The
WCTU originated in Ontario in 1874 and spread rapidly across
Canada; it was Cecilia Spofford who took up the cause in Victoria
in 1885. At 25 years of age Spofford was rather young to be so
committed to social causes, but she had a flair for organizing, was
energetic and used her congenial personality to win membership for
the WCTU. The WCTU was so successful that communities like
Moodyville prided themselves on being temperate family towns.

Spofford's mother, Jane MacNaughton, often worked side by side
with her daughter. Spofford was the first president of the WCTU in
British Columbia, and her mother the vice-president. Spofford
enjoyed her work with the WCTU and gave much of her time and
energy to the temperance movement. She had a good rapport with
audiences and often gave lively speeches from church pulpits around
the province. She exempted no one from this fight. She worked hard
at getting the women of the province to pledge their support to the
WCTU, thinking that the men would soon follow and then prohibition would be a reality.

The WCTU also promoted other reforms, such as female suffrage
and mothers' allowances. When mothers were finally allowed to
vote for school trustees in 1884, Spofford, afraid that they would
not take advantage of their right, canvassed the city of Victoria,
informing women of the upcoming election. The result was that
most mothers went to the polls to cast their vote. Mothers, she
believed, were the best authority on matters concerning their
children and should have a voice in their education.

*Cecilia Spofford.* (COURTESY BC ARCHIVES, I-51701)

In 1889 women became eligible for the first time to become school trustees, and the WCTU seized the opportunity to prepare women to be candidates in the next election. However, in 1892 there was a change in government attitudes and a new School Act disallowed women from holding office. Ever vigilant, Spofford fought back, setting up the Victoria Local Council of Women. She saw that such a council would operate as an umbrella organization, working with many of the women's groups to present a stronger united voice for women's issues. On January 18, 1895, the Victoria Local Council of

Women, on behalf of 20 women's groups, petitioned the government to overturn the School Act. They were successful, and by February, women could once again sit as school trustees.

In time the Victoria Local Council of Women was affiliated with the National Council of Women of Canada and proved to be a powerful champion for the rights of women and children. From working to ensure women's participation in the direction of their children's education it was a logical step for Spofford to put her energies toward getting women the provincial vote, and she presented many petitions for provincial suffrage through the WCTU and the Victoria Local Council of Women. She worked tirelessly for this cause, hoping that women who had the vote would then support the temperance crusade. Spofford also lobbied mothers to make sure that temperance women were on the school boards and in the classroom as teachers, and that temperance was an important subject on the curriculum.

After the turn of the century alcohol consumption went down and other social issues became more pressing so that by 1905, support for the temperance movement began to wane. Participation dropped by 50% and the existing unions were so scattered that it became difficult to maintain a united front. The Women's Christian Temperance Union rose to the challenge and sent Spofford around the province to promote the union and to start groups where possible. Once again, her organizational skills served her well and she was able to increase the number of unions from 12 to 26. Finally, through the combined efforts of all the temperance unions, her dream of national and provincial prohibition legislation came true. Prohibition became law in British Columbia in 1917 and federally in 1918.

Spofford participated in many other organizations and activities during her life of working for the betterment of society. The WCTU was also concerned about prostitutes, and reasoned that if they had a safe place to go they would leave their street life for one of virtue. Spofford spearheaded the building of a new Refuge Home which in fact ended up taking in single pregnant women, and poor, homeless women and girls. The home became a popular retreat for unwed mothers, so that in 1891 the WCTU opened a maternity ward. Spofford was a member of the British Columbia Political Equality League, was elected to the Victoria School Board in 1919, and was president of both the Children's Aid Society and the Provincial Council of Women. Spofford was also a member of the Social

Welfare Commission and the Minimum Wage Board in Victoria and was a candidate for the Woman's Independent Political Association in the 1918 provincial by-election.

By April 1937 Spofford was suffering from ill health and was confined to her home. Unable for the first time in her life to do for others, she wrote a history of the Baptist Women's Missionary Society in British Columbia. She also nursed her husband who was ill at the same time. His condition deteriorated, however, and he died. Spofford was badly shaken and her own health declined even further, although she felt somewhat better in February 1938 and attended a meeting in Vancouver. There she became ill again, and had to be brought back to a hospital in Victoria where she died; she was 79. Spofford had worked with women like Margaret Jenkins, Maria Grant and Helen Grant, all giving their lives to the service of women's organizations, and dedicating their energy toward social reform.

* * *

The part women played in the trades and labour movement in British Columbia is not well known. Perhaps this is to some extent due to the lack of early records about working women. Women working in the paid labour force, for the first half of the century, tended to hold jobs that were unskilled and low paying. They were domestic servants, teachers, nurses, stenographers, garment makers, telephone operators, waitresses, fish-plant workers, candy makers, cooks and shop assistants. The image of women staying at home languishing in their gardens or enjoying tea at an afternoon social was an upper-class notion only. Many women needed to work to supplement their family's income or to support themselves. In 1911 in Vancouver there were nearly 8,000 women working for pay, and few of those jobs allowed them to earn a living wage. They needed a collective base from which to voice their concerns but unions were male oriented; union policy did not reflect the needs of women, and there were few women among the working classes who had the connections or the backing to organize women and put forward their issues. Thus, it came to be that middle-class club women and early political activists, upset with the inadequate support for working-class women and the resulting growth of prostitution, stepped in and lobbied the provincial Liberals for wage legislation.

In 1918 the first women's minimum wage legislation was enacted, but it was double-edged for working women. The Act did raise the wages of working women and, as so few women were unionized, it was the only avenue of support for them. On the other hand, not all women were covered by the Minimum Wage Act; bank employees, federal workers, farm labourers, fruit pickers and domestic workers were excluded. Also, for women who were under 18 years of age, inexperienced or had a disability of any type, the board was empowered to set a lower minimum wage. Moreover, to help establish wages for working-class women, the government sought advice from middle-class women. Although these women had good intentions, their knowledge of the living necessities of working-class women was vague. For example, a local doctor's wife, while presenting a brief from the Local Council of Women to the Royal Commission on Labour Conditions in British Columbia in 1914, said that in her opinion young and inexperienced girls did not do enough work to entitle them to a living wage. In fact, these young women might be working, on the average, 60 hours a week.

The Local Council of Women, consulting with the royal commission's committee to establish wage guidelines, eventually decided that girls between 14 and 16 should start at wages of five dollars per week, with increases twice yearly until they reached ten dollars per week. This was below the wage needed to cover living expenses. The figure arrived at by the Local Council of Women was somewhat shocking for a few of the men on the committee, although they did decide to go along with the amount to avoid confrontation with the women. James Wilton, one of the members of the committee, felt the five-dollar figure was too low and said that $16.50 would be a more adequate sum. It is interesting that the very women who would benefit from the legislation were left out of the discussions and the resulting decisions. Women may have been gaining power but that power accrued only to middle- and upper-class women, not to the women of the working class.

## Helena Gutteridge
### 1880 - 1960

Helena Rose Gutteridge was a different kind of activist from her contemporaries. Women like Helen Gregory MacGill, Mary Ellen Smith or the women of the Local Council of Women came from the middle and upper classes of society and represented the British establishment that dominated the province. Gutteridge was a working-class woman who married late in life. She was gutsy and harboured a no-nonsense attitude. While she worked side-by-side with Helen Gregory MacGill for suffrage, equal guardianship and custody law, minimum wages for working women and pensions for needy mothers, Gutteridge's heart lay with working-class women. Her main focus in life was to see to the passage of legislation favourable to women, for the improvement of conditions for destitute, single-parent and working-class women. Gutteridge was a suffragist, a trade union activist and a pacifist.

Gutteridge came to British Columbia in 1911, already a confirmed activist. She was born in England in 1880 and displayed her independence early in life, for she left home when she was a mere 13 years of age. Even at such a young age Gutteridge knew she had important things to do and realized that to accomplish her goals, she would need an education. Her parents thought differently; they were of the opinion that girls should marry and raise children and did not merit higher education. However, Gutteridge was stubborn and her vision for her future was greater than any hold her parents had over her. She left home and broke off all contact with her family. She went to work to support herself and to pay for her studies at Holy Trinity Church School, the Regent Street Polytechnic and the Royal Sanitary Institute. Gutteridge eventually earned certificates in hygiene, sanitary science and teaching.

It is not known how Gutteridge became an activist, except that her desire for independence and self-fulfillment, coupled with her working experience, must have sensitized her to the plight of women. She admitted herself that she always had a militant streak, and she was obviously ripe for the suffragist movement in England. She waved banners and gave speeches about women's rights; she lectured at Speakers' Corner in Hyde Park, famous for its activist speakers. For her part in a suffragist demonstration at the House of Commons, Gutteridge was arrested, although not jailed. The jails were already too full and had no room for the likes of her. In 1911 Gutteridge sailed to Canada with a group of suffragists, intending to stay for only a short period of time. As chance would have it, she settled in British Columbia and led an active life in the province, working for reform.

Gutteridge's previous experience with suffrage and women's issues went a long way to helping improve conditions for women in British Columbia. Within a few weeks of her arrival Gutteridge joined the Political Equality League, an organization that was working for the vote for women. She felt the suffrage movement in British Columbia was too reserved and needed to embrace a more active and forceful methodology, and as well, that there was a distinct lack of interest displayed by the women themselves. Gutteridge believed that until women became a collective voting force, women's lives would not improve. While she threw her energies into the fight for the vote, for her it was just a means to an end.

At the same time as Gutteridge was working for suffrage, she was also involved in the labour movement. Two years after her arrival in BC, Gutteridge made herself known to the Vancouver Trades and Labour Council. Concerned about women's wages, she wrote to the TLC in July 1913, recommending that a meeting between the TLC and delegates from women's societies be convened to discuss the poor working conditions that women had to cope with. Impressed with her proposal and her audacity J. H. McVety, a member of the Vancouver TLC, suggested that Gutteridge join a labour organization. Needing no encouragement she began to help organize women laundry workers and garment workers; Gutteridge was a worker in the garment industry herself. Due to her organizational skills and zeal, the laundry workers became affiliated with the Vancouver TLC in 1914. One year later she was elected secretary-treasurer of the Vancouver TLC, the first woman to sit on the council's executive.

Gutteridge became very active in the TLC. She was sent as a delegate to provincial, national and international conventions, the first Canadian woman delegate to attend international labour congresses. She also devoted time to being a correspondent on women's labour issues for the *Labour Gazette*, a newspaper published by the federal Department of Labour. During the war years Gutteridge joined with representatives of Vancouver's women's societies to establish the Women's Employment League for the purpose of providing housing for destitute women and creating a job-registration service. Under her guidance, the league opened, on November 1, 1914, a house with 33 rooms, where unemployed women could live and learn a trade. The initial plan was to have the women manufacture toys for sale, and Gutteridge looked for funds to finance the enterprise. The sum of $1,500 was donated by private individuals and other sources but this was not enough. Using her considerable knowledge of political persuasion she obtained $2,000 from Vancouver City Council. The city council was particularly keen to help her when she explained the danger of women who were out of work and unable to support themselves turning to prostitution. Prostitution was becoming a considerable problem in

Vancouver and the council was under a great deal of pressure from the East End Improvement and Protection Association, the Vancouver Property Owners Association, the Vancouver Moral Reform Association and ordinary citizens to do something about it.

Concerned about working women's wages, Gutteridge began working toward a minimum wage bill with Helen Gregory MacGill. In 1917 the Minimum Wage League was founded, with Gutteridge acting as the chairwoman of the committee. She lost no time in pressing the case for a minimum wage standard with the provincial government. Finally, in 1918 Gutteridge's and MacGill's efforts were rewarded when Evlyn Farris' husband, Attorney General of British Columbia Wallace Farris, drew up a minimum wage bill for women and Mary Ellen Smith pushed it through the legislature.

Gutteridge also involved herself in pioneering social legislation for mothers' pensions. The idea behind mothers' pensions was to provide government assistance to destitute mothers. Mothers' pensions were to be made available to women with more than one child under the age of 16, whose husbands were not able to support them. Through the hard work of many women, the Mothers' Pension Act was passed in 1920. Although the Act has been criticized in retrospect for sidestepping the real issue of women's economic position, it was revolutionary in that it gave poor women money of their own — money that did not belong to their husbands.

Gutteridge went on to agitate for other reform legislation and continued her work with union organization but for unknown reasons, between 1921 and 1932, she ceased all of her reform activities and became a poultry farmer in the Fraser Valley. She was reported to have married during this time but evidently the marriage did not last and she was divorced within a few years. Again for reasons not known, she gave up farming and moved back to Vancouver where she added another dimension to her interests.

Politics had fascinated Gutteridge since 1918 when she was the secretary of the Federated Labour Party. With her experience of the political process she became active in the Socialist Party of Canada and when the Co-operative Commonwealth Federation was formed in 1933 she held various positions on the executive, including chairwoman of the Economic Planning Commission. When she ran for and was elected to Vancouver City Council in 1937, Gutteridge became the city's first alderwoman. She went on to run for a seat in the British Columbia legislature as a candidate for Point Grey in 1941 but was defeated.

*Helena Gutteridge, the first woman elected to Vancouver City Council, taking the oath of office, March 1937.* (COURTESY CITY OF VANCOUVER ARCHIVES, PORT. P. 276, N. 1125)

During the Second World War Gutteridge worked as the welfare officer for the Japanese-Canadians interned at Slocan. In the 1950s she began slowing down her commitments to trade unionism and politics but she did participate in the Provincial Council of Women's School for Citizenship and was a consultant to the United Nations on issues of women and peace. She died in October 1960 at the age of 80. The pioneering work that she did for suffrage, labour and the community has left a legacy for which the province is forever indebted.

\*\*\*

During the latter part of the first decade of the 20th century, women in British Columbia were beginning to share in a growing emancipation from restrictive moral and dress codes. Improving economic conditions along with better public health stimulated a major expansion in athletics. Sports heroines like 13-year-old

Audrey Griffin of Victoria drew thousands to watch her win a provincial women's swimming championship in 1915. She was vigorously cheered when she went on to become the Canadian champion in both the 45-metre and the 90-metre freestyle events. Such excitement drew many girls between the ages of five and 17 to join sporting groups and organizations such as the Girl Guides.

Guiding was important in the development of young women because it greatly enhanced feelings of self-esteem and purpose for many girls and it was unique in its approach to leadership training. The Girl Guides demanded non-traditional female behaviour on the part of its leaders. They encouraged vigour, ruggedness and self-sufficiency in camping and sporting activities, and adopted hiking and swimming as ways of developing strength. In fact, many young girls felt quite daring in becoming Girl Guides.

Critics of the Guiding movement have pointed out the inevitable contradictions inherent in the organization. It is true that Guiding maintained women's support role while at the same time advocating the more adventurous male role, but this did not necessarily mean that it was a retrogressive step for women. Bonnie MacQueen has looked critically into the Girl Guide movement in British Columbia and feels that Guiding was a double-edged sword for women. She wrote, "Only when people fully appreciate that such groups keep alive the contradictions of women's role in society can there be any kind of equality."[1]

Did the Girl Guide movement create confusion about self that ultimately pushed women back into the recesses of "women's place"? Or did it strengthen character by supporting the aspirations and well-being of young women and creating a place where they could work together to change the way the world saw them and the way they saw themselves? The answer to this is of course a matter of perception, but Phyllis Munday, a world-renowned mountain climber and one of the originators of Girl Guides in British Columbia, saw Guiding as a way to challenge young women in a spirit of fun, to develop a sense of well-being and to achieve a sense of pride in accomplishment.

Phyllis Munday
1894 - 1990

Rising from the depths of the Pacific Ocean, the Coast Range thrusts itself through the mist, exposing its ruggedness. Inspiring and enticing, it is a formidable adversary for those who seek to scale its peaks. It has claimed more than one life and shattered the hopes and dreams of many. Ringing the coastal communities of British Columbia for some 1,500 kilometres, with peaks rising to a towering height of 4,000 metres, it issued a challenge to one woman that was to shape the course of her life. That woman was Phyllis Munday.

The opportunities that life provides are often so random that to try to predict their course would be pure folly. How could anyone have foreseen that Phyllis Beatrice James Munday, born on a tea estate in Ceylon on September 24, 1894, would one day become known as "Dame of the Coast Mountains" for her exploration, mapping and photographing of the Coast Range in British Columbia? In her lifetime she would climb over 100 peaks, becoming one of the premier mountain climbers in the world and a role model for mountain climbers to this day. She was the only mountaineer to receive honorary membership in three international climbing clubs: the American Alpine Club, the Ladies' Alpine Club of England and the Alpine Club of Canada. It was the first time the American Alpine Club had ever honoured a woman mountaineer in that manner. To be invited as an honorary member of a climbing club is a special award for having demonstrated extraordinary talent in mountaineering.

Munday gained other awards during her lifetime. A massif on Mount Waddington was named Mount Munday in her honour and for her lifelong work with the St. John's Ambulance she was named Dame of Grace of the Order of St. John. She was given an honorary Doctor of Laws degree by the University of Victoria for her work in community service, mapping, glaciology, geography and botany, and was granted the medal of service of the Order of Canada. One of her lasting accomplishments was the introduction of the Girl Guide movement in British Columbia and the initiation of the worldwide Lone Guide program, for which she was awarded the highest decoration given by the Girl Guides.

If one were to have scripted a life for Munday, based on her background and her time period, by all rights she should have been a lady. The early 1900s were the age of Edwardian elegance. It was the time of the Tin Lizzie, George Bernard Shaw and elaborately designed mansions with overstuffed interiors and imported wood panelling. Women busied themselves with tea and garden parties, and propriety was sacrosanct. People of means were to be seen at the Vancouver Lawn Tennis Club or the Vancouver Yacht Club. But

Munday preferred forest denizens to tea cakes and pastries. She called herself a tomboy and wanted only to climb mountains.

It is difficult to know what motivates people to do the extraordinary; in many cases they do not know themselves. For Munday it was probably the love of the outdoors coupled with opportunity that determined her direction. Her father, Frank James, managed Lipton's and Ridgeway's tea estates in Ceylon. When Munday was seven years of age, she and her sister Esmée emigrated to Canada, their parents having gone ahead of them. (Their brother, Richard, was born after their move to Canada.) Living first in Manitoba, where James worked as an accountant, the family eventually moved out west to the Kootenays in British Columbia. The rigours that faced Munday and her family were far from the privileged life of servants and nannies that had surrounded them in Ceylon. Her mother, Beatrice, had lived her life as the mistress of an estate and was unfamiliar with the chores of housekeeping or the demands of the kitchen. Munday eagerly took up the challenge of frontier living and learned to hunt and climb. She loved nothing better than to harness up her old horse Titus, grab her .22, and take off exploring the bush, rousting out the occasional grouse for supper.

For the James family, British Columbia was planned as a temporary stopover on their way to New Zealand, so in 1906 they left the Kootenays and travelled to Vancouver to board their ship. However, they were quite taken with the city and decided to stay. Vancouver was a booming town and an exciting place to be. There were lots of jobs available for someone with Munday's father's skills and Vancouver offered an easier life for her mother. During the early part of the 1900s the population of the city expanded almost tenfold and modernization and house construction were evident everywhere. The roadside ditches and mud-caked wooden sidewalks were disappearing, replaced with electric street-railway lines which crisscrossed the city. Department stores like Woodward's, the Hudson's Bay Company and Birks became city landmarks. Stanley Park was crowded with people taking afternoon strolls among the tall trees, whirling around the dance floor of the new pavilion in the park, or listening to the ever-popular band music being played at the bandstand.

The Jameses settled into Vancouver quite happily. Munday's father joined the Vancouver Lawn Tennis Club and was a player of some note. It was his hope that his daughter would follow in his footsteps and become a tennis champion, but her attention was turned toward the mountains which sat so enticingly near the edge of the city.

At every available opportunity Munday would ride the streetcar to the end of the line for a climb up Grouse Mountain. "There was something about getting away often, in the wilds, that appealed to me more than anything else," she said. "We'd start off from home with a skirt on, you were never seen on the street with a bloomer, or a pair of pants. It just wasn't done in those days."[2] When they reached their destination, Munday and her friends would walk to the base of the mountain, and then exchange their high-necked blouses and full skirts for walking pants, stash their clothing under a log and spend the day hiking.

Munday enjoyed these times and was happy exploring Grouse Mountain with her friends but she was anxious to have a more organized outlet for her outdoor activities. She cast around for ideas and looked to the Boy Scouts for inspiration. She said, "I used to think all good things were for boys."[3] She could not understand why girls were not able to enjoy the same activities, so at 14, when she might have been concentrating on the science of homemaking, she started a troop of Girl Scouts. "We were as proud as punch," she wrote. "They (I don't remember who 'they' were) said we must have a Scout Mistress. This was easy as my Mum was always a good sport, and rather than see us stuck said 'yes'. She was really a figure head."[4] Munday became the Acting Patrol Leader.

At the time she started up her little troop of Scouts, Munday was unaware that the Girl Guide movement had been founded the previous year in England. When she was informed of this she was delighted but also a bit disappointed. "After our Company had been running a while we found out a Miss Mansfield had already a Company of about 40 at the big Church across from the Empress Theater. They called themselves the 1st Vancouver Company so we called ourselves 2nd Company, very reluctantly because we felt like pioneers as we had started on our own hook as the girls used to say. For some reason they soon broke up and a good many of their girls came to us."[5]

Munday helped organize her group under the framework of the British Girl Guides but had to mould the British Columbia Guides to the BC environment. Camping proved to be a popular activity, the first camp Munday organized being held at Bowen Island. "We were just a group of happy enthusiastic untrained girls shifting for ourselves," she wrote. "It was camping in the form of the good old days when there was real camping there, not dressed up with white shoes and fancy dresses [like] camping today [1980's]."[6]

Guiding was very dear to Munday's heart and it is possible that the Girl Guide movement in British Columbia would have been little more than a passing phase if it had not been for her perseverance. She lovingly nourished it through its lean years, at one point even advertising for girls. "In 1914 the Guides everywhere seemed to be dropping off as there was no interest whatever shown by anyone. No other active Companies then existed so I held meetings once a week just the same with the hope something would happen. When war broke out we advertised for girls and from that time on, they started to pick up."[7] By the 1920s her Guide Company was doing well and, wanting to have a program for younger girls, Munday started the 1st Vancouver Brownie Pack in the spring of 1920. She was very excited about this new direction. "I loved those dear little girls and sometimes wish I were still a Brown Owl with the same little Brownies as they were then."[8] When her Guide Company became too big to allow her the time to carry on with both, she turned the Brownies over to Nora Hunter, one of her Guides.

With the outbreak of the First World War the call to arms rang loud and clear throughout the streets of Vancouver, and a sense of sobriety and self-sacrifice gripped the city. Vancouver was transformed overnight as 26,000 young men and women went overseas. Women volunteered their time for the war effort, knitting socks for the soldiers, rolling bandages, raising money and working in factories to help meet war-time contracts. Munday desperately wanted to go overseas with the St. John's Ambulance and knowing that she was underage she falsified her birth date. Needless to say, she was rejected. Never one to be discouraged, Munday formed the St. John's Ambulance Brigade Nursing Division in North Vancouver and for many years served as a divisional superintendent.

In 1924 Munday took a year's leave of absence from Guiding to live up on Grouse Mountain with her husband, Don, who shared her passion for the outdoors. They couldn't have been better suited to each other; they both loved climbing and Don, a world authority on glaciology, was a renowned climber in his own right. Munday first met Don just after the First World War. She was employed as a clerical worker in the orderly room of the Military Annex of the New Westminster General Hospital, where Don was receiving treatment for an injured arm. When Don regained his strength they went on climbs together. They were a good climbing team, each sensing the other's needs, particularly in times of danger. After a few months of climbing together, a near-serious mishap made them realize how much they had come to rely on each other.

Munday related this incident in a taped interview. With gentleness in her voice she said, "We were on a climb on Mount Baker and the rocks were loose. It's a snow-covered area where the crevasses are really dangerous. The piece that Don was on didn't show any signs of going down. It was very steep and of course the whole thing began to move. I thought he was going to go, and it is just automatic for a person to do something to save a person's life. I stuck out my foot to save him from going down. You don't think about those things at the time."[9] Although Munday was able to stop Don from sliding, her own footing gave way. Don, having gained control, quickly came to her rescue and was able to support her while she gained a foothold before his ledge crumbled. Don later wrote: "The incident lends itself readily to being given a romantic aspect, like other occasions when we had stood together undismayed by the appraising eyes of danger, but it has mountaineering significance in showing how even at that time we relied on each other for rightness of action in emergencies, often without audible language between us."[10] They were married on February 4, 1920.

Climbing became a lifelong passion for them and little could keep them from their beloved mountains. Even after their wedding ceremony, when they should have been enjoying the gaiety of the celebration, they abandoned their guests and skipped their reception for a week-long honeymoon climb up Grouse Mountain. During another important event in their lives, shortly after the birth of their baby, when most new parents would be trying to cope with the rapidly changing circumstances of their lives, they packed up their 11-week-old daughter, Edith, and climbed with her to the top of 1,503-metre Crown Mountain.

It was very difficult for Munday to leave her Girl Guide troop but the experience did provide her with an opportunity to pioneer the Guides in a new direction. She wrote, "It hurt me very much to leave the girls but I did not realize at the time this was to mean Good-bye to them. I am still though a 1st Vancouver Company Guide in my mind as after all those years of comradeship, nothing can sever me from them, in spite of being away from active company Guiding."[11] The Mundays moved to Grouse Mountain initially to manage a resort that was to be built, but the financing fell through. In the meantime they constructed a cabin and became the first people to ski on the mountain. Grouse Mountain was quite isolated and it was while living there that Munday realized there were young girls who were equally isolated from active Girl Guide centres. Her response was to start the Lone Guides.

"I saw myself as a young rather distressed Guider having to give up my beloved Company because I was going with my husband and baby to live nearly 4000 feet above Vancouver on Grouse Mountain. This was too far to come to attend meetings. I soon became very lonely for Guides and as there were no Lones I started them. There were not many at first. We were scattered from Alaska to California and into Alberta."[12] The girls Munday referred to lived on lonely coast islands, in scattered communities, in lumber camps, on farms and ranches and in railway section houses.

She started a monthly newsletter which connected the Lone Guides with each other. It often took the bulletin a long time to make the rounds, for if a girl lived at the head of an inlet or up a mountain, she sometimes had to wait for good weather conditions before she could make the day or week trip to a place where she could gather the mail. One Lone Guide wrote, "I'm sorry this newsletter is late but it's been forty below here and no one went to the mail, five miles away, for three weeks."[13]

In addition to Phyllis Munday's extraordinary work in the Girl Guides and St. John's Ambulance she was also noted for her expertise in mountain climbing. Up until the time of her death many a mountain climber would confer with her about climbing paths or conditions. Munday conquered British Columbia's highest peaks and most of the mountains in the Coast Range, the Rockies, the Selkirks and the Premier Group, attaining a number of firsts. Although it was not her most difficult ascent, the climb Munday is most noted for is to the top of Mount Robson in 1924.

Mount Robson sits majestically in the verdant beauty of the Kananaskis country, the greatest peak in the Canadian Rockies, rising some 3,954 metres from the valley floor. Mount Robson is steep, with a pitch drop of 55 degrees. The climb was organized by the Alpine Club of Canada and even though Munday was a member, as a woman she had to apply to the club to gain permission to join the climb. Several mountaineers have underestimated this mountain and met their final destiny within its crevasses. Mount Robson offers slippery rocks, massive ice sheets, inhospitable weather and the ever-present danger of altitude sickness for the climber. There are no individual heroes on this mountain. Such a climb was thought to be beyond the physical endurance and mountaineering skill of a woman but Munday proved her critics wrong and became the first woman to reach the top. At the time of her climb, Mount Robson was believed to be the highest mountain in British Columbia, a notion to be disproved later by the Mundays.

Munday's description of the climb in her diaries offers some insight into the difficulties she encountered. The climbing party started their ascent before first light. "Up 2000 feet more. Now we had to work across the cliffs 200 yards under the upper ice-wall, and then actually climb its 150 foot face .... Perhaps a fairly steady head and foot is needed to trot rapidly along a ledge with 8000 feet of thin air immediately below you .... The slope above is unlike anything in the Rockies — an absolute chaos of ice blocks on a slope of not less than 45 degrees; domed with snow, and bristling with gleaming icicles, they were a never to be forgotten sight, fairy-like perhaps, but sinister, hostile, menacing."[14] As they reached the top one of her climbing partners extended his hand to her and said, "Well, lady, here is the top of Mount Robson." The time was 4:30 P.M. They had climbed for 14 hours that day to reach the top.

While Phyllis Munday helped reshape the boundaries for women she did not see herself as an active promoter of women's rights; the thought that women were merely "the fairer sex" never entered her mind. As far as women challenging themselves on the faces of mountains, Munday said, "If a person enjoys mountaineering and is strong enough, and well enough to do it, and can hold your own with a [climbing] party, then there is no reason in the world why a woman can't do it."[15] She had no equal among women mountaineers in the world and few among men. For her skills she was awarded the Alpine Club of Canada's Silver Rope Award for Leadership, the only Canadian woman to have received that honour.

Munday was also a photographer and always packed her camera, documenting previously undisclosed aspects of the natural environment for scientific purposes. She photographed ice-flooded valleys, raging rivers, deep crevasses, interesting ice formations and all the alpine flora and fauna that she could find, and many of her photographs won local and international awards. She published some of her wildflower photographs in a book she co-authored with her husband, appropriately titled *Wildflowers of British Columbia.*

Climbing in the 1920s bore little resemblance to the high-tech climbing of today. Much of the technology that exists today was not

*Phyllis Munday.* (Courtesy BC Archives, H-03440)

available when the Mundays were climbing. Lightweight, pre-packaged, dried food had not been thought of so the Mundays prepared their own. They had to pack in food for the whole expedition season which was quite an ordeal. A 40-day trip with six people would require, among other things, 42 k of flour, 9 cups of baking powder, 18 k of butter, 23 k of sugar, 22 k of jam, 7 k of potatoes, 9 k of cheese, 14 k of ham, and 23 k of bacon. It was quite a business figuring out the quantities of food and sometimes they found themselves stretched a bit thin. On one trip, with four days left to go, six people had to share one tin of sardines and one round of bannock.

Much of the food preparation began in the winter. While Don was supporting the family through his freelance writing, Munday drew up the lists of items needed for the coming climbing season. She would can butter and jam, dry fruit, and waterproof the cotton storage bags.

Munday designed and sewed the clothing and Don made the tent and packs. "We didn't wear heavy clothing, just a shirt and pants," she said. "I would make pants out of an old blanket. They were excellent and were practically rain and waterproof. We would carry an extra sweater and a bone dry coat."[16] For climbing shoes they designed their own edge-nail boots. Using a large nail with a long spike, they would push the spike through the sole and clip it over so that the two portions of the nail were just on the edge of the boot. Don made their backpacks out of packboards and canvas. Sometimes their entire living-room in North Vancouver was taken over with the preparations. Referring to their tent Munday said, "We shifted all of the furniture out of the living-room and laid it on the floor and cut it out. I sewed it up. It's made of sail cotton, very light and very waterproof."[17]

In addition to spending the winters preparing for the summer months, Munday continued her work with Girl Guides and the Lone Guides, as well as volunteering for the St. John's Ambulance. She was particularly fond of campcraft and served as Provincial Nature and Woodcraft Adviser to the Divisional Commissioner for the British Columbia Girl Guides for years. In 1947 she was awarded the Beaver Badge, the highest honour that the Canadian Council of Girl Guides could confer upon one of its members.

For a particularly daring mountaineering rescue, Munday was awarded the Bronze Cross by the Girl Guides. The incident involved a young boy who had fallen off a cliff while climbing on Grouse Mountain. When she got down to him she found that he had serious head injuries and realized that it would not be safe to move him back up the cliff. Munday decided that the best course of action would be to take him to the cabin she and Don had built on Grouse Mountain. It must have been trying for both as it was mid-winter and they were quite isolated. Owing to the difficult snow conditions it was impossible to get help and too dangerous to try to move the boy any more than necessary. Munday alone nursed him through his injury for three weeks and while he may not have known it at the time, he could not have been in better hands. This award was especially meaningful, for Phyllis Munday was the only mountaineer in Canada to have received it. She was modest about these honours, rarely referring to them in her writing or in interviews.

Through her work with the St. John's Ambulance Munday volunteered to teach courses in first aid and during a devastating flood in the Fraser Valley in 1948, she organized all the first aid. She spent many years as a divisional superintendent for St. John's. Munday's work with the St. John's Ambulance correlated nicely with her mountaineering. She was quite active in both the Alpine Club and the British Columbia Mountaineering Club and gave lessons in mountain rescue and first aid, as well as snow and ice climbing. She was often in demand as a speaker for various clubs in BC and gave countless illustrated lectures on alpine flora and fauna, glaciation and mountain climbing. Because of her record of mountaineering accomplishments she worked as the editor for the *Canadian Alpine Journal*, a magazine affiliated with the Alpine Club of Canada and known worldwide for its fine mountaineering literature.

While the Mundays spent some time in the Rockies and the Selkirks, the majority of their climbing career was exploring the Coast Mountains. They spent a memorable 12 years mapping and challenging the Coast Range. The Mundays were careful climbers and felt that no mountain was worth throwing their lives away. If a peak could not be reached or weather interfered, then so be it. They attempted 16 times to climb the 4,016-metre peak of Mount Waddington. Munday came as close as 18 metres to the top but the summit remained elusive for her. Only when a film crew documenting her life in 1982 flew her to the Homathko Icefield on the top of Mount Waddington did she dig her ice pick into the top. She was 88 years of age at the time.

Reminiscing about her life of climbing Munday explained, with all of the enthusiasm born of spending a lifetime rummaging around in the grandeur of the Coast Mountain range, "It certainly has been a great privilege to have climbed in this area. Those wonderful days will never come again, so I treasure them for what they are. That whole area was glorious country; full of high peaks, great glaciers, ice falls, seracs, small lakes and heathers, beautiful flowers."[18] She died in 1990, at the age of 96.

It was not so much all of her honours and accomplishments that made Munday special; it was more her zest for life. She seized life with vigour and exuberance and selflessly gave much of her time and energy to the Girl Guides and St. John's Ambulance and through her example shepherded the acceptance of women in sport within the province.

*\*\**

Since the latter part of the 1960s, there has been a significant shift in the way First Nations are viewed. Previous writing on First Nations people focussed on Native cultures as frozen in time and historically static: societies in decline and in need of salvaging. To assume this is not only presumptuous but invalid, as it would separate one group of people from the common experience of all humanity. The current literature is one of celebration, viewing aboriginal cultures as persistent, viable, and ongoing, and showing a people adapting to the march of history. This is not to deny that much has been tragically lost to indigenous groups over the last century. Their cultures were seriously disrupted: languages vanished, mythologies were forgotten, art and music neglected and theologies obliterated, all due to forced acculturation. But First Nations people have survived and continue to exercise a presence in British Columbia.

Some traditions remained and many were adapted with a creative energy that is truly inspirational. The great artists of the recent past, like Charles Edenshaw, Mungo Martin and Willie Seaweed, helped to maintain a continuity that today's artists have been able to draw upon. There has been a remarkable expansion of Northwest Coast art which employs the fundamentals of historical meaning and symbolism but exhibits new form and style. Marianne Nicolsen, a Kwakwaka'wakw from Kingcome Inlet, is an emerging artist whose works have appeared in the National Museum of Civilization in Ottawa and in "Alter/Native: Contemporary Photo Compositions" at the McMichael Canadian Art Collection in Ontario.

Leslie McGarry, great-granddaughter of Chief Mungo Martin, communicates her heritage as the Cultural and Recreation Director with the Victoria Native Friendship Centre and as the co-ordinator of the Royal British Columbia Museum's carving studio in Thunderbird Park. There are also many young women like Leigh

Joseph, a Coast Salish woman who provides a positive role model to other students. In 1997 she was an honour roll student at her high school on Vancouver Island, a member of the student government, active in sports and the performing arts and a member of a club which promotes multiculturalism and anti-racism. Both McGarry and Joseph received 1997 Women of Distinction Awards given by the YM-YWCA of Victoria: McGarry in the category of Communications & Public Relations and Joseph as Young Woman of Distinction.

Other cultural innovations are taking place at the same time. In Alert Bay, Gloria Cranmer Webster helped to start the U'mista Cultural Centre as a place to house the returning collection of Kwakwaka'wakw potlatch items, but also to make a place for the young to learn about their heritage. There still remains much to be done and while First Nations people may have been daunted they have not been subdued.

## Gloria Cranmer Webster
### 1931 - present

"If only the evil influence of the potlatch could be done away with," wrote Indian Agent William Halliday in 1903, "then the Alert Bay Kwakiutl would forge right ahead."[19] Halliday was not the only one to think the Kwakiutl and their customs troublesome. In the early part of this century, Canadian lay and missionary authorities held the Kwakiutl to be the most unmanageable and incorrigible of all British Columbia's First Nations. Even Reverend Alfred Hall, one of the founders of Alert Bay, wrote, "The testimony of everyone I have met is that they are a bad set." He later added, "a most difficult lot to civilize."[20] At the end of the 19th century most Euro-Canadians believed in a genetically inherent White superiority. Aboriginal people were typically regarded as feral and uncultured, and to help them was seen as a manifestation of the White man's generosity and burden. In a bent of paternalistic fervour, the potlatch, seen as a stumbling block to the process of civilizing the Kwakiutl, was banned in 1884. Much energy went into the assimilation process but the Kwakwaka'wakw[21] had a great sense of peoplehood and were tenacious in resisting attempts to change them. (Kwakwaka'wakw refers to Kwakwala-speaking people and is the now-accepted form of the former Kwakiutl and Kwagiulth.)

Gloria Cranmer Webster's work came out of this tussle between the controlling policies of the Canadian government and the Kwakwaka'wakw Nation's efforts to maintain its cultural and historical integrity. Cranmer was born into a strong family whose lineage has historically been involved with the guardianship of Kwakwaka'wakw treasures. She is the great-granddaughter of George Hunt, the famous field assistant to anthropologist Franz Boas, and the daughter of Dan Cranmer who was, until his death in 1959, the hereditary chief of the Kwakiutl people. George Hunt was the son of an English man and a Tlingit woman who lived among the Kwakwaka'wakw. Over a period of 40 years Hunt collaborated with Boas, often referred to as the father of American anthropology, to produce large volumes of material in the form of books, articles and photographs on the Kwakwaka'wakw, much of which is still used today by researchers. When government authorities arrested Cranmer's father and others for standing up to the government by holding an illegal potlatch, they took away a treasure trove of ceremonial accoutrements which defined social relationships and served as anchoring-points for their culture. Years later, it was Cranmer, working with others, who brought those treasures home and instilled a sense of pride and continuation in Kwakwaka'wakw heritage.

Cranmer was born on July 4, 1931, in the town of Alert Bay, on Cormorant Island, 288 kilometres upcoast from Vancouver. Alert Bay stands at the entrance to Queen Charlotte Strait and the Inside Passage, and as such it is rich in history. The island's curved beaches and lush forests were originally used as burial grounds by the Namgis people from the Winalagalis or Northern Kwakiutl community. With the coming of European settlers and the opening of a cannery on the island in 1870, Alert Bay became a central point for people travelling up and down the coast. The cannery attracted many people to Alert Bay, including a large number of Kwakwaka'wakw who came from the mainland of Vancouver Island and nearby islands. With this influx of people Alert Bay became one of the largest of the Kwakwaka'wakw communities. During the early 1900s it was the site of the governmental Kwawkewlth Agency and a residential school. Today it is a busy fishing community of around 1,100 people, graced by the U'mista Cultural Centre on the west end of the island and stately memorial poles that guard the century-old Nimpkish burial grounds at the eastern end.

Cranmer left Alert Bay when she was 14, moving to Victoria where she attended Victoria High School for grades 9 through 12.

Going to a high school with a student population of 1,100 was initially terrifying for Cranmer — her school in Alert Bay had only 37 students. Nonetheless, she persisted and after graduation she enrolled at the University of British Columbia where she received a degree in anthropology in 1956. During her years as a student at UBC, Cranmer worked in the museum there and in the summers went commercial fishing. After receiving her Bachelor's degree she had hoped to continue her studies toward a Master's degree in anthropology. Unfortunately, there wasn't the funding from Indian Affairs that there is now for education and, since Cranmer had spent a number of years already in university, the necessity to earn a living loomed large. Also her brother, who was living with her in Vancouver, wanted to quit work to go back to school.

Cranmer applied for a job through the Vancouver employment office and was told that Oakalla prison needed a counsellor. She was reluctant to go for the interview because Oakalla was where her people had been imprisoned, and up to that point in her life, all Cranmer really knew about prison was what she had seen in grade-B movies. So, with great reservations but motivated by financial need, Cranmer went for the interview and accepted the subsequent job offer. It was an opportunity, however, that would help her realize what a shock it had been for the old people who were imprisoned there in 1922 for the potlatch violations. Cranmer stayed at Oakalla for two years, working with young women who were first-time offenders. After she left Oakalla she was hired by the John Howard Society and worked with parolees for two years.

While working for the John Howard Society Cranmer met John Webster, who was the executive director of the society in Saskatchewan. They fell in love and married and Cranmer moved to Saskatchewan. Their daughter was born in Regina and after 18 months of shivering, as Cranmer expressed it, the family moved back to Vancouver. Cranmer then began working for the YWCA as a counsellor. Part of her job was with Travellers' Aid, which involved meeting Chinese and Korean orphans at the Vancouver Airport, and taking care of them during stopovers. After both of her sons were born Cranmer retired to raise her children. She was not one to stay at home comfortably, however, and when her older son, John, was four he asked his mother when she was going back to work. He thought it was time she did.

Taking this rather strong hint from her son, Cranmer returned to the work force, this time as the program director for the Vancouver

Indian Centre. She worked there for a year, and then in 1971, on her 40th birthday, as it happened, she read the headlines of *The Vancouver Sun* which reported that Ottawa was providing $2,500,000 for a museum at the University of British Columbia. She was elated; this was something that she had thought necessary for a long time. Cranmer immediately picked up the phone and called UBC to offer congratulations and was told that there was a job as an assistant curator waiting for her. She accepted. The work she did collating Northwest Coast artifacts for the museum was valuable in providing her with the knowledge and skills to help facilitate the building and development of the U'mista Cultural Centre in Alert Bay and bring home the potlatch items.

Since time beyond recollection the potlatch had been an important ceremony in the lives of the Kwakwaka'wakw, serving to reaffirm a person's status by presenting claims to invited guests in the form of gift giving. If the host's gifts were accepted and acknowledged in the accompanying speeches, and he was later included as a recipient of gifts at other potlatches and referred to by his potlatch name, then his status was recognized. Potlatches were held for the naming of children, for marriage, for transferring rights and privileges and for mourning the dead. As smallpox and measles, brought by explorers and settlers, swept through the aboriginal communities the Kwakwaka'wakw dropped in numbers from an estimated 19,000 in pre-contact times to just 2,370 by 1864. The population continued to decline into the 20th century. The Kwakwaka'wakw held onto their social system but one of the results of this decline in their numbers was a change in the scope and vigour of the potlatch. Though at one time there were too many men marked by heredity for high rank, now there were too few. This situation created a fierce competition for high status, particularly among lower-ranking people trying to emulate chiefs. Potlatching occurred on a grander scale than before, due to the new wealth earned from working in the White economy.

The practice of potlatching unsettled the European missionaries and Indian Agents. They reasoned that as long as such practices were allowed to continue, community control and development would not be possible. G.M. Sproat, an Indian Commissioner in the late 1870s, reaffirmed this thinking when he wrote, "It is not possible that Indians can acquire property, or become industrious with any good result, while under the influence of this mania."[22] Instead of assimilating to White society, the Kwakwaka'wakw were

using their money to buy gifts for their potlatches, thereby rein-
forcing their own social system.

There were other concerns expressed about potlatching. The
missionaries and Indian Agents were anxious about the health of the
potlatchers. They reasoned that two months of nightly winter
feasting during which families moved between villages, often living
in transitory housing, created a breeding ground for sickness. Then
too, some potlatches featured ritual cannibalism, either simulated or
in the form of superficial biting and this inflamed Euro-Canadian
opinion against the potlatch. First Nations people were seen to be in
a transitional state, needing protection until they became settled and
acquired European values and customs. The Indian Agents and
missionaries pressured the federal government to ban the potlatch.
Adopting what they thought to be a humanitarian attitude toward
aboriginal people, the Canadian government passed the first Indian
Act in 1876 and in 1884 Sir John A. Macdonald agreed to ban all
potlatching under the aegis of the Indian Act. Potlatching became a
criminal offence.

Initially, the law was not rigorously applied and it was not until
Duncan Campbell Scott became the Superintendent General of
Indian Affairs in Ottawa in 1913, and William Halliday became a
British Columbia Indian Agent, that the law was enacted. Impatient
with the slow speed at which assimilation to White society was taking
place, Scott moved swiftly to do away with potlatches, and under his
direction Halliday began the arrests. Both Scott and Halliday wanted
convictions but judges told them that they did not view potlatching
as a criminal offence, even if there was a statute banning it. At most,
the offenders received suspended sentences. Scott and Halliday were
only temporarily thwarted, however. By 1918 Scott managed to have
the potlatching ban changed from a criminal offence to a summary
conviction, which meant that Halliday could act as the official adjudi-
cator, trying and convicting the miscreants.

In 1920 and 1921, a few people were convicted and imprisoned.
Then in December 1921, Cranmer's father, Chief Dan Cranmer, gave
one of the greatest potlatches ever witnessed on the central coast. It
was said that Dan Cranmer's Village Island potlatch was 17 years in
preparation. Halliday wielded his judicial weapon and arrested 45
people. They were charged with making speeches, dancing, arranging
articles to be given away and carrying gifts to recipients. The sentence
was a term in jail, but the defence attorney pleaded for leniency of the
court. Halliday decided that the accused would be given suspended

sentences upon agreeing to surrender all of their potlatch ceremonial gear including masks, rattles, whistles and coppers.

Twenty-two people received suspended sentences, two were remanded for appeal and 20 men and women were sent to Oakalla prison. First offenders were to serve two months and second offenders three months. In the meantime, potlatch property was taken from Village Island, Alert Bay and Cape Mudge and sent to Ottawa where the collection was divided between the National Museum of Man (now the Canadian Museum of Civilization) and the Royal Ontario Museum in Toronto. Scott kept some of the items, which he added to his personal collection, and about 30 objects were sent to a private collector in New York.

Potlatching simply went underground and the ceremonies were often held during stormy weather when the Indian Agents were unable to travel. Frustrated, Agent Murray S. Todd, Halliday's successor, lobbied the federal government in 1936 to authorize Indian Agents or the Royal Canadian Mounted Police to seize any excess goods that they believed to be intended for potlatch purposes. The Minister of Indian Affairs introduced a bill to that effect, but the House of Commons found it offensive and said such an action was unreasonable and unjust. The minister withdrew the bill and from then on the Department of Indian Affairs left the potlatch alone. Potlatching continued illegally through the 1940s and then in 1951, a revised Indian Act was passed; section 149, which outlawed potlatching, was deleted, but not repealed as the Kwakwaka'wakw had hoped.

The first legal potlatch since 1884 was given by Chief Mungo Martin in 1953. In the early 1950s Martin was working at the British Columbia Provincial Museum, sculpting totem poles and teaching the art of carving. He and his students constructed a Big House at the museum and upon its completion hosted a potlatch. The success of this potlatch encouraged other groups to design and build their own Big Houses. In the 1960s First Nations people gained the right to vote in federal elections, and along with that came a resurgence in their cultures and language. Acceptance and renewal led the Kwakwaka'wakw of Alert Bay to begin the long process of repatriating their potlatch objects.

It was at this point that Gloria Cranmer Webster became involved. In the early 1970s she was team-teaching a course on First Nations of British Columbia for the Department of Anthropology at the University of British Columbia. She was also working as the assistant curator of the Museum of Anthropology at UBC. During this time a professor who was teaching a native law course came to her to solicit suggestions for class assignments. Cranmer had always wondered about the legality of the federal government's taking away the potlatch treasures. Did section 149 of the Indian Act, for example, rest on a legal foundation? Did it violate the legal rights of the First Nations people? Were the seizures and disposition of the ceremonial regalia provided for in the law and if so, was the law legally proper? (The answers to these questions are still being argued today: at a joint meeting of the Kwakiutl District Council and the Musgamgw-Tsawataineuk Tribal Council in May 1988 a resolution was passed to support a "Specific Claim" for the return of all potlatch regalia taken in 1922.) Cranmer's query proved provocative for one of the students in the law class: deeply shocked by his research, he encouraged Cranmer to tell the story.

In the late 1960s the Kwakwaka'wakw were negotiating with the National Museums Corporation for the return of their potlatch treasures, and the band council in Alert Bay asked Cranmer to attend the meetings as their representative. Accepting the invitation, Cranmer proceeded to work hard for their recovery. Finally, in

*Gloria Cranmer Webster, left, with her mother, Agnes Cranmer.* (COURTESY VICKIE JENSEN, VANCOUVER)

1970 the Board of Trustees of the National Museums agreed to return that part of the potlatch collection held by the National Museum of Man, conditional on the construction of museums at Alert Bay and Cape Mudge. In 1975 Cranmer resigned her position at the UBC museum and returned home to Alert Bay. Her family and the elders helped her to learn the kinds of things she needed to know to work toward the building of a cultural centre. Cranmer, with the community, orchestrated the development of the museum and after five years of fever-pitched work, the U'mista Cultural Centre opened on November 1, 1980.

The occasion was heralded with ceremony and dancing for it was a time of great joy; it was "U'mista," meaning the return of something important. In times past, people were sometimes captured by raiding parties. When they were returned to their homes, whether through payment of ransom or by a retaliatory raid, they were said to have U'mista. The return of the potlatch collections from distant museums is a kind of U'mista.

The museum itself is modelled on a traditional Kwakwaka'wakw Big House and is built of cedar post-and-beam construction with rough-hewn cedar walls and ceiling. The individual potlatch items, so long locked away, are placed around the sides of the Big House in the order in which they would have appeared in a traditional potlatch. The focus of the U'mista Cultural Centre, however, is much more than a museum. It serves as an educational and resource centre where the young people come to learn of their historical roots and study their language and culture. Cranmer acted as the curator of the U'mista Cultural Centre for over ten years; during that time, the centre produced two documentary films — *Potlatch: A Strict Law Bids Us Dance* and *Box of Treasures* — and published the translation and transcription of Kwakwala material for use in local schools, and a series of Kwakwala language books. Transcribing Kwakwala into textual material was not an easy task, for the Roman alphabet cannot script the sounds of Kwakwala. Cranmer, working with Jay Powell, developed the spelling system that is used by the U'mista Cultural Centre.

Today the centre acts as a resource and lending library. It also hosts an Aboriginal Cultural Stewardship Program, which trains First Nations people in the field of museum studies, and acts as a source of information on the establishment and operation of cultural centres and museums to aboriginal groups from all over North America and the Pacific Rim. The centre has developed a Talking Kwakwala

Dictionary and language-retention programs, and it is also featured as one of the Aboriginal Cultural Centres on Schoolnet, an on-line information service for students from kindergarten to grade 12. People come from all over the world to visit the centre. The guest books indicate that over 6,000 people went through its doors in 1997 alone. The Kwakwaka'wakw came very close to losing their language and culture and the U'mista Cultural Centre has become a place where they can rebuild their cultural heritage.

Cranmer is proud of the centre. "With the U'mista Centre perhaps we can help our children find their real identity and they will be proud of it .... When we look at the way our children are learning to dance we are proud .... This centre has helped us celebrate the fact that we are still here, that we survive, that we continue to survive. We will always be here."[23] Cranmer is now retired although she continues to work in cultural rehabilitation. In the early 1990s one of the most comprehensive collections of any North American aboriginal group was assembled in an exhibition at the American Museum of Natural History in New York. Cranmer assisted in the translation of the Kwakwala documentation and curated a major part of the exhibition titled "Chiefly Feasts: The Enduring Kwakiutl Potlatch." A magnificent book of the same name, showcasing the exhibit, was published in 1991. Cranmer also worked with a designer and curator on the exhibit for the interior of the Wakas House in the Grand Hall of the Canadian Museum of Civilization in Hull.

In 1986 Cranmer attended a conference on the relationship between museums and indigenous people, sponsored by UNESCO, in northern Sweden. There she met Shigeru Kayano, an Ainu leader who has contributed much to Ainu cultural revitalization. The Ainu are an aboriginal group in Japan who have suffered the same kind of cultural discrimination as Canada's First Nations. Kayano was interested in developing an Ainu cultural centre similar to the U'mista Cultural Centre. Cranmer visited him several times in Nibutani, a traditional Ainu village, and in turn Kayano, along with a group of Ainu, has visited Alert Bay to learn how to develop their own cultural centre.

In 1995 Cranmer received an honorary Doctor of Laws from the University of British Columbia for her work in the regeneration of Kwakwala language and culture. She continues to participate on museum planning boards across the nation and internationally, and to write articles on the potlatch and the Kwakwaka'wakw Nation. Because of Cranmer, people from all over the world are better able to know and understand the rich history of the Kwakwaka'wakw. Children from

Alert Bay can practise their traditional songs and dances, learn their language, attend potlatches and watch the dancers wearing the Crooked-Beak and Raven masks that snap their beaks crying out "Hap! hap!" And the old people now have a place to go to tell their stories, knowing that their narratives will forever be among the box of treasures that will serve to strengthen those who come after them.

On the occasion of the opening of the U'mista Cultural Centre, Agnes Alfred, a member of the Kwakwaka'wakw Nation, summarized her feelings about the potlatch by saying, "When one's heart is glad, he gives away gifts. It was given to us by our Creator to be our way of doing things, to be our way of rejoicing, we who are Indian. The potlatch was given to us to be our way of expressing joy."[24]

\* \* \*

During the first three decades of the 20th century thousands of women belonged to and supported women's organizations. Women hoped to show through their support of these groups that they had the knowledge to reform and nurture the basic institutions in British Columbia. Many believed that the best way to achieve their goals was to seek full political participation through citizenship and being able to vote. The push toward obtaining the vote was not necessarily the sole purpose of these organizations, but it was certainly viewed as a means to an end. Women throughout the history of the province have worked collectively, and some individually, for the betterment of their communities.

In the closing years of the 20th century women still struggle to reconcile activities outside the home with traditional roles, but we have also emerged as a powerful organized force for positive change in our communities and around the world. Today, women are dealing with issues around reproductive health and violence against women. We are bringing our unique life experiences, concerns and perspectives to the problems of the environment. Women are becoming consumer activists and are making connections with other women on a global scale, through organizations such as the Women's Congress for a Healthy Planet, the Women's Tribunal on Crimes Against Women and Women's Voices. We are helping to put women's concerns on the international agenda. We are still grappling with the issues of power and politics but we have pushed ourselves beyond the limits that once defined us and in so doing are changing ourselves and the world we live in.

CHAPTER THREE

# WOMEN IN ART AND LITERATURE

ALTHOUGH THE CRITICS debate the notion of what constitutes British Columbia art and literature, there is no question that when one looks to the artistic production of BC today, there exists a self-confident cultural community. This was not always the case, however. Isolation and marginality were dominant themes in the history of art and literature in the province until recently. The arts are basically an urban phenomenon, needing the intellectual stimulation found in cities for inventiveness, refinement and dynamism. Culturally, BC existed primarily as a hinterland until the 1960s, depending on imports for artistic nourishment. People did hang pictures in their homes and the province did have its poets and novelists but art and literature were basically activities of consumption, not of production.

\*\*\*

When Louis Jacques Mandé Daguerre of France succeeded in securing an image on silver-plated copper in 1839 and William Henry Fox Talbot of England developed a negative/positive process on paper at the same time, the art of photography was born.

Without established paradigms, photography became the province of the amateur. Women, who in the 1840s were not expected to have a profession or succeed at endeavours outside the home, found in this new medium a way in which they could employ their creative talents. Some women, despite the dictates of the time, were able to make their photography known; others worked in the obscurity of their homes, finding quiet satisfaction in their vocation.

These early photographers shared a fierce single-mindedness centred on their art. Photographic processes were cumbersome, needing long exposure times; they were sensitive to temperature variation, and lighting was guesswork. Nonetheless, women set up studios and took portraits of prominent citizens and workers alike, creating an archive for historical reference.

Photography has proved to be a productive medium for some of British Columbia's accomplished artists and will continue to be so as long as women keep on looking through lenses in the process of constructing creative vision.

## Hannah Maynard
### 1834 - 1918

In the British Columbia Archives sit 18 binders holding some 10,000 photographs, taken by Hannah and Richard Maynard, that document Victoria and its residents from 1862 to 1912. The Maynards were both professional photographers but, although they were husband and wife, they did not occupy the same studio. They sometimes worked as a team but each had their own style. Richard's main income came from the boot, shoe and leather store he owned but he also earned money as a landscape photographer. Maynard had taught her husband the art of photography and he in turn encouraged her to open a business of her own. She was widely respected as a portrait photographer and her studio was one of the most highly regarded in Victoria.

Photography was only 20 years old when Maynard began learning the labour-intensive art of applying guncotton and ether, which was a highly explosive viscous liquid called "collodion," to capture images on glass plates. She was the first female professional photographer in British Columbia and one of extraordinary talent and photographic vision, 20 to 30 years ahead of her time. Her work was often praised in newspapers and professional magazines. The *St. Louis & Canadian Photographer*, a highly esteemed journal, wrote,

"Mrs. Maynard is one of the most industrious and preserving ladies we have in our business. She stops at no impediment, in our Art, but is a regular go-ahead, even beating our Yankee girls two to one in photography."[1]

Maynard was a mother, wife, photographer, traveller and entrepreneur. She was robust in health and determined in character and had a good sense of humour. Always curious, she tested and stretched her skills, and people seemed to like her. She was prim and neat in her appearance but, while some of her clients may have dressed according to Weldon's Practical Fancy Dress for Ladies and Gentlemen, she did not, choosing instead to wear black which created a sombre appearance.

Maynard was born in 1834 in Bude, Cornwall, in the south of England. At 18 years of age she married her childhood sweetheart, Richard James Maynard, who was then a 21-year-old apprentice bootmaker. Richard loved wilderness and exploration and thought he would like to be a seaman. In fact, for a time he worked as a bootmaker in the winter and in the coasting trade in the summer. One of his dreams was to sail across the Atlantic to the New World, and soon after their marriage, in 1852, the Maynards emigrated to Canada. There certainly was opportunity for anyone willing to work in the new land but it was most likely Richard's adventurous spirit that was the motivating factor in their decision to move to Canada.

The Maynards spent their first ten years in Canada in Bowmanville, Ontario, and to all appearances they were happily settled in their new country. Richard opened his own boot shop and it was not long before there were four new sets of small feet running around: George, Albert, Zela, and Emma Jane. Lillian, their youngest, would be born later, a few years after their move to Victoria. The excitement of pioneering and trailblazing continued to be a source of wonder for Richard and when tales of the 1858 Fraser River Gold Rush reached Bowmanville, they sparked his dreams. The newspapers painted enticing pictures of the gold rush and captured the imagination of 30,000 North Americans. The instant gold towns of Fort Hope, Yale, Boston Bar and Lytton were filled with swaggering men, disgruntled miners, hurdy-gurdy girls, and get-rich-quick merchants who sometimes charged up to $100 for a bag of flour. Richard knew that he wanted to join the gold rush, so he packed his bags and bade his family a temporary farewell.

While Richard was panning for gold, Maynard set about developing her own talents and studied photography with, it is believed,

R. & H. O'Hara of Bowmanville. When Richard came home he had gold dust in his pockets, for he had done well in the gold fields. His experience had only served to whet his appetite, so it's not surprising that shortly after his return, they sold the family interests, packed, and moved to the frontier of British Columbia. This new colony, unpolished yet rich in resources, had much to offer someone of Richard's disposition. Maynard seemed not to mind the inconvenience or the hardship of the move, and said as much in a newspaper interview years later.

The family arrived in Victoria in 1862, via the Isthmus of Panama. When Maynard first set foot on the dusty streets of Victoria she had forever left behind the urban sophistication and civility of Ontario. Before her lay a small outpost town which boasted 37 brick buildings along with an array of wooden buildings, wooden sidewalks, a few gas lanterns, makeshift tent camps and a harbour full of three-masted schooners. This was a man's town, populated by miners, gold seekers, mariners and pioneers, mingling in the saloons and sporting houses with ladies of the night. Maynard left little in the way of personal journals and her recorded statements were generally matter of fact. Of Victoria, she said that the city consisted "of tents, gullies and swamps and the inhabitants mostly miners."[2] She had hardly dusted herself off and unpacked before Richard was off to the Stikine River to try his hand at placer mining.

Undaunted by being left alone in an untamed environment, Maynard proceeded to open her own portrait studio on Johnson Street near Douglas. She called it "Mrs. R. Maynard's Photographic Gallery." Maynard had a good business sense and was supported and encouraged in this endeavour by her husband before he left. Although she was one of several professional photographers in Victoria, there were many miners and sailors passing through who were eager to have their portraits done. Victoria was ripe for another photographic studio.

It is difficult to know how Maynard, as a businesswoman, was at first received. Her entry into the business world would certainly have been considered rather daring for a woman in 1862. There was a kind of ethereal mystique surrounding the women of the mid-1800s. They were considered to have fragile minds which were not easily given to intellectual discipline. It was thought that the demands of the business world would tax them beyond their endurance, corrupt them and lead to their demise. But this was the frontier, with transitory relations and shifting values, so there was some latitude for unusual behaviour. Maynard did admit that there were some objections to her being a woman in business, but she said she got around the disapproval by initially crediting her husband with her work. A journalist working for *The Victoria Colonist* interviewed Maynard upon her retirement, for by then she was quite a well-known and respected photographer. He wrote that when she opened her studio she "was for a long time boycotted by the public .... Until Victoria got used to a woman photographer, Mr. Maynard frequently pretended that he had taken the pictures, whereas in actual fact it was his wife who had done the job."[3] She claimed distress at having to hide behind her husband because as a photographer in her own right, she did not want to work in his shadow. However, she felt that until she became known, propriety dictated this gentle prevarication.

Maynard's story is intriguing for there is some speculation as to the truth of her account. Some modern critics believe that while she may have experienced discrimination during her early years as a photographer, she was overstating those difficulties in order to cover up the fact that she had taken credit for some of the landscape photos taken by her husband. In truth, Maynard did take many landscape shots along with Richard, and unfortunately, they didn't always sign their photographs. There are a few photos in the Maynard collection that are labelled "? Maynard," indicating uncertainty as to their authorship. Did she really take credit for pictures that Richard took? It's doubtful if the matter will ever be clarified but it doesn't much matter because her professionalism and her genius were well demonstrated.

When Maynard began taking pictures she did not have the benefit of automatic light meters or even a body of knowledge to draw upon to help attain consistency of exposures. The cameras of the late 1800s were gangly and heavy. As a portrait photographer Maynard used various kinds of fixed portrait cameras, her artistic daring and ingenuity co-existing with the fumbling and guessing that was inevitable with early photography. Her understanding of lighting was nothing short of extraordinary and her work reveals a gifted and inquisitive nature and an indomitable vitality. Initially, Maynard concentrated on conventional portraiture in the style of the time, but her work was engaging and her studio settings ingenious. She hand-crafted pastoral scenes, staged ocean and beach backdrops, and fashioned park-like settings, but always her camera focussed on the subjects, providing documentary evidence of their lives. In this she was different from her colleagues who often draped their portraits in artificial romanticism, which had the tendency to draw attention away from the person and toward the realm of the mythical.

Critics heralded Maynard's photography as being decades ahead of the style of her time. She had a remarkable ability to see and value the shape of a thing in itself. Through her photographs it is possible to sense the muddied and rutted streets in Victoria, the economic vibrancy of the community, the intemperance of miners coming out of saloons having spent their last dollar on whisky, or the cultural juxtaposition between the First Nations peoples, the British *nouveau* aristocracy, the merchants and the Chinese indentured workers, all mingling yet separate. Maynard photographed the young officers of the British Royal Navy with their straight-set caps, or bristling to attention to the commands of the master, and Victorian gentleladies enjoying a Monet-type picnic or sipping lemonade on the verandah on a warm summer's day. She recorded the turn-of-the-century bicycle craze and wrenched hearts with her photos of the 1887 mining disaster in Nanaimo. In reference to that tragic event, the *St. Louis & Canadian Photographer* wrote, "[Her] pictures are all well taken, but bring too vividly to mind the sufferings of the broken-hearted wives and children of the dead miners."[4]

In 1897 Maynard became the official photographer for the Victoria police department and for the next five years documented the likes of murderers, burglars, larcenists, muggers and fraud artists. All who were arrested were marched down the street to her studio. Among her customers were several tough and beguiling girls and a large number of children, many arrested for theft. Her portfolio was heavily loaded with Chinese men, who were considered antisocial. There was a Caucasian man who was sentenced to two years in jail for stealing eight dollars from a Native person; a woman charged with stealing $220 in 1902 from a man named Amos Coppermill; a Chinese man sentenced in 1889 to three years for breaking and entering and stealing ten dollars from three different stores on Fort Street; and a woman sentenced to six months for obtaining money by false pretences.

Perhaps Maynard's most famous client was the fashionable Belle Adams, convicted in 1898 of manslaughter. *The Victoria Colonist*, reporting the event in June of that year, wrote, "Nine o'clock last evening was the time of this latest tragedy of which unbridled passion and mad jealousy constitute the cause, and the scene of the horrible deed that cost Charles Kincaid his life was a first floor front room in the Empire Hotel on Johnson Street. Here the woman, frenzied by the fear that her unrestrained and unnatural affection for a man not of her own race or color was no longer returned, half-severed his head from his body with a razor. Kincaid, Charlie Brown, as he was called in Victoria, was wounded to death, staggered down the stairs and into the street, where he fell, and within a few moments gave up his life."[5] Despite the deed, when it came time for Belle to have her picture taken she made sure she was well dressed for the photo. She wore a large hat, smartly tilted to one side, and her hair was neatly turned back and secured with a large bow. She was sentenced to five years in jail.

As Maynard's infamous clients posed for their photographs they were paying silent testimony to a city in a state of transition. By the early 1890s Victoria gave the impression of being a city of prosperity. There was street lighting and streetcar service (free to new home-owners), downtown had changed from a small collection of wooden buildings to a city constructed of brick and stone, a wealthy class had emerged and Oak Bay had become an exclusive suburb. But underneath this apparent prosperity lay a city in crisis. Its traditional economic base in maritime shipping was threatened and the bottom of the market dropped out of the manufacturing industry. The city was hit by a depression. Businesses closed their doors, people found themselves without employment, and crime was on the rise.

By the time Maynard reached middle age her photographic style had changed. She began investigating different techniques, improvising as she went along. From about 1880 to 1895 she experimented with double images, collage photography, photomontages, photosculpture and bas-relief. Her critics were contemptuous, referring to her images as freaks and tricks, nothing more than recreational photography which was allied neither with commercial concerns nor with art. By the late 19th century artists were beginning to stretch the boundaries of art, searching for new and innovative forms, but if their work did not follow conventional design they were not able to exhibit in official salon showings. If photography was to be an art it must look like established art, and multiple images and photomontages were not considered art by the pundits of the time. Even Maynard's longtime supporter, the *St. Louis & Canadian Photographer,* referred to her multiple images as being "of the freak order."[6]

In spite of such insults, Maynard persisted and eventually burst forth with a creative vitality that put her in the forefront of photographic and technical imagery. Her critics now referred to her as a genius. Maynard's talent was most evident in her photomontages of children. She made minute tintypes of children that could be mounted in a ring or brooch and, beginning in 1880, she produced an annual series which she called "Gems of British Columbia." She re-photographed all of the portraits of children she had taken during the year, composing them into fanciful images. She had hundreds of tiny faces peering out of cornucopias or shaped into sprays of droplets shooting from a fountain. One of her Gems included 22,000 little faces, some so small that to see them people needed a magnifying glass. Maynard became well known for her Gems and mailed them to the parents of the children whose pictures appeared in the montages.

Maynard also experimented with photosculpture in which the model appeared to be a living statue. She referred to these photos as "Living Statuary." These photosculptures were eerie and surreal. Her technique was clever. Maynard had her models pose behind a white paper-maché bust, and covered their hair, eyebrows and clothing in a white powder. She used a black cloth to cover up various parts of the body, creating a truncated effect. Maynard also added photo embossing to her portfolio. She hand-tooled the backs of the prints with a bone or ivory paper knife and then filled the raised portions with plaster-of-paris or paper maché. These "photos" are particularly interesting because there are very few successful examples of bas-relief in existence.

Maynard's step into the surreal was not only a natural expansion of her technical and artistic talents but also a move into the realm of the spiritual. White ghostly or spirit figures started showing up in her montages. She portrayed young boys as grave diggers and weeping girls as spirit figures. Several tragedies befell Maynard that could easily have sent her in this direction. She first lost her youngest daughter Lillian to typhoid in 1883. Lillian was only 16 at the time of her death. Five years later Emma, her second daughter, died in a drowning accident and then, in 1892, her daughter-in-law, Adelaide, also drowned. To Maynard death must have seemed relentless, stripping her of her loved ones one by one. After Adelaide's death the Maynards took their grandson in to live with them because his father was an alcoholic. Lilly, Emma and Adelaide appeared in nearly all of Maynard's later surreal work. Her studio was an icon to the deceased; there were pillows with embroidered portraits of Lilly and Emma, their images were imprinted on plates

*Hannah Maynard's "Gems"* CA. *1891, on a dieffenbachia plant. The little faces are from Maynard's earlier Gems from 1881 to 1883. The scene on the pot is a photograph of The Gorge, a local waterway.* (COURTESY BC ARCHIVES, E-09401)

and they were immortalized in a framed portrait juxtaposed with a photo of the family burial plot. After the death of Lillian, Maynard started attending seances and joined the very popular Spiritualist movement. Perhaps this attempt to reach out to her loved ones in seances, and memorializing them in surreal artistry, helped sustain her in her bereavement.

It would not have been considered eccentric to attach oneself to Spiritualism, since as a movement it was quite trendy; even the mayor of Victoria was a member of the Spiritualist cult. The late 19th century was an age when artists, writers and others were exploring the accidental and the incongruous. People felt free to expand their once-rigid cultural boundaries. Spiritualism was something new and part of this exploration. Not all people were comfortable with this new direction; some felt it a threat to their established views of the world and it was firmly denounced from church pulpits. Edward Cridge, Dean of Christ Church Cathedral in Victoria, delivered a stinging address about Spiritualism from the pulpit, one Sunday in July 1870. He preached, "We need not enter into the question whether the professed intercourse with departed spirits is real, or pretended; or whether modern 'spiritualism' is only a system devised by men to obtain notoriety, procure gain, or to

*Hannah Maynard and her nephew, Maynard MacDonald (who is also the white bust), in a collage. The framed portraits are of deceased family members. Top to bottom: Lillian, Adelaide and Emma Maynard.* (Courtesy BC Archives, F-05095)

prejudice godliness. It is sufficient for the thoughtful mind to know that the practice is impious, and unlawful, displeasing to God, and destructive to religion in the soul."[7]

Maynard's most ingenious photos were her multiple images. For these she often turned the camera on herself and produced several delightful series of whimsical pictures. She must have been heavier than she desired, for in her self-portraits she executed her photographic wizardry and gave herself an hour-glass figure. It was said that she had a mocking, even gallows, sense of humour. In one well-known photo, depicting afternoon tea, she is the genteel server, the somewhat arrogant guest and the perpetrator of a practical joke in which she appears as a painting leaning outside the frame to pour a cup of tea on the head of her guest self. Canadian photo-historian David Mattison called her multiple exposures the most accomplished of her experimental work. He felt that she had a technical and artistic maturity that few of her contemporaries in Canada could equal.

Maynard was a good businesswoman and an active promoter of her photography. She made sure the Victoria newspapers received many samples of her work and was a regular contributor to the *St. Louis & Canadian Photographer*. Maynard continually perfected her advertising and she moved her studio four times, always to a better location. On one occasion she ran an ad for two years, notifying people of her new address. Maynard's gallery was described in an 1888 edition of the Winnipeg *New West Magazine*: "She possesses superior facilities for executing all orders in the promptest and most satisfactory manner, and her photographic work cannot be excelled for brilliancy of expression or harmony of effect .... She is recognized as one of the foremost representatives of the profession in the country."[8] A photograph of the interior of her Pandora Avenue studio shows a friendly and welcoming waiting room, not unlike the proprietress. Vases filled with lilies are set about the office, and pots of plants and a large dieffenbachia add to the decor. A hand-carved screen by her desk has hundreds of photos displayed on it. Various statues grace the office and a fur rug softens the floor.

It is easy to concentrate solely on Maynard's photography and forget her travelling adventures. She sailed from England to Canada as a newly married young woman, pregnant with her first child, and later from Toronto to Victoria with four young children in tow. In a newspaper interview she said, "Even today it is rather remarkable to hear of a woman going into the great beyond of the interior country, but then I thought nothing of it."[9] In September 1875, she and

Richard went on a holiday by the mail steamer *Salvador* to San Francisco. In August 1884 they booked passage on the steamer *Princess Louise* for a trip around Vancouver Island to photograph the scenery. Richard travelled a great deal, even going as far as the Pribilof Islands in the Bering Sea. Not to be outdone by her husband Maynard sailed on her own in 1888 to the Queen Charlotte Islands.

While she kept diaries of these trips they were mostly cryptic writings about the weather, places visited or people's state of health aboard the ship. Richard apparently was prone to seasickness and on their journey to San Francisco she wrote in her journal, "[Richard] sick to-day, I have not been yet."[10] Her writings on her circumnavigation of Vancouver Island were a bit more descriptive. The entry for Saturday, August 16, was, "Lovely morning so we were called early to get up. We are now on top of a high rock taking a view of the indian camp whilst [Richard] down to his tent, me on the top with the cameras. 3 indians came up with nothing on but a piece of old blanket, however they did not kill me. We took two negatives when the whistle blew for the starting, so it was pack up and off for the steamer."[11]

When Richard retired from his photography and the boot business in the late 1890s he lived the life of a gentlemanly patriarch, being cared for and fussed over by his family, and died in January 1907 at the age of 74. He left his business to their son

*Hannah Maynard in her studio,* CA. *1894.* (COURTESY BC ARCHIVES, F-05033)

Albert who was well qualified, having managed it for 30 years. Albert was also a photographer. Maynard continued working until 1912 when she disposed of her photographic equipment to a Chinese photographer named Peter. At the end of her 50-year career she said, "I think I can say with every confidence that we photographed everyone in town at one time or another."[12] Hannah Maynard died on May 15, 1918, at the age of 84.

It is possible that without Maynard's determination and dedication, much of Victoria's early history would not have been so carefully documented. There are numerous books that describe the city's growth, but to really understand a community in the making it helps to look beyond those time-worn annals and study its imagery and form as reflected in the photographs of its early residents. Among the best documentation of those early times is the photographic images taken by Hannah Maynard.

\* \* \*

In the late 1800s, amateur and touring companies were the mainstay of the arts for many early British Columbians. It was a hard life, travelling by buckboard over washboard roads, sleeping in dingy hotels, never sure where the next meal was coming from and performing in less than desirable places like barns, church halls, tents, saloons and grain elevators. Pauline Johnson, dressed as an Indian princess, entertained her way through much of the province's territory, and of the many musicians, magicians, comics and lecturers who travelled beyond the reach of the railway, she alone is remembered, not so much for her verse but for her allure. She was the darling of the stage and for British Columbians she symbolized the energy of the frontier.

Although Pauline Johnson spent only the last few years of her life in Vancouver, her stage presentations throughout BC endeared her to the people of the province and they claimed her as their own.

Pauline Johnson (Tekahionwake)
1861 - 1913

She sleeps betwixt the mountains and the sea,
In that great Abbey of the setting sun:
A Princess, Poet, Woman, three in one;
And fine in every measure of the three.[13]

It has been 85 years since Pauline Johnson died, and yet her legacy as a poet, storyteller and balladeer lives on. She is something of an enigma for late 20th-century critics who tend to look for reality in their poetry, and demand a literature that is full of intellectual and philosophical messages. Although highly regarded, Johnson has never been venerated as a first-rate poet. She left no lasting messages nor did she endeavour to change the world. She was a lyricist and her poetry was expressive, exuding a vitality that evoked great empathy and passion among her audiences. Through her literary recitals Johnson was able to whisk her listeners away from the mundane to ethereal planes. She sang about the beauty of Canada and the richness of its colour, and celebrated its diversity. She wrote of honour, truth and pride, and deftly entwined Native lore with British culture. Her own objective, she always said, was simply to "set people on fire."

Johnson was a mistress of the soliloquy and a genius in stage presentation. Her audiences adored her and the mere mention of the famous Pauline Johnson would have the public competing for tickets. Although she would appear in beautiful gowns that were the height of European fashion and enchant theatre-goers with her rhymes, alliterative music and sweetly flowing rhythm, she was just as likely to sweep onto the stage with a war whoop, costumed in full Native regalia. Her audiences loved it and would erupt into clamorous applause.

One of Johnson's costumes consisted of a buckskin outfit which she wore over a red cashmere dress. She trimmed the sleeves with ermine, fastened silver brooches to the bodice and wore a red blanket casually over her left shoulder. Although this costume was a fabrication of her own design and not an authentic copy of her Métis heritage, most of the decorative items were of special significance to her. The brooches were family heirlooms that had been crafted from silver coins. The red cape was a ceremonial blanket used when her father and grandfather initiated the Duke of Connaught into the Council of the Six Nations. Around Johnson's waist was a belt of wampum, given to her by the Blackfoot, into which she tucked her father's knife. Whenever Johnson recited "Ojistoh," a ballad about a woman who stabbed an enemy warrior with his own knife, she would pull out her knife and brandish it for effect. She sported a necklace of bear claws and hung two human scalps from her waist. One was Huron, which she had inherited from her great-grandfather, Jacob Tekahionwake, and one was

Sioux, given to her by a Blackfoot chief. It was with this manner of adornment that Johnson would begin to weave her spell.

As the audience hushed she would raise her voice with a force that was reported to "hold the echoes of both the forest and river"[14] and recite "The Red Girl's Reasoning," or "Cry for an Indian Wife," or her most famous poem, "The Song My Paddle Sings." Her eloquence, beauty and gentle swaying would mesmerize the audience and move them into the characters of her text. One of Johnson's contemporaries said of her effect, "A graceful figure, and pleasing face, prepossess the audience at once. The warmth of feeling, the unstudied utterance, the alternate fire and softness of her intonations, the apt appealing gestures, all tell of the hereditary instinct of eloquence, which has come down to her from a line of chiefs and councillors with whom persuasive oratory was the very life and mainspring of tribal policies."[15]

Pauline Johnson was Métis, born in 1861 of a Mohawk father and an English mother. Her father, George Henry Johnson, was a chief and a distinguished leader of the Six Nations. He was an accomplished orator, fluent in several languages, and served as an interpreter for the local Anglican mission near Brantford, Ontario, where he met Johnson's mother. Emily Howell was an English-born Quaker who gave Johnson her love of Keats, Scott, Longfellow and Byron. Both her parents were well read and encouraged Johnson to read and memorize poetry.

Johnson grew up on the Six Nations Reserve with her three siblings. She spent her early years happily roaming around Chiefswood, their home of 200 acres, overlooking the Grand River valley. Early formal schooling was reserved for her brothers so Johnson stayed at home and refined her needlework, honed her archery and worked at becoming skilled in canoeing and woodcraft. One of her favourite pastimes was listening to the stories told by her grandfather, Chief John "Smoke" Johnson. Chief Smoke Johnson had a reputation as a great orator and often regaled his young granddaughter with tales of battle and courage, and Mohawk legends and history. It was from him that Johnson developed her understanding of the rhythm and drama which her audiences came to love. She treasured the times that she could spend in reading and writing poetry. She could often be found floating down the river in her canoe, reading a book of verse or reciting her own poems to her dog, Chip.

In 1884, when Johnson was 23, her idyllic life came to an abrupt end because her father died. The family received a small inheritance but it was not enough to maintain their beloved Chiefswood. Johnson's mother decided that the best course of action would be to rent their home and move into a small apartment in Brantford. It also became imperative for all members of the family to seek some form of employment.

For Johnson there could be only one thing: writing. She began sending her poetry to magazines and newspapers, and found that her poems were readily published. It was not long before she was known as a poet but the money she earned was not enough to enable her to be self-supporting. Until she became financially independent, Johnson had to look to her sister and mother for her livelihood, and she and her sister had many arguments over her choice of profession. Her sister was more practical and felt that Johnson should seek employment in an office where she could be assured of a steady income. Johnson demurred and the ensuing disagreement created a rift between the two sisters that lasted the rest of their lives.

Shortly after her father's death, Johnson was asked to write a poem by the Iroquois for a ceremonial re-burial of nine Seneca chiefs. She felt deeply honoured, particularly as one of the chiefs, Red-Jacket, had been among the most famous of the Seneca orators. For the occasion Johnson wrote "The Re-Interment of Red-Jacket." The poem represented the notions of nobility and rightful redress of past wrongs, a theme that was to fill some of her later work. The final stanza reads:

> And so ere Indian summer sweetly sleeps
> She beckons me where old Niagara leaps;
> Superbly she extends her greeting hand,
> And, smiling, speaks to their adopted land,
> Saying, 'O, rising nation of the West,
> That occupy my lands so richly blest;
> O, free, unfettered people that have come
> And made America your rightful home —
> Forgive the wrongs my children did to you,
> And we, the red-skins, will forgive you too.
> To-day has seen your noblest action done —
> The honored reintombment of my son.'[16]

In 1889 Johnson vaulted into the limelight when two of her poems were included in a Canadian anthology edited by William Lighthall of Montreal. Lighthall's book, *Songs of the Great Dominion*, was reviewed by Theodore Watts-Dutton, an important literary critic in England. Watts-Dutton praised Johnson's poetry for its freshness in *The Athenaeum*, a well-known literary magazine whose harsh criticisms were world renowned. To be acknowledged

*Pauline Johnson.* (Courtesy BC Archives, A-09684)

and accepted in a journal of such distinction was an important step for any writer. Johnson's path as a poet was assured.

The event that sent her on her way as a literary performer was an appearance she made before the Young Liberal Society of Toronto in 1892. In an attempt to stimulate interest in the social functions of the society, Frank Yeigh, then president of the Young Liberals, invited several eminent Canadian poets to give readings of their works. Although Johnson had been publishing her poetry in the leading journals of the time she had not participated in a literary recital outside Brantford. She accepted the invitation but was apprehensive about her ability as an orator. The evening was going slowly until Johnson's recitation. As she glided onto the stage she immediately captivated her audience with the sweetness of her voice; she began with,

> They but forgot we Indians owned the land
> From ocean unto ocean: that they stand
> Upon the soil that centuries ago
> Was our sole kingdom and our right alone.[17]

Johnson electrified the audience with her readings and she alone was recalled, to thundering applause. *The Vancouver Province* must have had a writer at the performance for it reported, "Thrilling was the effect, dramatic the appeal of this dark-hued girl who seemed to personify her race. It was the Indian who spoke, the Indian woman, as with intense passion she voiced the cry of her kind."[18] Because the night was so successful, Frank Yeigh arranged a series of 125 recitals for Johnson during the 1893-94 season. She crisscrossed the country many times, giving shows in opera houses as well as local saloons. Her changing room might be a makeshift nook covered with Hudson's Bay blankets or a permanent theatre dressing-room flowing with silks and satins. It was not long before Johnson became the darling of Canada and was referred to as "the Mohawk Princess." She eventually added Tekahionwake, the name of her great-grandfather, to her own.

In 1893 Johnson travelled to England for the publication of her first book, *The White Wampum*. To become successful as a Canadian author and avoid the stigma of a colonial usually meant being published by established foreign companies. Johnson took London by storm. For Londoners who thought of Canada as a physical and cultural wasteland, Johnson brought the voice of a cultured and talented country. She played to sold-out houses, and society women vied with each other to have her perform in their drawing rooms.

Upon her return to Canada, Johnson continued to work hard, performing and publishing. Her second book of verse, *Canadian Born*, was published in 1903 and sold out within the year. Perhaps her two most notable books were *Flint and Feather* and *Legends of Vancouver*. *Flint and Feather* was a complete edition of her published poems. It was, she said, her gift to the Canadian people. "Flint suggests the Redman's weapons of war; it is the arrow tip, the heart-quality of mine own people; let it therefore apply to those poems that touch upon Indian life and love. The lyrical verse herein is as a 'Skyward floating feather, Sailing on summer air.' And yet that feather may be the eagle plume that crests the head of a warrior chief; so both flint and feather bear the hall-mark of my Mohawk blood."[19] Her book was exceedingly popular, going though several reprints. *Legends of Vancouver,* a compilation of stories about the mountains, forests, rivers and streams of Vancouver, honoured her long-time friend, Chief Joe Capilano of the Coast Salish. Still in demand, *Legends of Vancouver* was published in its latest edition by Douglas & McIntyre in 1997.

Johnson's love of British Columbia drew her time and again to perform here. She played to many audiences in the province, often giving her proceeds to charity. In 1903 she travelled 140 kilometres up the Cariboo Trail, giving performances at roadhouses, taverns and small communities. By this time Johnson had spent 17 years on the road and was becoming weary of her nomadic life. She yearned to settle down, continue her writing and perhaps give an occasional performance, and in 1909 she gave her last show, in Kamloops. She moved into a room on Howe Street in Vancouver and unpacked her trunk for the last time.

Unfortunately, Johnson's life in Vancouver was brief. Breast cancer forced her into a Bute Street hospital for care. Her illness began taking its toll and, unable to write as much as she had hoped, she became desperately short of money. She had been working toward the publication of *Legends of Vancouver* but was too ill to complete the task. Johnson never complained and in fact, spent her time worrying over others less fortunate. As for her impending death, Johnson was pragmatic. She said, "When we are born into a world of sorrow, everyone rejoices; but when we die and go to the happy hunting grounds everyone mourns. Well, I don't want even my best friends to mourn for me. If now and again the people of

*Pauline Johnson, 1903.* (Courtesy City of Vancouver Archives, Port. P. 1633, N. 957)

Canada read some line of my work, which brings home to them the love I have for this great country of mine, then they may remember me as having done my best to share with them something that the Great Tyee had given to me."[20] The only regret she expressed during her illness was her inability to write. She said that she was full of ideas but knew that she would never write again.

Knowing that Johnson's independence and strong pride would never allow her to accept any financial aid, her friends rallied around her and devised a way to help. A small group of newspaper people and representative members of the Vancouver Women's

Press Club and the Women's Canadian Club got together and established the Pauline Johnson Trust Fund. Through the fund they raised enough money for the initial printing of *Legends of Vancouver*. Out of the proceeds of the sales they were able to finance a larger publication, and the money earned by *Legends of Vancouver* was enough to sustain Johnson until her death. She lived long enough to enjoy the many letters she received from fans expressing their enjoyment of her new book, and never learned of the activities of her friends.

Pauline Johnson died on March 7, 1913. Flags were flown at half-mast in Vancouver and condolences came from the Prime Minister, the Royal Society of Canada, the Vancouver Women's Press Club, the Canadian Women's Press Club, the IODE and the Women's Canadian Club and many others. Thousands thronged the streets of Vancouver to watch the funeral cortege of "the Mohawk Princess."

Johnson's burial site is appropriately in a grove of trees at Ferguson Point in Stanley Park. Her expressed wish was that her ashes be buried in Stanley Park overlooking Siwash Rock, the sentinel at the First Narrows entrance to Burrard Inlet. Permission to bury Johnson within the park grounds had to be granted by the federal government and the Parks Board, and came just one day before her death. For Johnson, Siwash Rock epitomized her love of Vancouver, because it stood as a lasting monument to the beauty of British Columbia, her beloved province. Of Siwash Rock she wrote,

> Unique, and so distinct from its surroundings as to suggest rather the handicraft of man than a whim of Nature, it looms up at the entrance to the Narrows, a symmetrical column of solid gray stone. There are no similar formations within the range of vision, or indeed within many a day's paddle up and down the coast. Amongst all the wonders, the natural beauties that encircle Vancouver, the marvels of mountains, shaped into crouching lions and brooding beavers, the yawning canyons, the stupendous forest firs and cedars, Siwash Rock stands as distinct, as individual, as if dropped from another sphere.[21]

Johnson knew of British Columbians' love for her and requested that "... no tombstone or monument be raised in my memory, as I prefer to be remembered in the hearts of my people and my public."[22] Her ashes, together with copies of *Flint and Feather* and *Legends of Vancouver*, were placed between two white silk cushions in a concrete box. A boulder carved with her name marked her resting spot, and in 1922 a cairn was unveiled as a memorial to her. On it is a profile of Johnson embellished with a crossed feather, an arrow and a canoe. On the right side of the cairn is a reflective pool.

It might be tempting for literary authorities today to classify Pauline Johnson as merely a seductress of the stage, a pop diva of the late 1800s. Indeed, some of her harshest critics have tried to do just that but Johnson offered much more than simple enchantment. Perhaps more than any other person, she excited a feeling of Canadian national consciousness, long before such a thing was viewed as important. Her writings, laced as they were with patriotism and Native traditions, enabled Canadians to view themselves less from their parochial perspectives and more as part of a country rich in varied history and traditions. She helped her public see themselves as an integral part of a multicultural heritage, one to be explored and nourished. In 1961, 100 years after her birth, Pauline Johnson became the first Canadian writer to appear on a five-cent stamp.

* * *

In literature the first British Columbia women to achieve recognition were Emily Carr and Ethel Wilson. Emily Carr turned to writing when ill health curtailed her painting. She won the Governor General's Award for non-fiction for *Klee Wyck* in 1941, and before her death she had written three more books: *The Book of Small*, *The House of All Sorts*, and *Growing Pains*, all well received by an appreciative public. Ethel Wilson was celebrated as one of the best writers of English fiction of the 1950s. Wilson was particularly noted for her stance on the place of regionalism in writing. "I feel very strongly that the writing of Canadians should and must be Canadian in aspect," she once wrote, "but not deliberately so ... that is second-rate. But region — that's a different matter. I'm all against conscious nationality in a novel (for a novel is about people and is universal), and for regionalism, if region means a lot to the writer."[23] Wilson wrote in a regional sense, incorporating Lillooet, the Gulf Islands and Vancouver's West End into her novels. She won popular acclaim for *Hetty Dorval* published in 1947, *The Innocent Traveller* in 1949 and *Swamp Angel* in 1954.

Other women gained recognition as writers, critics and poets. In 1941 Dorothy Livesay, Anne Marriott, Doris Ferne and Floris McLaren produced *Contemporary Verse: A Canadian Quarterly*, among the best Canadian poetry magazines of the decade. In 1959 Sheila Watson ushered in contemporary writing in Canada with the publication of *The Double Hook*, a powerful novel set in the community of Lillooet which still commands literary attention to this day. The 1960s witnessed a new creative energy in poetry from a group of graduate students at the University of British Columbia. They mimeographed and distributed an innovative poetry newsletter called *Tish*. Its success in turn fostered *Canadian Literature, Prism*, and *The Malahat Review*. These literary magazines were uniquely British Columbian and underscored a significant change in the province. Fine literature no longer had to come from elsewhere. British Columbia was becoming known for its own literary tradition.

## Dorothy Livesay
## 1909 - 1996

Dorothy Kathleen May Livesay was born in Winnipeg on October 12, 1909, in a snowstorm. Livesay was a poet of prodigious talent who has been described as one of the finest lyricists of her generation. With her poetry, radio scripts, verse, plays and documentary studies, she helped forge a strong Canadian literary culture for over 60 years. She had a legion of persona; she was a poet, teacher, social worker, literary critic, anthologist, editor, fiction writer, social historian, journalist and activist.

Livesay lived at a time when there were few women poets and when being a woman meant having to contend for standing in the literary arena. Of this she wrote, "The other Canadian artists of my era were those men born soon after the turn of the century. No companion women poets were born until the end of the First World War .... So until they began to make their mark in the forties, I always had the feeling I was struggling alone to make a woman's voice heard. I admired the men, particularly those who encouraged me ... but I felt curiously detached from them in a literary and life-style sense."[24] Throughout her life Livesay received many honours, including the Governor General's Literary Award for Poetry, first in 1945 and then again in 1947, the Lorne Pierce Medal for Literature in 1947, the Order of British Columbia and the Order of Canada.

Livesay was a complex, multi-dimensional woman who lived a life of contrasts. She was at times Cinderella hoping for her Prince Charming to rescue her from the trials of life, and at other times a determined feminist fashioning new territory in the literary world.

Schooled to honour the values of conservatism and laissez-faire economics, she instead embraced the tenets of Marxist ideology and became a social activist who spent her time fighting for the rights of the working people. She was shy and socially awkward but sexually liberated, having taken many lovers; she grew up before the pro-choice era and yet went through the agonies of an abortion. She had a wanderlust, studying at the University of Aix-Marseilles in France, working in London and teaching in Zambia but when she first attended secondary school she was terrified. Because Livesay suffered from fragile health as a youngster and was considered delicate and high strung, she was kept at home and had little early formal education, yet she studied at top universities and earned many degrees in her lifetime. She received a BA from the University of Toronto, studied at the Sorbonne in Paris, earned a diploma in social work from the University of Toronto, received an M.Ed. from the University of British Columbia and was awarded an honorary Doctorate of Literature by the University of Waterloo.

Livesay's love of poetry and storytelling, her humanity and her stubborn refusal to give up in the face of calamitous events were inherited from her family. Both her parents were professional writers and for Livesay, typewriters clacking and manuscripts cast about the house were normal fare. Her early home life was intellectually stimulating, filled with a continual stream of visiting poets and writers who had concentrated discussions of literary works. Her father, John Frederick Bligh Livesay or JFB as she called him, was Livesay's strongest ally, encouraging her writing and giving her support when it most mattered. JFB was a newspaperman who worked as a reporter for the Winnipeg *Telegram* and as a general manager with the Western Associated Press. He was a war correspondent during the First World War and a founder of the Canadian Press agency where he was the manager for 20 years.

Despite an outwardly authoritarian manner, JFB felt very strongly that gifted women should be encouraged and appreciated. He was a liberal romantic who introduced his young daughter to progressive women writers. Referring to her father Livesay wrote, "Indeed, he was probably the only parent in the city of Toronto in the twenties who combined a passion for Henry James with a passion for women novelists: Jane Austen, Charlotte Bronte, Virginia Woolf and Katherine Mansfield. It was a somewhat precious, specialized reading. The social frustrations women faced in the nineteenth century were no less galling than the social freedoms of the twentieth; in neither case could a woman be wholly a human being. For an Englishman, my father was unusually sensitive to this problem."[25] This environment created in Livesay an independence of thought and the conviction that she was the equal of any man.

Livesay's mother, Florence Hamilton Randal Livesay, was appropriately Victorian in her manner and staunchly religious. She was educated in English, French and music, and had been a teacher of Latin and French. In her own way Livesay's mother was a feminist, but one restricted by time and circumstance. Before her marriage to JFB, Florence Randal was a reporter for *The Ottawa Journal.* In March 1902 at the age of 27 she exhibited her independence when she went to South Africa as a teacher but continued writing for the *Journal,* sending articles home about the Boer War. Randal became involved with several Boer families who were held as prisoners in a concentration camp during the aftermath of the war. This experience awakened in her a social consciousness which affected her choice of research and writing in the years to come. After Randal returned to Canada she worked as a reporter for the *Winnipeg Free Press* and met JFB in 1903. During her marriage vows, when faced with pledging lifelong obedience to her husband, Randal refused to utter the word "obey." She may have been bound by custom to male authority but she asserted herself when she felt it was necessary.

Livesay's mother was the quintessential poet, forsaking household duties and her personal appearance for her writing. She was content to live among dustballs, misplaced tea cups and the piles of paper that were strewn about the house. At a very early age Livesay was used to seeing her own words in print, as her mother would often add her childhood sayings to a column she wrote for the *Free Press.* When most children were out chasing butterflies and creating finger-painting masterpieces, Florence took Livesay under her wing and began sharing her own writing and research with her daughter. Both of her parents encouraged their daughter in her writing and helped her hone her skills, but she was uncomfortable writing under their watchful eyes. While she had a passion for verse and poured her soul into her writing, she was a shy and reclusive girl, reluctant to share her innermost feelings with her mother. She would hide her poems and stories in her bedroom drawer. When Livesay was 13, her mother came upon a selection of her hidden poems; she edited them and sent them off to be published.

Remembering this time Livesay wrote, "This was a time in my youth when I hoped for love and understanding, but instead was encouraged to seek public acclaim. Secretly, I poured out my feelings in my diary and poems. Those poems were such personal expressions it seems strange now to think that they were made public! I did not will it, but I went along with it .... I must have been feeling, in my unconscious, that I was being made an object to appease my parents' frustrations."[26] Eventually, Livesay would come to believe that poetry must be social and public and serve as a witness to life, but she was not at ease with this for some time. By the time she was 16 she began to have the confidence to send out poems on her own. She sent them to the Canadian Authors' Association and to magazines such as *Saturday Night*, *Canadian Forum*, and *Canadian Magazine*.

Although Livesay had not gone to school as a small child, she did attend St. Mildred's School in Toronto for her high school years. In spite of the fact that her parents were considered middle-class, sending Livesay to private school was a financial stretch for them. Comparing herself to her schoolmates she felt deprived and drably dressed. Her mother bought clothes for her at Simpson's "on the bill." The term "poor" became a real word for her. By the time she was at university her father was earning a larger salary as general manager of the Canadian Press, though they still found themselves short of money. It seems that JFB was a poor money manager and lived beyond his means.

When Livesay was studying at the University of Toronto in 1928, her first book of poetry, *Green Pitcher*, was published; her second book, *Signpost*, was published four years later. What she did not know at the time was the extent to which her father was pushing the books with his newspaper friends, and when she found out, she was devastated. Livesay had always been careful not to be seen by editors as father's pet. She seemed to be always struggling against the ever-persistent influence of her parents.

While she was a student at the University of Toronto, Livesay won the Jardine Memorial Prize of $100 for a poem she titled "City Wife." Despite her successes and her growing reputation as a serious writer, Livesay found herself on the outside of the hub of writers at the university. Writing was still regarded as a male preserve and the role of women writers was questioned. Because Livesay wrote poetry she was saddled with the reputation of being an intellectual and her social life took a dive. She hated the gender imbalance and longed for a time when women and men would be looked on for their achievements and abilities. As a young student Livesay was feeling dissatisfied with poetry as a means of literary expression and began to question her direction in writing. Journalism appealed to her so she took a summer job in 1929 as a junior reporter for *The Winnipeg Tribune*. She quickly found the journalistic style and the time constraints of deadlines entirely too compromising; this was not the avenue that she was searching for.

In the late 1920s Livesay was approaching the cusp of adulthood and feeling the need to assert her independence, so for her third year of university, she studied at the University of Aix-Marseilles in France. Her year in France would prove to be just what she needed for her personal development. Recounting this time Livesay wrote, "I was existing on three fronts: learning how to break with the family and be on my own, absorbing and evaluating manners and ideas outside my Canadian experience; clarifying my views on being a woman and finding some challenging ideas through my reading and through my friendship with a girl my own age; and being obliged to face the future — how to earn a living?"[27]

When Livesay returned to Toronto she delved into academic life, working toward graduation. She was beginning to develop an interest in the philosophy of ideologies. She joined a circle of students meeting with a professor of economics, Otto van der Sprenkel, who supported left-wing political thought. Livesay was intrigued by his political opinions but was also drawn to him because of his sophistication and his cosmopolitan outlook. They spent many an hour discussing poetry and politics and he introduced her to the writings of Karl Marx and the objective discipline of T.S. Eliot. For the first time since she had entered university, Livesay felt comfortable and at ease within this small group of intellectuals. Here was a group that accepted men and women as equals. As her social life became brighter her studies correspondingly suffered. "In my fourth university year," Livesay wrote, "my academic standing collapsed completely because I got in with a group of young people who were centred around a Professor of Economics .... He had been to Russia and we had great arguments about why he wore silk pajamas because if he was communist he ought to wear cotton!"[28]

Livesay did graduate, with a degree in French and Italian studies. She hoped to go to the Sorbonne for graduate work in French and English contemporary poetry, but without a scholarship she had to wait until she could earn her way. Canada was in the grip of the Depression and jobs were hard to come by, particularly for a graduate in arts. Livesay ended up running Charlotte's Coffee Shop near the U of T campus with her sister, Sophie, for the summer but by the end of that time, she still did not have enough funds to pay for her passage. Her mother and sister were fully supportive and both contributed to her fare, so that by August of 1931 Livesay was on her way back to France.

The year in Paris was to be a turning point in Livesay's life. She did indeed study at the Sorbonne and wrote her thesis on "Symbolism and the Metaphysical Tradition in Modern English Poetry." But Paris was much more than studying. There were art galleries to visit and theatres to experience. She fell in love that year with a young man she had known in Toronto. For a year they shared their hopes and dreams as well as their life together; it was a very intense relationship. Livesay continued to write poetry but began to add a social consciousness to her writings. It was the "dirty thirties" back home, Fascism was afoot, Nazism was gathering steam and the Spanish Civil War was threatening. Individuals felt that they could make a difference and political activism became a common theme among the young. "The depression and the Nazi movement and the feeling of war was all abroad in Paris in 1931 and 32," Livesay wrote. "I remember coming out of one meeting and the police were there waiting. Everybody coming out of the building was forced to go right down into the Metro .... They just took their sticks and whacked us until we went the right way. Oh, but we saw the brutality of the French police — there were workers killed and wounded who had been demonstrating and parading in March, celebrating the Paris Commune, at the cemetery of Père-la-chaise."[29] These experiences left a deep impression on Livesay and fueled her growing need to help improve the circumstances of people caught in poverty. Toward the end of her year in France, Livesay's *affaire de coeur* ended sadly. Her feminism and need for independence met head-on with her growing desire for marriage and children. It was a dichotomy that she could not handle, so she reluctantly broke off the relationship.

Excited by her year of study and political activism, Livesay returned to Toronto intent upon a career in social work, and entered the School of Social Work at the University of Toronto in 1932. As a result of her experiences in Paris, Livesay became dedicated to socialist principles. She was extremely concerned about the poor and dispossessed in her own country and wanted to involve herself in some way on their behalf. Canada had few socialist policies and organizations at the time, except for the Young

Communist League, the only group helping the destitute. Livesay found their activities to her liking and became a hard-working member of the League. She also joined the newly formed Progressive Arts Club in Toronto, an acting group that specialized in guerrilla theatre. Livesay was first introduced to revolutionary theatre in Paris and admired the style of mass chants and group voices. The Arts Club put on plays that dealt with social inequality and the lives and struggles of Canadian workers; its members were generally dissatisfied with the cultural values of Canada. It was while working with the Arts Club that Livesay wrote her first play, *Joe Derry*, which focussed on the suffering of underprivileged children and the uncaring attitude of the bourgeoisie.

For her second-year practicum in social work, Livesay went to Montreal to work in the Family Service Bureau. The conditions of the Depression were appalling in Montreal, worse than anything she had witnessed in Paris, and while there Livesay participated in demonstrations and political rallies. "I was active mostly on the cultural front, writing 'agit-prop' plays and by spring, becoming involved in the anti-war movement," she wrote. "I learned a great deal about communist tactics of penetration and camouflage; but I was too committed to be shocked .... I believe I let myself be duped because no one else except the communists seemed to be concerned about the plight of our people, nor to be aware of the threat of Hitler and war."[30]

Livesay's growing radicalism upset her father, who was afraid that she would be branded a revolutionary. In 1931 the Communist Party had been outlawed and anyone with leftist leanings was subject to close scrutiny by the state. Her father had encouraged Livesay to be a free thinker and, for him, the tenets of communist ideology were too inflexible in thought and single minded in purpose.

In Montreal Livesay was befriended by a man she met at a communist meeting. The two quickly became lovers and Livesay found herself pregnant. Other than their political philosophy they had very little in common. Don had only a grade-school education and had no job nor any hope of finding one. Livesay had always thought that one day she would love to have children but not at this point in her life. She admitted that she was not in love with Don, although she did consider him a true friend. She felt that her only option was an abortion, and went to her father for help. He not only provided her with the emotional support that she needed but also paid for her abortion.

Abortion was a clandestine operation in the 1930s, so secrecy was of utmost importance. Livesay was not allowed to bring anyone with her for the abortion, and it was cruel, performed without anesthetic or pain relievers. When she arrived home she felt terribly alone and frightened and she was beginning to experience complications from the procedure. "Alone upstairs I panicked," she said. "I telephoned my father. It's done, I said. But I am scared. Can you come? Right away .... Tell Mother I have a fever."[31] The abortion was a secret that they both decided to keep from Florence who would not have approved. The fact that Livesay felt comfortable going to her father for help was an indication that they had achieved an amazing sense of maturity in their relationship as father and daughter.

In 1934 Livesay headed off to New Jersey for a job as a social worker serving a block community. There were concerts, plays, and films to attend and picket lines to march in. She despaired over the racism but found the American scene refreshing. In Canada, Livesay felt that political tension was high and anyone with left-wing tendencies was suspect, and she enjoyed the freedom from suspicion that the United States offered her. She also thought that the American government was progressive in tackling the social and economic problems of the 1930s. Roosevelt was then president and had established the National Reconstruction Administration; Canada had no equivalent. A progressive socialist labour party, the Co-operative Commonwealth Federation, was new to Canadian politics, having just become a legitimate political party in 1932. And while the CCF was eventually responsible for helping to create social welfare programs like universal pensions, health and welfare insurance, children's allowances, unemployment insurance and workers' compensation, at this time Canada was behind the United States in dealing with Depression issues.

During the time when Livesay was achieving scholastic success and working for the Communist Party, she maintained her writing only as a secondary interest. But this was to change. While rummaging through a bookshop in Greenwich Village Livesay came across the poetry of Auden, Spender, MacNeice and Day Lewis. For the first time she found poets who offered political thought in a poetic style, with lyrical modes and the mellifluous rhythm that she so enjoyed. This was exactly what she had been looking for, for years: the melding of the personal with the social, the documentary held together by lyrical elements. It would take time for her to establish a new writing style but this union of the political and the lyrical became the key to her poetic genius. In "Lorca," one of the early poems she wrote in this new genre, Livesay celebrated the Spanish poet and dramatist, his drive against Fascism and his subsequent assassination in the Spanish Civil War. In the last few stanzas Livesay highlighted her new-found sense of political drama:

> You dance. Explode
> Unchallenged through the door
> As bullets burst
> Long deaths ago, your heart.
>
> And song outsoars
> The bomber's range
> Serene with wind-
> Maneuvered cloud. [32]

While Livesay was in New Jersey she became involved in another romantic adventure with a man who belonged to the same communist cell. This particular relationship took a quite unexpected turn for her. "After our unit meetings, Ben would give me a ride home to Englewood," she related. "Eventually, he became my sleeping partner. I thought of us as being comrades rather than lovers. Nonetheless I enjoyed his slow, undemonstrative companionship. We had no way of meeting socially other than at the party cell, and so we never became really personal or intimate. I began, however, to take it for granted that he was my man."[33] She received the biggest shock of her life when Ben invited her to what she believed to be a Jewish fund-raising dinner. In fact, the dinner was a surprise celebration of their engagement. Ben's parents, friends and relatives were all there, toasting their forthcoming union. "What a trauma I went through, striving not to cry and to look normal," she wrote.[34] A young man at the dinner helped her out of this sticky situation but then he too declared his love for her. Suddenly Livesay was tired and felt far from her roots. Not unexpectedly, she became ill; she was told that she had an ulcer and that it would be best to return home. She quit her job and went back to Toronto.

Back home, Livesay began to put her life together and take stock of her direction. She had been away from writing in earnest for a long time and wanted to get back to her poetry. While she was recuperating she wrote prodigiously. She published a number of short stories, a long narrative lyric entitled "The Outrider," a ballad, a radio play and a book of documentary poetry, *Day and Night*. It was for *Day and Night* that she won the most prestigious literary prize in Canada, the Governor General's Award.

In 1936 Livesay received a small inheritance from an aunt. Never having been west of Winnipeg she decided to use the money to move to British Columbia. She wanted very much to meet the literary crowd on the west coast and saw her move as an opportunity to popularize a left-wing literary journal with which she was involved. Livesay was passionate about *New Frontier*, for it was the only publication of its kind in Canada. The journal was begun in Toronto in 1936 with the intent of encouraging a Canadian literature; the publishers hoped to rally middle-class intellectuals and artists to write articles of social criticism. Before leaving on her trip, Livesay arranged several stops across the country to give readings of her poetry. Up until this time she had never really considered her poetry as a means of oral communication but she loved every minute of it. The tour was a success and her audiences found her social criticism welcome and refreshing. They called it the "new poetry." Newspapers on the prairies devoted columns to Livesay, heralding "Miss Livesay" as a concrete example of the growth in Canada of young writers with progressive ideas.

When she arrived in Vancouver, Livesay was intent upon finding someone who could help her market *New Frontier*. A friend suggested an out-of-work accountant named Duncan Macnair. Macnair was a member of the Vancouver Poetry Society and had just returned to BC after a long trip around the world. He seemed an adventurous soul and he and Livesay began working together. They quickly found they had similar interests and experience, and it was not long before they fell in love.

"On a bright blue and gold May afternoon," Livesay wrote, "we set out to walk to the University of British Columbia, calling on the way on a list of progressive professors .... We walked all the way to UBC and back, talking our heads off. It was then Duncan told me that his favourite novel was *Diana of the Crossways* by George Meredith. This convinced me that he was a supporter of women's rights and of women artists, just as my father had been .... I guess the first gesture I made, as a good comrade, was to invite him for supper at my flat on Haro Street."[35] They were married the following year, in August 1937. Livesay was ready for marriage and children but was reluctant to commit to a lifetime together. "I cannot promise you that I will stay married when I am fifty," she told Macnair. "I might want to start another life."[36]

Shortly after her marriage, Livesay was forced to give up her job with the BC Welfare Field Service because married women could not be employed as social workers, teachers or nurses. She could work as a journalist but the job would not be rewarding or challenging for there were very few topics that women were allowed to write about. After five years of working for the benefit of the unemployed, for women and for peace, she found herself temporarily rudderless and became depressed.

There was, as always, her writing, but Livesay was quite disillusioned with the literary scene in Vancouver. While she did help to create a writers' group at the West End Community Centre, she still felt bereft of serious literary criticism. The intellectual commentary and analysis among the poets in the east, which Livesay was used to, did not happen among the writers of the West End Community Centre; poetry was not the main concern for the mostly male members of the group.

Wanting an outlet for her creative talents Livesay soon befriended three women poets, Anne Marriott, Doris Ferne and Floris McLaren, in Victoria. Together they numbered just four but they had the ambitions of a dozen or more. Anxious to rally the cause of poetry for western Canada they launched, in October 1941, *Contemporary Verse: A Canadian Quarterly*, a journal devoted to poetry. *Contemporary Verse* was quite successful and became a well-known and respected magazine, drawing subscribers and publishing many of the new modernist poets from across Canada, including Miriam Waddington, Earle Birney and P.K. Page. Livesay herself published over 23 works in the journal. By the time Livesay was in her 30s she was recognized as an outstanding Canadian poet.

The marriage between Livesay and Macnair was reported as being unhappy. They did love each other and Macnair certainly supported his wife in her poetry and all of her political causes, but as time moved on he became more authoritarian in his relationship with her. In response Livesay became rebellious and obstreperous. An exasperated Macnair committed the unforgivable sin and became physically violent toward Livesay. She fled with their two young children, vowing never to come back. It was only when friends intervened that she agreed to return to her husband. Macnair never hit his wife again but their marriage was never the same. In a poem she wrote in 1972, she revealed her inner frustrations about marriage. The last lines read:

> And our two souls so left
> Achieve no unity:
> We are each one bereft
> And weeping inwardly.[37]

The war years were intense ones for Livesay. In 1940, her son Peter was born. Not too long after his birth, Livesay took the baby to Toronto to see her parents, and while there she registered for a course in day care and early childhood education. In 1941 the Japanese attacked Pearl Harbor and the evacuation of Japanese-Canadians from the BC coast took place. Livesay, back in BC by this time, was asked to go to the interior to work as a social worker and teacher for the Japanese-Canadians in the internment camps. But her second child was due, and as well, Livesay was in the process of setting up a day-care centre in North Vancouver. She declined the job offer. When Marcia reached toddlerhood Livesay tried taking a job as a part-time social worker but her small daughter was distraught at being cared for by a housekeeper. Livesay stayed home and turned to writing.

After the war, Livesay entered the most productive writing period of her career. *The Toronto Star*, for which she had worked in the 1930s, sent her to England for a few months to report on post-war reconstruction. Pleased with her stories, they then sent her on to Cologne and Dusseldorf to write about rehabilitation programs in the Ruhr. By 1947 Livesay had written *Poems for People*, which earned her a second Governor General's Award. That same year she also received the Lorne Pierce Medal for distinguished service to Canadian literature. Livesay began writing for British Columbia's *Star* newspaper and the *Star Weekly*, all the while writing poetic documentary for radio. She came to think that poetry should be spoken, sung or chanted, for only then could people feel the life that was bound up in the written word. In her view, radio, a relatively new medium for literary presentations, helped to reinforce literary culture.

Radio became the focus of all live professional drama production in Canada. Livesay saw radio broadcasting as a challenge to writers to develop new techniques. She was able to present poetry as a performance with rhythm, melody, song and dance. The kind of documentary that she wrote was based on her earlier experience with mass chants. Livesay developed a montage of successive voices which entwined the poetic and the conversational into a single voice. One of her outstanding works was a 30-minute performance entitled "Call My People Home," which was produced by CBC Montreal with the Montreal Symphony. In 1947 the federal government was due to lift the National Emergency Transitional Powers Act, which served as an extension of the War Measures Act. The Act pertained to the regulation, internment, deportation and resettlement of Japanese-Canadians after the war. Livesay wrote "Call My People Home" with a view to helping Canadians understand the treatment and plight of the Japanese-Canadians during and after the Second World War.

In addition to her writing Livesay began a new career, teaching creative writing at the University of British Columbia's Extension Department and English at the high school level. She also worked at the YM-YWCA as a supervisor for young adults.

In 1958 Livesay was 49; her children were grown, she was tired of teaching and her marriage had been a constant struggle. She was starting to think about her earlier pre-nuptial pronouncement about wanting to do something else with her life when she reached the age of 50. Rather than go through another crisis in her life, Livesay decided that she would like to qualify as an adult-education teacher. As there were no such courses offered at the University of British Columbia, she applied to London University. She needed financial support for her studies so she also applied for a Canada Council fellowship. She was awarded the fellowship in 1958 and left to study in Britain. It was exactly what she needed. Livesay had a wonderful time, enjoying her courses and even becoming romantically involved with a fellow student. However, any decisions about the future of her marriage were taken out of her hands when in February 1959 she received an unexpected telegram from her son, saying that Macnair had died suddenly.

"I stood in the hall, shaking," Livesay remembered. "Instead of going upstairs to my room, I went outside again, stumbling long into the twilight street. The only words that would come to me were, 'I'm free ... I'm free ....' "[38] And yet of that May and June in London she wrote, "Could I have left it there, my life? I began to feel loss and guilt regarding Duncan's death. Had I stayed at home in North Vancouver would he have had that fatal attack? This mystery I will carry along with me, ever after."[39] At this point in her

life Livesay had worn four hoods: childhood, girlhood, womanhood and motherhood. Now there were two more waiting:
widowhood and selfhood.

After Macnair's death Livesay contacted the Department of
External Affairs to inquire into the possibility of working for them
in India or Africa. Instead, she landed a job as a teacher in Northern
Rhodesia with UNESCO. "A new start had to be made," she wrote.
"I had no thought of aging, or dying. I had predicted that at age fifty
I might want to be done with marriage, done with family care or
free-lance jobs. I wanted a taste of professional life, financial
security; above all, I longed to experience the lot of young people in
the third world, a world headed for independence from colonial
domination."[40] Peter was studying anthropology at UBC and Marcia
had been accepted at Queen's University so family responsibilities
were not an issue. She was free to go to Northern Rhodesia. Livesay
taught at Kitwe Training College which was on the outskirts of a
mining town, Kitwe, in the centre of the Copperbelt. Unfortunately,
she began having problems with her health. She contracted malaria,
and was plagued by periods of gout and arthritis. She began
drinking to ease her pain but, fearful that continued drinking could
easily become a pernicious problem, as it had been with her father,
she gained control of the situation before it got out of hand.

By the summer of 1963 Livesay had returned to Vancouver and
bought a house in Kitsilano. Her children were attending classes at
UBC and living at home with her. She had been away from the
Canadian literary scene for five years and upon her return found that
poetry had taken a new turn. The new poetry was oral in style and
focussed on form and rhythm. Livesay was excited by this new direction and applied to take a Master's degree in Education at UBC. She
wrote her thesis on "Rhythm and Sound in Contemporary Canadian
Poetry." After receiving her degree in 1965 Livesay experienced a
resurgence in her writing, and the form of her poetry began to open
up. As she was enjoying this renaissance she started suffering health
problems. This time she was diagnosed with lung cancer.

Livesay's cancer was controlled and she continued to write
throughout the 1970s and 1980s, publishing two autobiographical
books, a novel and several works of poetry, and became a writer-in-
residence at universities across the country. Of all her writing,
perhaps her poetry about women best epitomizes her pilgrimage
through life. Her early pieces depict women as trembling, wanting
to avoid hurt and suffering. Her middle poems burst into fierce and

*Dorothy Livesay.* (COURTESY JURGEN VOGT PHOTOGRAPHY)

intense love stories in which the women were swept up in a wind-
storm of emotion. As Livesay became more confident and at peace
with herself, her poetry basked in sunshine, with women metamor-
phosing into earth mothers, taking in and protecting men. In the
final stages of her writing, Livesay's female characters, like herself,
are no longer fearful or dependent on men.

In the 1990s Livesay quietly retired from public life, devoting
her time to her family and friends. Her health was failing and she

died in her 88th year, at Glengarry Hospital in Victoria, on December 29, 1996. She is survived by her son and daughter and seven grandchildren.

In all, Dorothy Livesay was a writer for 68 years and published 24 books, as well as poems too many to count. Her writing took her audiences on a journey with her "many selves," starting from her early transcendentalism and moving to the dialectic of the political in the 1930s and 1940s, through the documentary of the 1950s, and on to the flowering of the self-realized conscious agent of her later works. Livesay was an individualist and an iconoclast who always challenged and pushed her readers and colleagues to accept different styles and techniques as well as new forms of content. To honour her memory, one of the annual British Columbia Book Prizes has been established in her name: the Dorothy Livesay Prize for Poetry.

\* \* \*

Beginning in the 1960s, British Columbia writers could have their works published in their own province with the growth of publishing houses like Gray's Publishing, Talon Books, Pulp Press, Douglas & McIntyre, Harbour Publishing, Oolichan Books and Sono Nis Press.

Also in the 1960s, the visual arts expressed the new modernism through neo-Dadaism, minimalism and funk. Visual arts and literary expression grew enthusiastically with artists like Gathie Falk who turned away from her funk art to produce easel painting. Playwrights like Joy Coghill, who did pioneering work with the Bastion Theatre in Victoria, and Beverly Simon, who wrote *Crabdance*, encouraged the growth of drama.

The issues of racism and discrimination became the focus of the 1970s and 1980s for some artists. Sharon Pollock, a playwright, wrote the *Komagata Maru Incident* in 1978. Her setting was unique in that she utilized a circus atmosphere to comment on Canada's handling of a shipload of Sikh immigrants who had travelled to Vancouver aboard the *Komagata Maru* in 1914. Other writers began to document BC's multicultural heritage. Anne Cameron wrote about coastal Native legends in *Daughters of Copper Woman* and Ruth Kirk won the 1987 Roderick Haig-Brown Regional Prize for *Wisdom of the Elders: Native Traditions on the Northwest Coast*. Joy Kogawa wrote *Obasan*, about the Japanese evacuation from the coastal regions of British Columbia during the Second World War.

Sky Lee's *Disappearing Moon Cafe*, published in 1990, was the first novel about Vancouver's Chinatown that was written from a woman's perspective.

It is the variety of experience and heritage of its writers, artists and dramatists that has led British Columbia into being an important centre of artistic and literary merit in Canada.

# Chapter Four

# WOMEN IN PUBLIC HEALTH

As IMMIGRATION TO British Columbia increased in the 19th century, so did the incidence of life-threatening epidemics. Cholera ravaged the countryside in 1832, 1834, 1849 and 1850. Influenza, measles, scarlet fever, typhoid, typhus and tuberculosis were constants in the lives of the early settlers. Control meant isolation. Unfortunately, there were few hospitals in the province until Sister Frances Redmond established St. Luke's Home in Vancouver. St. Luke's was run as a charitable institution, relying on donations and volunteers. Trained nursing staff was difficult to obtain, for there were only a few nursing schools in the country. Sister Frances trained her own nurses, but it was imperative, as the population increased, that training be implemented on a national scale. To remedy the situation Lady Aberdeen started the Victorian Order of Nurses in 1897 but opposition by doctors to the VON was sufficient to restrict the nurses' activities. Nonetheless, the VON eventually built and operated over 40 hospitals throughout the country.

Initially, nurses had no status as professionals and securing nurses' registration was not easy. The schools of nursing at hospitals were run by male doctors and administrators who were reluctant to relinquish control over their nursing programs. By 1910 all provinces

had passed a Nurses Act which effectively raised nurses to professional standing, but it took nine more years before a university
degree program in nursing was offered. The University of British
Columbia became the first in the British Empire to establish such a
degree. This was a daring step for the university and it was not taken
without opposition. The provincial College of Physicians and
Surgeons was wary of the program and suggested that two years of
training was sufficient. "The over training of nurses is not desirable
and results largely in the losing of their usefulness," they said.[1] Since
that time women have excelled in all areas of medicine; by the
1990s women comprised 80% of paid health-care workers in the
province and 27% of physicians and surgeons.

Sister Frances Redmond
1854 - 1932

Referred to as Vancouver's "Little Florence Nightingale," Frances
Dalrymple Redmond was Vancouver's first public health nurse. She
founded one of the earliest hospitals in Vancouver, St. Luke's
Home, and acted as the superintendent for years. Sister Frances was
devoutly religious and was a deaconess at St. James Church in
Vancouver. Wounded in the Boer War, she became one of the few
women in the world to receive the Victoria Cross.

Frances Redmond came to Canada from England with her
husband, Dr. William Charles Redmond, and their two sons, early
in her married life. She eventually lost both of her children; one
died in infancy and the other, William Charles Dalrymple Redmond,
was killed in the First World War, at Festubert in 1915. Years later
she adopted an infant baby girl and fostered two young boys,
although little is known about them. The Redmonds settled first in
Winnipeg, and when their son Charles went to university in
England, Frances Redmond decided to study nursing and midwifery
at Laval University in Montreal. It meant a separation from her
husband for a time but her training provided her with the nursing
certificate she desired. On completion of her course work Frances
Redmond assumed the title of Sister Frances, a designation
commonly accorded in England and eastern Canada to women who
entered a life given to nursing, social service or religious devotion.

On July 13, 1886, Vancouver experienced a devastating fire
which destroyed most of the fledgling city. Clearing fires to the west
of the city were caught by a wind and minutes later Vancouver

exploded in fire. On Powell Street Reverend H.G. Fiennes Clinton sounded the alarm, ringing the bells of St. James Church. Twenty-one lives and over a thousand buildings were lost in the tragedy. Father Clinton knew of Sister Frances through her church activities in Winnipeg and in 1887 wrote to her, requesting help to rebuild the church and minister to the sick in the wake of the fire. Her skills, he said, were desperately needed. She agreed, seeing her new job as a challenge and a duty.

When the Redmonds arrived, Sister Frances was welcomed by the doctors in Vancouver. They were pleased to have someone with her

*Sister Frances Redmond, founder of St. Luke's Home, Vancouver, 1894.*
(Courtesy City of Vancouver Archives, Port. P. 128, N. 128)

training and made good use of her services, keeping her busy day and night tending to the ill. Although Vancouver was rebuilding its commercial centre, it seems that saloons, office blocks, hotels and stores took priority over hospitals. Vancouver needed a hospital and Sister Frances set out to do something about it. She and Father Clinton worked on plans for the construction of St. Luke's Home. Obtaining funding for the hospital was no problem for Sister Frances, an active fund raiser; she was reported to be able to raise money when no one else could. St. Luke's became known as an institution of outstanding benevolence and good will and Vancouverites were proud of their hospital and of Sister Frances.

After the hospital was built, Sister Frances undertook to develop a training school for nurses. It was another first for British Columbia and young women from all over the province came to attend the school. Despite the services at the hospital there always seemed to be many people who needed home care, so during her off-hours Sister Frances visited the sick around the city. She lived her life always thinking of others and was devoted to improving the welfare of the community. During one particularly cold winter she opened a soup kitchen in the basement of Market Hall to feed the needy. In the late 1890s Vancouver and Victoria experienced a smallpox epidemic, and once again Sister Frances stepped in and, with her nurses, took care of those afflicted.

St. Luke's was not the first hospital in the province. In 1864 the first maternity hospital had been established in Victoria and by 1869 it had merged into the Royal Hospital. After the building of St. Luke's, other hospitals opened and by 1899 there were 20 hospitals in the province, with more being built every year. Unfortunately, they were unlicensed, so many were unsupervised and uncontrolled, and known to be dirty and crowded, and it was not uncommon for outbreaks of infection to occur among the patients. The reaction to these conditions was the Amendment to the Hospital Act passed by the British Columbia government in 1913. The Act specified that all private hospitals and maternity homes be licensed and employ qualified and certified staff. The following year, in 1914, the Board of Health closed down 14 hospitals and issued licences to 35.

Father Clinton and Sister Frances had become good friends and when his health declined later in his life, Sister Frances accompanied him to Pasa Robles in California hoping that the warm climate might help him. Unfortunately, his health continued to fail and he died there in 1912.

*St. Luke's Home, 309 Oppenheimer (now East Cordova) Street, Vancouver, in 1889.* (COURTESY CITY OF VANCOUVER ARCHIVES, BU.P. 671, N. 554)

St. Luke's was demolished in 1925 and another built in its place. The "new" St. Luke's functioned as a nursing home and Sister Frances worked to ensure the ambiance was like that of a "real home." Sister Frances was much loved and appreciated and in her later years she opened her home to travellers, nurses, social workers, and visiting clergy, including Dr. Winnington-Ingram, Lord Bishop of London. In 1929 she was presented with the medal of Good Citizenship for all her years of nursing service to Vancouver. One journalist wrote, "There are no women in British Columbia braver and more devoted to their calling than is Sister Frances. She is a very bright, cheery, charitable lady, and makes hosts of friends where she is known."[2]

In the spring of 1932 Sister Frances' own health began to fail and she died in Vancouver General Hospital on April 15, at the age of 78. The little white-haired nurse, who had been unflagging in her self-sacrificing service to the sick and needy, was laid to rest in Mountain View Cemetery.

*\*\*\**

Ignorance about public health and lack of knowledge of how to deal with the problems and challenges of pioneer homemaking condemned more than a few isolated families to sickness and death. In 1889 Adelaide Hoodless of Ontario was severely shaken when she lost an infant son to drinking impure milk. Realizing she was ignorant about home safety, and not wanting other young mothers to go through the loss of a child due to lack of knowledge, Hoodless devoted her life to ensuring better education for women in the spheres of motherhood and household management. In addition, to ensure the place of domestic science in the lives of rural women, she founded the first Women's Institute in 1897. Not surprisingly, rural women were eager for information that would help them secure the health and well-being of their families It was not long before Women's Institutes spread across Canada, establishing a system for women to learn about the scientific methods of homemaking.

In 1909 the Department of Agriculture in British Columbia hired Laura Rose, a dairy instructor in Ontario, to organize Women's Institutes. Under her leadership 15 Women's Institutes were begun in rural areas across the province. Rose's duties demanded that she travel throughout BC explaining to women the aims and benefits of the Women's Institutes and the necessity of learning domestic science for the improvement of their lives. In 1911 Alice Ravenhill, one of the leading school medical officers in England and one of the best authorities on hygiene, was also hired by the Department of Agriculture to help in organizing the Women's Institutes in BC.

As a new and growing organization the Women's Institute had a considerable amount of work to do. The members of the board gathered information concerning domestic science from around the country. They developed courses and programs and wrote pamphlets on a diverse range of topics such as cookery, gardening, poultry, fruit farming, preserving, the extermination of flies and mosquitoes, dressmaking, the correct procedure for the running of meetings and laws covering British Columbia women. Ideas flourished within the organization and Madge Watt, the secretary of the provincial Women's Institute, proposed that the Department of Agriculture establish a Farm Settlement program for women. The idea was to build a curriculum to help women farmers learn about local conditions before starting farms of their own. As part of the program, Watt helped to create temporary residences where women could stay while they were looking for land to purchase. The Women's Institutes were involved in every aspect of agriculture that concerned women. They organized a fruit-shipping department for women in Summerland and developed an exchange program through which women in BC would trade commodities like fruit, butter and cheese products, with women from the prairie provinces.

After the First World War new concerns arose about women's health, and the Women's Institute was there to support women. The Institute was in the forefront of teaching women about sex hygiene, public health, and recreation. In 1926 Evangeline Shaw MacLachlan was appointed the first woman superintendent of the Women's Institute, bringing with her considerable experience in health. Fifteen years earlier MacLachlan had developed a Well Baby Clinic on Vancouver Island, as well as the South Saanich Anti-Tuberculosis Society. She came to the Women's Institute with a background in nursing and was one of the founders of the Victorian Order of Nurses in Vancouver. Under her direction the Institute went on to launch the Othoa Scott Fund, named after a girl who suffered a disability from a tubercular spine. It was set up to help disabled children, and led into the Fund for Crippled Children of BC. As a consequence of these funds, two very important institutions for the support of children's health were built. In 1927 the Children's Hospital in Vancouver was constructed and at the same time in Victoria, the Queen Alexandra Solarium was established.

The Women's Institutes were originally set up for women living in rural or remote areas and have had a long history of serving the needs of those women. There was a time, stories say, when women would walk ten miles through snow, heat or mosquito infestations to attend a Women's Institute meeting. With the urbanization of Canadian society and universal education, membership in the Women's Institutes has declined considerably. In 1987 there were 43,000 members and in 1995 the number had dropped to a low of 29,000. But as needs change so do organizations. The important thing is that women's organizations are continually generating new platforms with which to support the health and well-being of the women of the province.

## Alice Ravenhill
### 1859 - 1954

British articles about Alice Ravenhill always comment on what a pity it was that she chose to leave a promising life in England to live with her sister in the untamed and culturally starved wilds of British Columbia. Even she admitted great trepidation at the thought of coming to Canada and at the beginning committed herself to not more than four or five years at the most.

Alice Ravenhill was the middle child of seven in an affluent family in England. She had nurses and governesses to watch over her, to make sure she was brought up in a manner befitting the daughter of a famous naval architect and marine engineer. The only anomaly in this Victorian upbringing was that she was allowed to attend school, an unusual activity for girls of her social standing. She excelled at school and upon her graduation at 17, she hoped to continue her studies at the National Training School of Cookery in England. Her father forbade it, wishing her instead to find the right young man and marry. Ravenhill was not so easily put off and bided her time.

Ravenhill educated herself in literature, language, history, geology, biology and physiology. She transcribed T.H. Huxley's *Lessons in Elementary Physiology*, as well as some of Sir John Lubbock's books on natural history, into Braille. Her bedroom was a testament to the scientist that she was to become. Besides her lessons and books she kept worms and cows' eyes that she used to study and dissect. Seeing the dedication of his daughter to science Ravenhill's father eventually agreed to let her engage in further studies. She went to school at the National Health Society and was awarded a diploma in National Health in 1892. Ravenhill immediately set out on a path of lecturing and teaching about personal health, hygiene, nutrition and child care. She ignored social boundaries. She gave classes in universities in London and Cambridge and talked to factory girls' clubs and working men's clubs. She especially believed that men should be responsible about their paternal duties and that boys should attend continuation courses to learn about parenting.

Ravenhill's message was simple: blind instinct in terms of public health, home economics and hygiene must give way to trained intelligence. She worked to promote women's health and better conditions for mothers and babies. Ravenhill maintained that all work connected with the home was worthy of intellectual study. Nutrition, hygiene, domestic affairs, physiology and psychology and the care of children were all important for the general welfare of the family and the community. In a book she co-edited with Catherine Schiff in 1910, Ravenhill emphasized that domestic arts were not a collection of social conventions learned by imitation or exercised by instinct. She set about developing courses for teacher-training colleges on physical development in childhood and thousands of teachers went through her programs. For her extraordinary work in England she became the first woman Fellow of the Royal Sanitary Institute of London.

Ravenhill never married. As a young woman she was engaged to be married but her father terminated the relationship just three days before the wedding, asserting that her fiancé would never make anything of himself and was therefore not worthy of her. Her father turned out to be wrong; her fiancé went on to become an eminent surgeon. In 1910 Ravenhill moved to British Columbia with her sister to help establish a new family home. Their brother and his son had preceded them to homestead at Shawnigan Lake. In preparation for her arrival in Vancouver, Ravenhill took a course at Studley Horticultural College to learn, among other things, dairying and carpentry.

England's loss was British Columbia's gain. Ravenhill was immediately critical of the education system which she felt ignored the intellectual ambitions and economic needs of the many women who would remain unmarried. Not every woman, she said, would marry and to support those women, education should be aimed at equipping them with the tools they would need to be capable, practical and intelligent citizens. A year after her arrival she went to work for the BC Department of Agriculture, helping with the newly established Women's Institutes. The BC Women's Institutes were one of the pioneering organizations promoting women's social and educational advancement and Ravenhill was a vital force in their development.

Ravenhill lobbied for the inclusion of home economics as a discipline worthy of study in university. In 1915 she was appointed to an advisory board and headed a committee for the purpose of establishing a Chair of Home Economics at the University of British Columbia. Three years later, the Department of Education recognized the need for a system of industrial training to maintain economic prosperity; the teaching of domestic science became an important component of that training.

Ravenhill travelled all over BC for the Department of Agriculture to give talks on home management to the various Women's Institutes. Seeing a need for written material on the topics she was lecturing on, she induced the department to publish a Women's Institute quarterly journal which she edited. She also prepared a series of bulletins for the Women's Institutes on food preserving, child care, and the place and purpose of family life. Ravenhill was becoming known as one of the leading experts in home hygiene and her expertise was sought by many organizations. She gave courses and lectures at the Normal School in Vancouver and to teachers in

*Alice Ravenhill, 1949.* (COURTESY BC ARCHIVES, F-07219)

Nanaimo. She taught at Oregon State College at Corvallis and lectured at Salt Lake City, the University of Nebraska, Texas State University and Kansas State University.

In 1917 Ravenhill accepted the position of Director of Home Economics at Utah State University. Her duties as director and teacher were more taxing than she had imagined. Each of her five weekly courses was attended by several hundred students which left her with a massive amount of marking. She felt there was a need to have students engage in practicums so she established a "practice house" for students taking the Home Economics program. In 1918 the Spanish influenza hit the college; Ravenhill was presenting a lecture at Colorado State University when she collapsed. She spent some time in a sanitarium in Colorado but, anxious to get back to Utah and resume her duties, she left Colorado in a severely weakened state and quickly fell ill once again. Her doctors advised her to resign her position and rest.

Ravenhill heeded their advice and left Utah in 1919 to go back to British Columbia. Her health had been seriously compromised by the flu and she was ill for the next four years, requiring the assistance of a nurse for three of those years. Anxious to justify her continued existence, Ravenhill donated several hundred of her books to the library of the newly established University of British Columbia. She felt a deep connection with the university for she had spent time on several committees, working to develop plans for it.

As her health improved she started to lend her support and expertise to a number of organizations. Ravenhill became a member and sometimes served on the executive of the Sociological Society, the National League for Physical Education and Improvement, the Penal Reform League, the Infant Mortality Conference, the National Froebel Union for the training of nurses, the Child-Study Society and the Queen Alexandra Solarium committee. She often served as a substitute for the Dean of Christ Church Cathedral, taking over the services during his occasional absences, and was asked by friends to lead a study group on the historical background of the Bible, which she enjoyed immensely.

In addition to the field of home economics, the love of Ravenhill's life was the art of British Columbia's Native people. She first became interested in Native arts when she was asked by the Women's Institute to adapt Native designs to the making of hooked rugs. From there she expanded her knowledge to include Native methods of tree felling, house building, food preparation, drama, and oratory. By the 1930s Ravenhill had become a local authority on the arts and crafts of British Columbia's aboriginal people. She wrote a book for the provincial museum which included photographs she had taken of the arts and artifacts of BC Natives. She aroused a great deal of interest in Native arts and formed the Society for the Furtherance of BC Indian Arts and Welfare.

Still vital at the age of 87 Ravenhill campaigned for educational equality for Native people in 1946 and was most distressed that Canada denied midwifery training to Native girls. Recognized for her pioneering efforts to make known and preserve Native cultures, she received an honorary Doctor of Science degree from the University of British Columbia in 1948. Dr. Norman MacKenzie, the president of the university, said, "A distinguished scientist who, after devoting many years of energy to the advance of social welfare in Great Britain, has won the lasting gratitude of this Province by her pioneering efforts to make known and preserve its native cultures."[3]

Alice Ravenhill retired to a home for aged women in Victoria in 1948. She died in 1954 at the age of 95. She was a brilliant woman, courageous and scholarly, who gave much to her adopted country.

\*\*\*

By the 1850s Canadian women had begun to demand access to medical schools. It would not be until 1883, however, that the Women's Medical College would open its doors to students. For women in British Columbia this meant travelling to Queen's University or the University of Toronto to obtain their training. Up until 1949, when the first BC faculty of medicine opened at the University of British Columbia, all physicians practising here came from outside the province. These women brought with them expertise on congenital heart disease, anesthesia, immunology, nutrition, pharmacology and the treatment of cancer. Many of them would become leaders in their areas. In 1951 Dr. Ethlyn Trapp introduced new treatments for cancer to British Columbia, changing the course of cancer therapy in the province. She pioneered the way for women like Dr. Julia Levy who, in 1993, developed an innovative cancer treatment that combines drug therapy with laser light to destroy abnormal cells while leaving healthy tissues unharmed and intact.

Dr. Ethlyn Trapp
1891 - 1972

Dr. Ethlyn Trapp was a pioneer in radiotherapy treatments for cancer. She received the Order of Canada for her work in cancer and was the first woman officer of the Canadian Medical Association. In her time she was President of the Canadian Federation of Medical Women, President of the BC Medical Association and President of the National Cancer Institute. Dr. Trapp received many awards in her lifetime, among which were an honorary Ph.D. from the University of British Columbia in 1954 and a citation from the Canadian Medical Association for her cancer research in 1963. Dr. Trapp was responsible for spearheading radiology clinics in British Columbia and she also launched the first clinical research project on breast cancer.

Trapp was born in New Westminster in 1891, and at three years of age she permanently damaged her hip while climbing on the hills near her home. She never let her limp bother her and she matched energy with her two sisters and four brothers. In fact while at university she skated, played hockey and tennis and could dance the evening away. Trapp studied medicine at McGill University, graduating in 1927. She then travelled to Europe to take post-graduate studies in medicine in Vienna and Berlin. Upon her return to British Columbia she set up practice as a pediatrician in her home city of New Westminster.

Described by friends as unassuming and gentle in character but strong in purpose, she was nominated by her colleagues from the Vancouver Medical Association as the "Prince of Good Fellows."

During her years in private practice, Trapp became interested in radiotherapy as a treatment for cancer, and went to Berlin, Stockholm, Paris, London and Manchester to train in this particular branch of medicine. Her plan was to set up radiation therapy centres in British Columbia for cancer treatment. As radiotherapy was in its infancy, Trapp had a long way to go to convince her colleagues in Canada of its benefits. In 1937 she opened a new practice and, taking a chance, she incorporated the new radiotherapy equipment, untried till then in this part of the world, in her own work. She was quite successful and her clinic developed into a private treatment centre for cancer. With Dr. Margaret Hardie and Dr. Olive Sadler, Trapp launched the first clinical research project on breast cancer.

Upon the outbreak of the Second World War, the director of a private cancer institute in Vancouver, Dr. Max Evans, called upon Trapp to take over his post while he was serving in the war. Trapp did double duty, working as director in the mornings and in her practice in the afternoons, until his return in 1945. In 1947 she was elected president of the British Columbia Medical Association. Still anxious to have radiotherapy accepted by BC doctors, Trapp, using her own money, set up the first treatment centre in 1951 to prove its usefulness. She evidently had some impact on the medical establishment for in the following year she was honoured by being asked to be an Osler lecturer for the Vancouver Medical Association.

This was the first time, since the annual memorial to Sir William Osler was established in 1921, that a woman had been invited to present a paper. The requirements for an Osler lecture were rigorous and it was not just anyone who was asked to give a talk. Her discussion of radioactivity and radiotherapy was enthusiastically received by her colleagues; she gained their interest and commitment. *The Vancouver Province* reported on her talk stating, "A woman was Osler lecturer at the Vancouver Medical Association Tuesday night for the first time .... Dr. Ethlyn Trapp, radiologist, was applauded by 252 doctors as president Dr. J.C. Grimson presented her for the singular honour. Demands for an Osler lecture are that it be highly scientific, philosophical and cultural in tribute to the Canadian honoured in many countries as the father of modern medicine. Modern Alchemy was the title of Dr. Trapp's lecture, which dealt largely with radioactivity."[4]

Owing to her constant lobbying efforts for a provincial cancer treatment centre, in 1952 the Vancouver General Hospital opened the BC Cancer Institute. A story in *The Vancouver Province* on October 7, 1952, announced the formal opening. The newspaper said that "High tribute was paid Dr. Trapp in a welcoming address by Dr. Shong who said it was the latter who stimulated the BC Medical Association to active interest in providing cancer services in 1935."

Trapp retired from practice in 1959 but stayed active, studying horticulture, anthropology and sociology at the University of British Columbia. In 1968, at the age of 76 she was the recipient of the Medal of Service of the Order of Canada. Always full of humility Trapp said that there was no reason she should get anything. She felt that there were many people who deserved a medal far more than she. Dr. Trapp died in 1972 at the age of 81. As a parting gesture, she left her beautiful home, with its accompanying 27 acres on the banks of the Capilano River, to the municipality of West Vancouver, to be used as a park for all to enjoy.

\*\*\*

*Dr. Ethlyn Trapp receiving an honorary degree from the University of British Columbia, May 1954.* (COURTESY CITY OF VANCOUVER ARCHIVES, CVA 78-48, AND THE ASSOCIATE VICE-PRESIDENT, ACADEMIC AND LEGAL AFFAIRS, UBC)

Public health care in the province is indebted to women like Sister Frances Redmond, Alice Ravenhill and Dr. Ethlyn Trapp. There have been others, however, who have aided the cause of public health in British Columbia. Vivian Dowding, for example, drove the backroads of British Columbia in the late 1930s, teaching women about ovulation, fertilization and contraceptive methods at a time when many doctors knew nothing about contraception. She operated constantly under fear of imprisonment as birth control was illegal under the Criminal Code of Canada, and had been since 1892. Anyone found breaking the law could face a two-year prison sentence. It was not until Grace MacInnis worked to get birth control removed from the Criminal Code in 1969 that dissemination of this information became legal. Unlike the fight to obtain the vote, there were few advocates to help women avoid repeated pregnancies; it was simply not a topic of discussion in polite society. Until the Society for Population Planning was formed in Vancouver in 1960 Dowding remained alone in her advocacy of family planning. Her work was important because in the first half of the century, complication from child-bearing was the second-greatest cause of death for women (tuberculosis being the first) in BC.

While many advances have been made in women's health there remains much to do, particularly in the areas of access, research and education. Women generally live longer than men and use the health-care system 25% more than men, in part because normal occurrences in a woman's life, such as pregnancy and menopause, are treated as medical conditions. Research and clinical practice, however, have more often focussed on men and use males as the standard by which to measure women.

When the British Columbia Ministry of Health issued a report in 1993 on women's health, it pointed out by way of example that women are often treated quite differently from men when they present symptoms of a heart attack. "Women in emergency," they reported, "are less likely to receive 'clot-busting' medication that stems damage to heart tissue and less likely to be referred for advanced investigative procedure or coronary by-pass."[5] The consequences are that heart attacks are more often fatal in women than in men and when their heart disease is diagnosed they tend to be sicker and less likely to recover.

On the whole, women are much healthier than they were when Sister Frances began her hospital over 100 years ago. Women born in 1921 could expect to live until they were 61; in 1998 that figure stands at 81. There are, however, other pressing issues in health care in the 1990s that concern women. Low income is disproportionately associated with higher incidents of death and disease, and in British Columbia, more women than men live below the poverty line. Women's groups, politicians and health-care professionals are currently working to create a system that understands and cares about women's health.

We Love You, Mom !

# Chapter Five

# WOMEN IN POLITICS AND LAW

ON MAY 24, 1918, all women who were citizens of Canada aged 21 years and over became eligible to vote for the first time in federal elections. In July 1919 they gained the right to stand for election to the House of Commons but they were still excluded from the Senate. It was not until after the Persons Case of 1929 that women could be appointed to the Canadian Senate.

For decades, women had been pressuring the federal government to appoint a woman to the Senate but three prime ministers in a row refused, using the British North America Act of 1867 as their excuse. The BNA set out the powers and responsibilities of the provinces and the federal government and used the word "persons" when it referred to more than one individual and the word "he" when it referred to one person. If only a man could be considered a person, then only men could be appointed to the Senate. This was not changed until Nellie Mooney McClung, Irene Marryat Parlby, Louise Crummy McKinney and Henrietta Muir Edwards challenged Canada's highest court, the Privy Council in England, to define women as "persons." An earlier ruling from the Supreme Court of Canada had found that according to the BNA Act, only men could be considered "persons." So it was a great relief to the women of Canada when the Privy

Council reversed that earlier decision and announced on October 18, 1929, that Canadian women were indeed "persons" under the law. In its announcement the Privy Council referred to the exclusion of women from public office as an inhuman relic of days past.

In the mid-1800s, the laws in British Columbia generally excluded women from public life. They were not able to hold public office, to vote or sit on a jury, nor did they enjoy the right to advanced education. Married women could not own property nor could mothers claim custody of their children. A husband owned his wife and children as he did his material possessions. If a husband chose to send his children to live elsewhere, his wife was legally defenceless to object.

After a lengthy campaign by women that spanned 50 years, the government of British Columbia passed a bill in the legislature on April 5, 1917, that gave women the right to vote in provincial elections. Many debates ensued among women's groups as to how best to use their vote. Helen Gregory MacGill offered this observation: "Many women felt they should organize to avail themselves of their new won power in order to obtain better laws for women and children."[1] Others questioned whether women should create a new political party or should work within the framework of the existing parties. The Victoria Local Council of Women had a meeting in February 1917 to discuss this issue. Maria Grant, a long-time campaigner for suffrage, spoke with intensity when she said, "The women's vote and a party aloof from either faction would be the thin end of the wedge that would crack the skull of party government."[2]

A seat in the BC legislature has been a rare occurrence for women. Of the 225 constituencies contested during the inter-war years, only four percent were held by females. Since Mary Ellen Smith's groundbreaking entrance into the legislature, 52 women have been elected as MLAs, 50% of them since 1986. It was not until 1991, with Rita Johnston, that British Columbia and Canada had a female premier for the first time.

\*\*\*

## Mary Ellen Smith
### 1861 - 1933

Mary Ellen Smith was a teacher, suffragist, politician, author and mother. She was the first woman MLA in British Columbia and later, the first woman cabinet minister, which made her the first woman cabinet minister in the British Empire. Smith was born in Devonshire, England, and came to British Columbia in 1892 with her husband and their four children. In England, Smith had been a school teacher and her husband, Ralph, worked as a coal miner. When his health began to fail they moved to the west coast of Canada, living for a time in Nanaimo. In her new home in Nanaimo, Smith joined and worked with a number of community organizations. A dedicated believer in the vote for women, she joined the Women's Christian Temperance Union. Her scope of interests took her beyond women's groups, however; she sang in the church choir, was a charter member of the Nanaimo Hospital Auxiliary and founded the Laurier Liberal Ladies League. The Smiths were a popular couple in Nanaimo and were both honoured by the community with suppers and testimonials when they left in 1911 to move to Vancouver. Ralph served as the president of the Trades and Labour Congress of Canada for five years; he was a provincial MLA from 1898 to 1900 and again from 1916 to 1918 when he was Minister of Finance. He served as a Liberal MP in Ottawa from 1900 to 1911.

Smith had grown up in an environment filled with politics. Her father, Richard Spear, was a coal miner and the Spear household was constantly humming with coal miners and their wives, meeting to discuss political affairs. She and her younger brother were often encouraged to listen in and to participate in these discussions. As a consequence she became politically astute and quite passionate about achieving justice for the disadvantaged in society. Smith worked hard in BC to bring about the franchise for women and gave well-attended speeches in which she talked about the benefits of equality between the sexes. As her message of social equality spread, she became a popular speaker on the lecture circuit across Canada. Her sober manner enabled her to project her beliefs about equality to her audiences in a manner that appealed to men and women alike.

After settling in Vancouver, Smith joined a number of women's groups in which she began laying the foundation for a political career. She enlisted in the Women's Suffrage League of Canada, was President of the Vancouver Branch of the Women's Canadian Club and the Women Ratepayers Association, Vice-President of the Political Equality League, and a member of the University Women's Club. She helped found a free nursery for the children of working mothers and campaigned for a new penal institution for women prisoners. She also worked alongside her husband during his 20 years as a politician, and this training was invaluable for her future career as a politician in her own right.

Upon her husband's death in 1918, a by-election was called; Smith was a candidate and she won by a wide margin. She was immensely popular and received a standing ovation from all sides of the Legislative Assembly when she made her first appearance.

Smith's first order of business was helping to pass into law the Female Minimum Wage bill. She worked at getting mothers' pensions for poor widows, deserted wives and unmarried mothers, and pushed for the passage of the Juvenile Court Act to allow the appointment of women judges in Juvenile Court. She worked on and saw passed the Maintenance of Deserted Wives Act, the Maternity Protection Act, the Act for Registration of Nurses, which served to legitimize the nursing profession, and Old Age Pensions. The 1920s were a decade of social legislation, and Smith, as a

*Mary Ellen Smith, CA. 1920.* (COURTESY BC ARCHIVES, B-01563)

cabinet minister without portfolio, was often in the forefront. She also helped to ensure family maintenance, widows' inheritance, the protection of neglected and delinquent children, the regulation of night employment and the implementation of a Workman's Compensation Act.

In 1923 the government sent Smith to England to encourage emigration to Canada. She appeared to have made a good impression in England as she received good coverage in the press. She was also honoured with membership in the Royal Colonial Institute and was presented to King George and Queen Mary.

In 1928 the provincial Liberals were defeated and Smith lost her seat, but she continued to offer her service for the betterment of Canada. She was sent to the League of Nations in April 1929 as the Canadian delegate, and she continued to serve as President of the provincial Liberals. She chaired the Liberal Party convention of 1932, just one year before her death. Smith died in the spring of 1933 after having suffered a stroke. She left a legacy of social legislation which acted as the foundation of the political welfare state Canada was to become.

\*\*\*

The momentum and experience women gained during the suffrage movement was channeled into social reform. There was much that needed to be done. Women's groups advocated minimum wages for working women and sought job protection for women on

*Mary Ellen Smith with other members of the BC Legislative Assembly, CA. 1918.* (Courtesy BC Archives, F-09918)

maternity leave. They pushed for responsible public health and education, laws guaranteeing women's rights in marriage, mothers' pensions and laws ensuring child welfare. They formed voluntary organizations for children and young people like the Girl Guides and church-related youth groups. Women assisted in bringing in legislation to ensure the purity of milk and compulsory immunization. They worked to amend the Jury Act to enable women to sit on juries and helped to create a new system of juvenile courts and flexible sentencing, with the accent on probation and parole. Individual women began to be seen in positions of leadership. Judge Helen Gregory MacGill worked with Attorney General Wallace Farris in drafting legislation and suggesting administrative improvements. She set up a special department to safeguard the "neglected child" and introduced a program of foster homes. The achievements of the women reformers were substantial and the progress of today's social legislation owes a lasting debt to these pioneers.

Helen Gregory MacGill
1864 - 1947

Being a young lady of privilege, Helen Emma Gregory, at the age of 16, was presented to Ontario society during the dizzying round of the 1880 social season. For her debutante ball MacGill was elegantly dressed in a long gown complete with bustle and train. She carried a fan, and wore long gloves that were delicately fastened with 18 tiny buttons. With her petite, five-foot stature, her rosy cheeks and taffy-coloured hair, MacGill was every bit the image of a mid-Victorian beauty. Her speech was clipped, a hallmark of good breeding; she had a disdain of gossip and insisted on courteous behaviour. In her decorum MacGill followed the code of a proper gentlewoman.

It was in her thinking that she parted with the constricted notions of the day. The women of MacGill's background were groomed to be obedient and submissive to their fathers and later their husbands. They were to think of themselves as inferiors in intellect whose status and authority came from marriage to a man of the "proper" background. MacGill recoiled from such assumptions and believed them to be not only absurd but disgraceful. Women, she often said, should have complete freedom to pursue their individual talents and when married should share power and responsibility equally.

Throughout her life, MacGill would encourage women to realize their potential. She once said, "Most of us do not attempt to realize a fraction of our capabilities. Yet most of us could live not one but many different kinds of lives, each full, intense and complete."[3]

MacGill could easily have been a misfit, to be gossiped about within the confines of genteel society, but she was skilful in handling people and possessed such an air of self-assurance that she drew

*Helen Gregory MacGill, 16, at her debut in 1880.* (From *My Mother The Judge*, by Elsie Gregory MacGill)

people to her and her ideas. She was well liked and was a popular role model for many women. MacGill's demonstrated independence, and her passion about women's intellectual parity with men, stemmed from her family. She was raised in a family of judges, physicians and politicians where discussions of social and political issues were commonplace. Her mother, Emma, was a strong figure in MacGill's life and brought her up to believe that women should have choices. Through her work in various politically motivated women's groups, Emma showed MacGill that there was purpose in life beyond children and homemaking.

MacGill was passionate about music and very much wanted to study at Trinity College. Before she could do so, however, she had to first overcome her father's strenuous objections. He was not as positively predisposed toward the "new woman" as were his wife and daughter. Silas Gregory was concerned that a profession would preclude matrimony for his beautiful daughter but with enough persuading from Emma and MacGill, he came to realize that gentility and a music vocation were not necessarily incompatible. Trinity College was not so easily swayed. Music was considered a gentleman's profession, and women were simply not admitted into the hallowed halls of Trinity; women were able to sit for exams at Trinity but they could not attend classes nor earn a degree. This meant that women wishing for a profession in music had to secure their training outside the university. There were teachers who gave classes to prepare candidates for the examinations set at Trinity.

In order to prepare for Trinity, MacGill entered a private music class in Toronto. Her teacher, Arthur Fisher, recognized that as a pianist, she had exceptional talent. MacGill worked hard at her studies, practising the piano eight hours a day. The hard work paid off because when she took her first set of examinations in 1884 she earned a first-class standing. The exams were difficult and MacGill was one of only four students out of 30 to succeed. Encouraged by her achievement she studied even harder and took her second set of examinations a year ahead of schedule. This time she secured a second class.

Armed with her success MacGill applied to Trinity but was turned down. The provost was sympathetic — recognizing her talent he knew her to be an excellent candidate for Trinity — but there was a "no women" policy. Never one to give up, MacGill began a letter-writing campaign, sending letter after letter to anyone who had power of admissions at Trinity. Eventually, she was allowed to enroll and received her Bachelor of Music in 1886. Her degree gave her the distinction of a number of firsts. MacGill was not only the first woman to receive a Bachelor of Music from Trinity, but also the first woman anywhere in Canada to receive such a degree and in fact, the first woman in the British Empire to do so.

MacGill continued her studies at Trinity, this time working toward a Bachelor of Arts. Not all went smoothly for her. She seemed to be struggling always with society's notions of women's place. One of her second-year professors, teaching a class in philosophy, informed his students that he deplored MacGill's presence and while he was compelled to accept her into his class he did not intend to help her in any way. If she wanted to attend class, he told her, then she must move her chair away from the other students. This was certainly uncomfortable for MacGill but she would not be undone by him or anyone else. She graduated magna cum laude in 1889. Once again, MacGill was Trinity's first and only woman graduate, this time with a BA. Wanting to continue her studies, she read for her Master of Arts degree and, in 1890, she walked the convocation platform to the melody of "She's My Sweetheart." Her accomplishment appeared in leading newspapers across the country, heralding MacGill as the first woman to obtain an MA from Trinity.

While MacGill was working on her Master's degree she met John Walker, the celebrated editor of *Cosmopolitan* magazine, on a trip to New York. Intrigued by the independent and well-educated woman, Walker invited MacGill to submit articles to him for possible publication. He was so impressed with her writing that he hired her as a correspondent for *Cosmopolitan* and its sister magazine, *The Atlantic Monthly*. One of the issues Walker wanted MacGill to cover was the new national constitution in Japan. Since 1868, Japan had been going through an eventful period in its history. The Meiji Restoration brought to an end the military governments that had dominated Japan since 1185. Under the Restoration Japan had formed a constitutional monarchy, and by 1890 a representative government was established. Walker thought MacGill would do a good job of reporting on such political changes.

MacGill was elated but once again came up against prejudices toward women. Her proposed trip was thought not to be wise for a virtuous young woman of 26. MacGill had to withstand reproaches even by the newspapers which wrote of her coming trip as "A preposterous proposal for a young unmarried girl!"[4] MacGill had been this route before, though, and had learned tenacity. Her family

*Helen Gregory MacGill, Bachelor of Arts, 1889.* (FROM MY MOTHER THE JUDGE, BY ELSIE GREGORY MACGILL)

relented only when she agreed to travel in "style befitting a lady." Letters of introduction were provided by the Prime Minister, Sir John A. Macdonald, a family friend, to Canadian and British officials in Japan. She was presented to the Governor General of Canada who also granted her support. When her travel preparations were completed MacGill was free to trek across the country to Vancouver where she would board a liner sailing to Japan. As she would be travelling across the Canadian west, MacGill made arrangements with *The Toronto Globe* and newspapers in Great Britain and the United States to write about the west. MacGill took her time and visited trading posts, Indian reserves and trap lines. She toured many of the small settlements inhabited by the crofters, Scottish labourers and fishermen who had settled in Manitoba in 1888, Mennonites, Hungarians, Scandinavians and Icelanders. Her trip around Lake Winnipeg caused quite a stir: she was the first "lady" many of the inhabitants had ever seen.

MacGill's journey to Winnipeg held more for her than mere writing and discovery. While she was with her appointed escort, Lee Flesher, on her trip around the lake, the two fell in love and were secretly married, within a week of their first meeting. To Lee, MacGill was beautiful, brilliant and gifted. To MacGill, Lee was perceptive, liberal and well educated, and held progressive views about female independence. Lee's energy crackled with the free spirit typical of frontier communities and MacGill possessed an air of self-confidence and independence. They were a match. The exchange of their vows remained a secret for only a few months because a doctor the couple had visited in Killarney, Manitoba, mentioned "the young Flesher couple who are expecting a baby." Both sets of parents were shocked and hurt at the deception. MacGill and Lee had not intended to keep their marriage a secret but MacGill's beloved grandfather had just died and she thought that an announcement of marriage during a time of sorrow would be unseemly.

There was still the question of her trip to Japan. Both MacGill and Lee had decided that she should continue with her plans, as so much energy had already been expended in preparation for her trip. Leaving Lee in Winnipeg, MacGill travelled to Vancouver by train. She stepped off the Canadian Pacific Railway and onto Granville Street in the fall of 1890. Before her lay an array of crowded houses, indicating the rapid growth of the city. Looking toward the harbour's edge MacGill could see a row of mansions built by wealthy CPR executives. Vancouverites were interested in MacGill's journey and had been looking forward to her visit, headlining her as "A Talented Authoress." MacGill boarded Cunard's 3,000-ton *Abyssinia*. Although the *Abyssinia* was noted for its speed, the voyage across the Pacific was an arduous one. The ship was caught in a storm the second day out and with the tossing and rolling, MacGill lost her balance, fell down a companionway and broke her left foot. She spent the remainder of the trip immobilized.

All of this might have served as some sort of bad omen for MacGill but her visit went smoothly and she was able to glean enough information about the new constitution to sustain her reading audience for a long time. Her time in Japan was extremely busy. She toured the islands of Honshu and Hokkaido, she was present at the opening of the Diet (or Parliament), she learned how to perform a tea ceremony and was honoured with a performance of No dances, a privilege not often allowed foreigners and rarely women. In Tokyo MacGill found life quite western and in between interviews for *Cosmopolitan*, she attended balls and banquets.

As MacGill was preparing her return trip to Vancouver her father was working himself into a temper. He felt that his daughter had acted scandalously by marrying a stranger, especially after such a brief acquaintance. In order to assuage his feelings, Silas Gregory set about planning a second ceremony for MacGill and Lee in Hamilton. The family was aghast; this simply was not done. In the first place, Emma told Silas, people would think that the first set of vows was invalid and secondly, with a baby coming soon, comments and rumours would be sure to circulate. But Silas was a stubborn man and much to the displeasure of the family and the embarrassment of MacGill and Lee, the wedding went on. Hamilton society was astonished and many of the invited guests registered their disapproval by sending their regrets, a disappointment for a couple who had proclaimed their undying love in a buckboard while jogging over 900 kilometres of dusty prairie roads. After the ordeal of the wedding the couple quickly moved to California.

Lee had rented his homestead in Winnipeg and now leased a fruit orchard in Santa Clara. Lee and MacGill set about making their new home while awaiting the arrival of their baby. MacGill wrote voluminously about Japan and her articles were well received. Before long she had made a name for herself among the literary crowd in California. When it came time for the baby to be born, MacGill went through a traumatic labour for her baby was too big for such a petite woman. During most of her labour MacGill barely clung to life. Lee stood by trying to soothe her but neither he nor the doctor thought MacGill would pull through. However, she was strong in spirit and eventually delivered Eric Herbert Gregory, a strapping 12-pound boy. Needless to say, MacGill was severely weakened by the ordeal and it was assumed, according to the medical theories of that time, that she would be permanently debilitated.

Lee was so overwrought that rather than being caught in such a helpless situation again he vowed to study medicine. In the meantime MacGill's mother, Emma, came to live with the family to help out, leaving Silas at home to take care of himself. MacGill slowly regained her strength and when she was able to manage their young son, Lee enrolled in a three-year medical course at the University of California. In 1892 the family packed their belongings, said their good-byes to Santa Clara, and moved up the coast to San Francisco.

While Lee was studying, the family needed an income, so MacGill took a steady job earning $25 a week writing for the *San Francisco Morning Call*. She also freelanced for a variety of American and Canadian newspapers and magazines. Many of MacGill's assignments took her into the underworld of San Francisco. She visited opium dens, and wrote about the tong wars, gang warfare and organized crime. In 1894 her second child, Frederick Philip, was born.

In the meantime Emma, who missed her husband but felt that her daughter still needed her, was drawn to the burgeoning clubs of women focussing on social reform. She joined the Women's Christian Temperance Union and the Women's Alliance. Emma also studied law and joined the Portia Club, a society of women lawyers. She became a well-known suffragist and a leader in the reform movement. When Emma's father died in 1890, she had received an inheritance; with the money she bought Lee a pharmacy and, for herself and her daughter, she purchased two small weekly newspapers. All three acquisitions proved to be successful ventures, so it was not long before the family was able to end their years of struggle and enjoy some of the small luxuries that they had previously denied themselves.

In the midst of this renewed prosperity Lee was invited to work with a group of doctors at the Mayo Clinic in Rochester, Minnesota. Honoured and excited by the prospect, Lee accepted. It meant that he would have to sell his pharmacy and close his medical practice and that Emma and MacGill would sell the newspapers. Lee and MacGill decided that a chance to work at the Mayo Clinic would be worth the upheaval. Once again the family packed their belongings and moved to Minnesota, arriving in 1897. Unfortunately by the time they arrived the offer had fallen through. The Fleshers were crushed but they were used to adversity; they could manage. Not having the same opportunities as in San Francisco, Lee had to settle for the long hours and meagre fees of a midwestern town doctor. More misfortune was about to befall them. While Lee was performing an emergency charity operation, a cut from his own surgical knife caused a serious blood infection. He eventually recovered but he never regained his previous energy.

MacGill started writing again to support the family. Taking up where she had left off in San Francisco, she looked into political graft, impropriety and illegal schemes that prevailed in many Minnesota state institutions. Her articles slowly captured political attention and MacGill was asked to work on a committee to help in the development of a regulating body managing all such institutions. The result was the creation of the Minnesota State Board of Control, of which MacGill was quite proud.

In the winter of 1901 Lee's health began to fail. He suffered bouts of delirium and hemorrhaging, and died quite suddenly. Bereft, MacGill had to sustain her family. She received a small life insurance and through her writing she was able to earn a good living for her mother and her boys. Two years after Lee's death, MacGill was visited by an old admirer from her university days at Trinity, James Henry MacGill. They had known each other while they were at university but drifted apart after their graduation in 1889. After MacGill's marriage to Lee, Jim had kept up a steady correspondence with her so that his visiting her in Minnesota was not surprising. Jim was a successful man of 33, a lawyer, writer, deacon, Mason and Lieutenant of the Sixth Regiment of the Duke of Connaught's Own Rifles. Following a short courtship they were married in 1903.

After a honeymoon that took them back to Trinity, Jim and MacGill, with Emma and the boys, moved to Vancouver where Jim had been living. MacGill joined a number of women's groups. She became a member of the University Women's Club, the Vancouver Women's Press Club and the Women's Musical Club. Because she had a keen understanding of the law, due to her past involvement in women's issues, and an interest in issues involving the status of women and children, she was elected chairwoman of the University Women's Club Committee for Better Laws for Women and Children in British Columbia. Jim opened a law office across from the provincial court house in Vancouver. Their marriage soon produced two daughters, Helen Elizabeth Gregory and Elizabeth Muriel Gregory. The two were often referred to as HelNelsie. Jim found raising stepsons an onerous task and while he loved his wife, all was not peace and harmony in the MacGill household. A few years after the move to Vancouver, MacGill's mother suddenly died after an emergency operation for cancer. MacGill missed her mother fiercely; the two had been constant companions in the home and in the work of social justice.

When MacGill assumed the chair of the Committee for Better Laws for Women and Children she threw herself into the study of law. She spent long hours reading statute law, case law, English common law, private law and criminal law, and the more she read, the more uncomfortable she became with what she learned about the laws concerning women and children in the province. MacGill felt that the laws were antiquated and inhumane, and that they treated women as inconsequential. Although women were not allowed to practise law in British Columbia at the time, MacGill had such an excellent grasp of social law she was often asked by other lawyers for her interpretation of the law as well as for information on previous cases. She also gave legal advice freely to women who found themselves in situations of distress. Many who sought her advice came with heart-rending stories. MacGill helped women who had lost their children to the families of their estranged husbands because, under the Infants Act, mothers had no right of guardianship. She advised women who had lost their homes to the Crown upon the death of a husband for, under the law of Intestacy, Escheats and Crown Procedure, women were not allowed to receive their husbands' estates if there was no will.

MacGill's campaign to awaken citizens to the wrongs of existing social legislation was having its effect in the realm of public opinion but not in the domain of the political bureaucracy. It seems that Victoria's parliamentarians were content with the way things were. Never one to sidestep her beliefs, MacGill rolled up her sleeves in preparation for battle. One of the first things she did was to inform women, through her writing and through giving talks at women's clubs, of the laws affecting them. She wanted to equip women with knowledge of their legal rights, and the lack of them, and to encourage them to seek reform through political action. After many speaking engagements she took all of the dog-eared notes that she carried from speech to speech and compiled them into a book; *Daughters, Wives and Mothers in British Columbia: Some Laws Affecting Them* was published in 1912. In it MacGill outlined all of the laws which influenced the lives of the women and children of the province. She paid for the printing herself and sold the book for

25¢. *Daughters, Wives and Mothers* was very popular and MacGill quickly recouped her initial financial investment.

MacGill added to her sphere of legal pursuits the Juvenile Courts Act and the Juvenile Delinquents Act. In some areas of the province, children were treated as adults in terms of the courts and imprisonment. British Columbia had no provisions for rehabilitating juveniles over the age of 16. Children caught on the wrong side of the law were sent to industrial schools, which acted more as detention houses and did little in the way of training. In the industrial schools girls were taught domestic skills and boys learned farm work, but MacGill felt that this was not enough and would not help these children to re-enter society as productive members. She pushed for skills training and education programs to be established in the industrial schools. MacGill also wanted the age of committal to the industrial school to be raised from 16 to 18 years in order to separate the more malleable from the seasoned offenders. She recommended a supervised probation for accused juveniles and asked that society pay attention to providing foster homes for homeless children, in order to give them the comfort and security of family life.

The judicial system could only see the cost of MacGill's scheme and wanted no part of it. Besides, the prevailing attitude at the time toward delinquent children was one of punishment. It was commonly believed that children were inherently either bad or good and no amount of intervention would help them. For MacGill, the only way to change such attitudes was to change the court system and the only way to do that was for women to gain the right to vote. The connection between legislation and suffrage was becoming apparent to MacGill, and to others engaged in the reform movement. There was ample evidence to suggest that changes in social legislation occurred only after women's suffrage was politically sanctioned: it happened in New Zealand in 1893, in Australia in 1902, in Finland in 1906 and in Norway in 1913. In all of these countries, social legislation improved remarkably after the introduction of female suffrage. MacGill joined Frances McConkey, Cecilia Spofford and Maria Grant to head the Victoria and Vancouver delegations to push for female suffrage.

It must have been an exhilarating time for MacGill. With the attainment of the provincial vote in 1917 and the federal franchise in 1918 came a flood of social legislation. One milestone for MacGill was the passage of the Equal Guardianship Act, a piece of legislation which had her stamp on it. MacGill had drafted the original Act and lobbied for its passage. The Act allowed women equal footing with their husbands in terms of all rights, responsibilities and guardianship of their children. In the case of separation, the child was no longer the property of the husband alone. Guardianship was decided by the court which was to be guided by the best interests of the child. With the franchise in place it was now time to get women elected to positions of political power.

Women's groups in British Columbia petitioned the government to appoint a woman to the Vancouver Juvenile Court. Because of her understanding of the law, MacGill was the obvious candidate so on July 9, 1917, Helen Gregory MacGill became the first woman judge in the province and the third in Canada, behind Emily Murphy and Alice Jamieson, both of whom were juvenile court judges in Alberta. MacGill had 53 years of experience behind her at the time of her appointment and although she was never formally admitted as a student of law in a university, her own reading and study were the equivalent of what law societies everywhere in Canada recognized as qualifications for a solicitor.

MacGill became one of the most successful juvenile court judges of her generation, bringing energy and integrity to the juvenile justice system. MacGill did have to dodge the arrows of narrow-mindedness that were aimed at women in positions of power, but in general she was seen by colleagues and the public as a talented breath of fresh air. Her decisions were seen as considered, well thought out and humane, and she was recognized for raising the court to a high level of moral responsibility and accountability. She sat for 25 years on the Bench and in that time championed many reforms in the handling of delinquent children.

When she first became a judge, the juvenile court system parallelled the adult or police court, except that it was viewed as inferior to the police court. MacGill set about changing that perspective. In her jurisdiction, arrested juveniles would no longer be viewed as mini-adults. To MacGill they were children who had individual personalities, needs and circumstances. In a booklet discussing the juvenile justice system she wrote that "... each delinquent is to be dealt with as an individual. He or she is to be regarded not as a case, but as a human soul in difficulty, in need of aid, discipline and encouragement."[5] According to MacGill the work of the courts should be preventive in nature and offer programs of treatment. It was important, she believed, that delinquency should be stopped before the behaviours became habitual.

In her court MacGill sought a full investigation of each child, including psychological assessments, home studies and medical records, but the justice system was not set up for the extra work and training that she was demanding. Complaints swirled through the ranks, but with her characteristic finesse MacGill persuaded some of the more experienced court workers to undertake the job of probation officers. She asked a select group of school teachers to assess the type of education that would be needed for each child, and she appealed to the business community to provide apprenticeship training. Anna Sprott, for example, provided bookkeeping and typing skills through her Sprott-Shaw Business School, and hairdressing schools taught beauty training.

Over time, MacGill set forth the aims and ideals of the juvenile courts, outlined the duties and qualifications of judges and probation officers, recommended planned budgeting for the juvenile court system, and compiled a reference guide to the federal and provincial Acts that were relevant to juvenile justice. She also kept the public informed, through articles and speeches, about the concerns and the machinery of the juvenile court system. MacGill eventually put all of her thoughts down in a book which she published, titled *The Work of the Juvenile Court and How to Secure Such a Court in a Canadian Community.*

Public minded, MacGill was always looking for a chance to promote social reform. She was a member of the Women's Institute, the Imperial Order of the Daughters of the Empire, the King's Daughters, the Women's Canadian Club, the Canadian Daughters' League, the Women's Benefit Association, the National Council of Women, the American Women's Club, and the Phi Delta Delta, and a founder of the Vancouver Business and Professional Women's Club. MacGill served on many boards including the Welfare Sub-Committee of the United Nations. She was on the executive of a penal reform group, chaired the Vancouver Mothers' Pension Board in 1920 and was a member of the Mayor of Vancouver's Unemployment Committee during the Depression in 1930.

A popular speaker, MacGill was in demand from a variety of different groups in Canada and the United States. She had a gift for ad-libbing and carried a sense of fun into her instructive talks. She gave classes on public speaking and parliamentary procedure and eventually produced a small text, *How to Conduct Public Meetings in Canada and Where to Find the Rules.* She re-edited and expanded the text several times, taking into account new procedures.

MacGill wrote extensively about reform, social legislation, juvenile delinquency and child labour. She wrote for the government, the League of Nations, social service organizations, and the media, as well as for learned journals. Her booklet, *Laws for Women and Children in British Columbia,* was extremely popular, going though eight editions and revisions between 1912 and 1939. In each edition she addressed the new laws affecting women and she always had a final chapter of suggested amendments for discussion. MacGill often called for a family court, and a health and unemployment insurance program.

She was a perceptive writer and certainly a wise one but the effort of getting a finished copy was an ordeal, for she was not inclined to strict organization and tidiness. Her writing desk was always heaped with a confusion of clippings, folders and notes, and written drafts were gone over so many times that they often became illegible through the pasted, clipped and pinned notations. MacGill's eyesight was never very good and she laughingly admitted that as she got older, she had to scrub the page with her nose to read the print.

As MacGill's time on the Bench lengthened so did her fame and when she was removed as judge of the Juvenile Court in 1929 for political reasons, there was an unprecedented outcry from admirer and foe alike. In 1928 the provincial Liberals were defeated by the Conservatives. Simon Fraser Tolmie, the newly elected premier, came into office with a group of businessmen who were inexperienced in the realm of politics. MacGill had been a Liberal appointee and the Conservatives wanted Liberal heads to roll. To remove a judge for political reasons, however, was not a popular move. The businessmen tried to think of some way to get rid of MacGill and when that didn't work, the attorney general dismissed all justices and magistrates of the Juvenile Court and reassigned them under a new name. MacGill alone was not reappointed. Tolmie's cabinet got more than it bargained for. Headlines about MacGill's treatment were front-page news across the entire country. In an organized protest, women's groups petitioned with over 4,000 names to have her reinstated. The uproar over her dismissal generated more protest than had been witnessed in British Columbia politics over the previous three decades and it continued to plague Premier Tolmie until his lacklustre administration gradually disintegrated due to internal squabbles and the Depression.

Despite this wrenching disappointment for MacGill, the interlude proved fortuitous. Her daughter Elsie was seriously ill and MacGill herself discovered that she had a cancerous growth on the scar tissue formed from the difficult childbirth she had had years earlier. She received radium and X-ray treatment at St. Paul's Hospital in October 1930, and after her release continued to receive X-ray therapy throughout 1931. The medical regimen was apparently successful for her energy returned and she was soon ready to get back to work. In 1932 another provincial election took place with the Liberal leader, Thomas Dufferin Pattullo, forming the government. MacGill was immediately reinstated as a justice of the Juvenile Court to cheers from the public and the media.

Back as a magistrate MacGill continued to be the architect of a more modern juvenile court system. She pressed for a family court that would encompass all aspects of domestic relations. She worked toward a reformatory for girls who were first-time offenders and were too old for committal to the Girls' Industrial School. Work had finally begun at Oakalla prison on a new building for women prisoners, something MacGill had worked toward for years. In the summer of 1936 she travelled to Montreal as a delegate to the first Canadian Penal Conference.

The year 1938 was a memorable one for MacGill. She ended up back at St. Paul's Hospital with a broken leg; she had been crushed in between her car and another. This was also the year that the University of British Columbia conferred upon MacGill an honorary degree of Doctor of Laws. MacGill was the first woman so honoured by UBC, and she was deeply touched by the recognition. In a letter to her children MacGill indicated her excitement: "All hold your breaths!" she wrote. "You are going to have another Doctor in the family! Not just one of those Ph.D's! Far from it! But a genuine honest-to-goodness LL.d [*sic*] ..."[6]

MacGill's family was excited for her and her son Freddy wrote a charming letter of congratulations in which he said, "It is eminently fitting that the first woman to receive an honorary degree from the provincial university should be the one who through her preeminence in social legislation has done so much for the welfare of the province of British Columbia. Some of us have felt that when you put on the insignia of the degree on May the twelfth you should be able to feel that the crimson folds of the gown are enveloping you not only in colour and dignity but also in a mantle of respect, admiration and affection ...."[7]

MacGill's degree was talked about across the country. The Quebec *Chronicle* wrote "No single woman in Canada has made a greater contribution to the solution of social problems of children than Judge MacGill by her education of public opinion and her personal work in juvenile courts."[8] *The Vancouver Province* wrote, "A woman of broad culture, wide sympathies and unquestioned capacity, Mrs. MacGill has practically devoted her life to making conditions better for women and children in British Columbia .... In honouring Mrs. MacGill the University has rewarded a lifetime of courage, devotion and self-sacrifice on the part of one of the city's most prominent citizens, and has done itself credit in the process."[9]

There was more to come that year. MacGill was nominated as Woman of the Year and chosen for the Canadian Hall of Fame. She was appointed to serve on the executive of the International Juvenile Court Judges Association and was elected the National Conveyer of Laws for the National Council of Women. She received many invitations to be the guest of honour at various clubs and associations.

The ensuing years, however, were more difficult for MacGill. She lost her beloved husband to cancer quite unexpectedly. In 1939, Jim went into the hospital for tests complaining that he was not feeling well, and he died before the family could come to grips with his illness, just 12 days after his diagnosis. In the fall of 1944 her son Freddy died, of a cerebral hemorrhage. A few months after his death the Vancouver Women's Building shut down, due to financial difficulties; this had been a project very dear to MacGill, one she had helped spearhead in 1910, and to which she had given a great deal of energy.

All of these misfortunes challenged MacGill physically so that in 1945, at the age of 82, she retired as a judge of the Juvenile Court. One month later she suffered a heart attack. She survived, but only as a shell of her former self. Over the next two years her body withered, her mind wandered and she became nearly blind, and she died peacefully in her sleep in 1947. MacGill was buried in the family plot in Mountain View Cemetery next to her loved ones who had long since departed. The Vancouver University Women's Club, to which MacGill had devoted so much of her time, held a memorial service for her at the library of the University of British Columbia. Her children bequeathed her doctoral robes to the university. The President of the University Women's Club and the President of the Canadian Federation of University Women presented a memorial tablet which was eventually set in the east wall at the southern end of the Reading Room of the library.

MacGill's daughter, Elsie Gregory MacGill, went on to become a woman of note, taking after her mother. She was the first woman in Canada to graduate with a Bachelor of Science, specializing in electrical engineering in 1927 and became the first aeronautical engineer in the world. During the Second World War, Elsie

Gregory MacGill oversaw the Canadian production of the Hawker Hurricane, the airplane made famous in the Battle of Britain. In 1955 she wrote *My Mother The Judge* in which she relates the life of her famous mother.

\*\*\*

Not all women who shaped the politics of the province belonged to women's groups. There were a few political trailblazers who stood apart from the crowd and resisted feminist sisterhood. These women preferred the fellowship of their political party, tying their goals of equality to their party platform. Grace Winona MacInnis was one such woman. She was a feminist who fought for women's rights both inside and outside the elected assemblies. She had little time for sexist attitudes and laws but as a socialist and member of the Co-operative Commonwealth Federation she blamed capitalism, not patriarchy, for women's oppression.

### Grace MacInnis
### 1905 - 1991

Many great women in British Columbia have served at the forefront of the body politic, and standing tall among them was a politician of extraordinary talent: Grace Winona MacInnis. She was born in Winnipeg on July 5, 1905, daughter of the famous J. S. Woodsworth, a founder of the Co-operative Commonwealth Federation. She married Angus MacInnis, a federal Member of Parliament, and then became a politician in her own right, serving as an MLA in the British Columbia legislature from 1941 to 1945 and as an MP in Ottawa from 1965 to 1974.

A socialist of long standing, MacInnis thought the proper job of government was to help people do collectively what they were not able to do by themselves. In her time, MacInnis developed a reputation as a fighter for equality and social justice, championing the rights of the disenfranchised, the poor, and women. In MacInnis' opinion, women and the disenfranchised were the major sufferers from poverty, and poverty was a major hurdle to achieving the full rights offered by Canadian society. In her fight against the ravages of poverty she pushed to the forefront of the political agenda consumer protection, day care, affordable housing, maternity leave, job training for women, equitable pay, unemployment insurance, medicare, birth control, a guaranteed income system, family allowances, and abortion rights.

The 1950s were ripe for women like Grace MacInnis to further the political, social and economic rights fought for by the first generation of feminists. Legislation dealing with social and welfare issues had been piecemeal and sporadic, and the social deprivation wrought by the Depression and two world wars had wakened the Canadian public to the need for the state to take a more active role in ensuring an adequate standard of living for all Canadians. Unemployment insurance became law in 1940 but universal medical coverage, the Canada Pension Plan, equality of access to education, the vote for Japanese, Chinese, East Indians and First Nations people and other social reforms were not. Equality became the banner word from the 1950s through to the 1970s; however, the practical implementation of political theory was still largely beyond public political will. While poverty and equality of opportunity were topics often discussed in Parliament, the old ways of judging women and their place in the world remained. MacInnis had to overcome an all-male Parliament. She once remarked that as the only woman in the House, her colleagues mostly regarded her as one of themselves, but whenever she got on to her pet subjects of birth control, family planning, and abortion, they would become just like little boys in a washroom, nervous and behaving raucously in every way they knew.

MacInnis' political direction stemmed from her socialist philosophy. She felt strongly that capitalist economies were responsible for human degradation and misery. She admired social-democratic countries like Sweden and Denmark, which she thought were on the right path to economic equality, and hoped that with the right amount of attention to humanitarian principles, Canada would gradually evolve toward a co-operative system. She often told her audiences that the comforts and security of the individual ought to be the main point around which the whole economy revolves and to which the efforts of the government should be bent.

The central core of MacInnis' humanism grew out of her early family background. She came from a long line of visionary philanthropists; her grandfather and great-grandfather were both ministers in the Methodist Church and her father, J.S. Woodsworth, was a politician, Methodist minister and author, as well as a founder of the CCF party. MacInnis grew up learning about the unemployed longshoremen on the west coast, the poor immigrants in Winnipeg's north end, Nova Scotia miners who led hard and insecure lives, the poverty of women, and the elderly who ended up destitute. "Our family grew up thinking that people and people's ideas were much more important than what colour of carpet they had in the living room or if they had a car in the garage or two cars," she declared.[10]

Within her family MacInnis learned that poverty can distort people to the point where there isn't much humanity left. The Woodsworths' thanksgiving prayer before meals reinforced their concern for their fellow man. "We are thankful for these and all the good things of life. We recognize that they are a part of our common heritage and come to us through the efforts of our brothers and sisters the world over. What we desire for ourselves, we wish for all. To this end, may we take our share in the world's work and the world's struggles."[11]

J. S. Woodsworth was an ardent pacifist who had a strong sense of social commitment and believed that the welfare of one is the concern of all. It was this belief in social commitment that frequently got him into trouble. His support for the Winnipeg General Strike in 1918 led to his arrest on charges of seditious libel. MacInnis had tremendous respect for her father and admired his actions on behalf of the poor and needy. "We children always felt our father was different," she said. "We could not have put the difference into words, but it was there. Other children called their father 'Daddy' and looked on him much as one of themselves, only older. We called ours 'Father' and there was formality and a shade of awe mixed with our affection for him."[12]

Woodsworth came to feel that social service left to the initiative of scattered individuals and organizations was no longer good enough. He became restless with his ministry and began doubting his decision to continue the tradition indicated by his heritage as well as his effectiveness as a preacher. In the meantime, the family moved to Gibson's Landing on the Sunshine Coast of British Columbia in 1917, where Woodsworth ministered to a small parish. He eventually left the Methodist Church to take up the life of a politician. This move would eventually open opportunities for MacInnis and affect her direction in life. Leaving his family secure in BC, Woodsworth hit the campaign trail, running as a candidate for the Independent Labour Party in Winnipeg Centre. He won the election, taking a seat in the House of Commons in 1921. As it was logistically too difficult to move six children in various stages of school, the family decided to have MacInnis, as the eldest, join her father in Ottawa. Just 16 at the time, MacInnis first attended the

French convent, La Congrégation de Notre Dame, in order to study French, and later studied at the Ottawa Normal School. More intent upon scholarship than politics at this time, MacInnis was not particularly interested in the political drama unfolding around her. She was, however, drawn to the debates in the House of Commons and enjoyed going to listen to the business of Parliament. This experience was to serve her well for as an MP, MacInnis would be touted as the doyenne of debaters — the equal of any and ever ready to engage in a battle of wits.

Woodsworth established a home in his riding and in 1924 the family moved from British Columbia back to Winnipeg. MacInnis went to join her family and while there attended the University of Manitoba. She graduated with a BA in 1929 and won a French government scholarship for a year of study at the Sorbonne. After her studies in Paris she returned to Canada to take up a position as a French teacher in Winnipeg in September 1931. Her mother had been a teacher and MacInnis had always assumed that she would follow in her mother's footsteps. However, teaching was not quite what she expected.

MacInnis was an intense young woman who loved learning and the challenge of probing the unknown. She found that her students were more interested in socializing and saw taking French as a nuisance. Lacking patience and classroom experience, MacInnis would lose her temper and her students would respond by becoming unruly. The experience levied a heavy toll on her emotional health and she resigned. "My experience was lagging behind my qualification," she explained, "and I really got next door to a nervous breakdown over trying to handle six roomfuls of French."[13] She felt like a failure, and it was years before she forgave herself.

Her father came to her aid and had MacInnis join him in Ottawa as his unpaid secretary. It proved to be an exciting time for MacInnis. It was while working with her father that she learned the art of "backroom" politics for which she later became famed. She worked tirelessly for her father, lobbying, typing, organizing and giving speeches as they moved toward building a new federal political party, the Co-operative Commonwealth Federation. Her work kept her extremely busy and any thought of social life for this very serious woman was out of the question. It was while she was working in Ottawa that she met an interesting older man.

Angus MacInnis was the Independent Labour Party member for Vancouver South. He was exactly right for MacInnis. He was sincere, hard working, and certainly her equal intellectually. MacInnis liked his proletarian background: Angus came from humble beginnings and his formal education was stopped when he was just 14. His father had died and Angus needed to work to help support his family. He had been a motorman in Vancouver's city transit system and active in civic politics. Because of their busy schedules and Angus' extensive travelling as an MP, their courtship took place primarily through the mail. They wrote 98 letters, outlining their love and respect for each other. They talked of politics and the growing Depression as well as MacInnis' increasing recognition in the political arena. They became completely devoted to each other. At times though, Angus despaired over their age difference. He was 20 years her senior. In one letter to MacInnis he wrote, "To be quite frank, I too, am almost unnerved at times by the immensity of the prospect before us. I think mostly of you. You are yet so young and have a right to demand so much of life ...."[14]

Angus was also very aware of MacInnis' need for equality within their relationship. In another letter to her he wrote, "My first impression of you was very favourable, I mean the first time we had dinner together I felt that here was a woman who if she wanted the company of men at all, wanted it on an equality basis. And if there is any quality I like in a person more than any other [it] is that of insistence in taking a full share of all obligations."[15] Their wedding plans were made through the mail and in January 1932, Grace Winona Woodsworth married the very popular MP.

"I don't think I could have married anyone but Angus," explained MacInnis. "He was everything I believed in, and that is so fundamental to a marriage. He was an idealist, an activist, hard working, and above all a kind and decent man. I could never have married someone who did not share my enormous love of politics. It would have been suicidal for both of us. And he could never have been a Liberal or Conservative!"[16]

Their marriage signalled the beginning of a political partnership and loving relationship that survived until Angus' death 32 years later. The first year of their marriage was an extremely busy one for both of them. The United Farmers of Alberta, the League of Social Reconstruction, the Canadian Labour Party and a loose confederation of other socialist and farm groups came together to create a new political party, the Co-operative Commonwealth Federation. MacInnis' father was chosen as their first president and Angus became one of the provisional officers. Angus and his wife were often separated during this time, both busy with speaking engagements in support of the CCF. People flocked to MacInnis' speeches because they wanted to see the daughter of the famous J.S. Woodsworth but it wasn't long before their attention shifted to her message of social responsibility.

MacInnis gradually stepped into the front-line activities and took over many of the duties important to the running of the CCF, eventually becoming the caucus secretary. She worked hard at bringing all of the differing elements in the party together in order to create a common platform. She also helped start the youth wing, which became a strong player in the CCF party. Her early activities in the founding of the CCF proved to be good training for learning the world of politics. She was also beginning to form her opinion of what constituted good leadership. Mackenzie King, she said, was unable to make a statement without equivocating; Lester Pearson was a good diplomat, she felt, but a poor prime minister because he lacked strength of conviction and suffered from too much pomposity. "It is very easy for certain types," she said, "like Diefenbaker did, to confuse himself with the lord. The thing that keeps you from doing that is your dedication to your belief that what you are after is a lot bigger than yourself."[17]

Up until the Second World War MacInnis had been an ardent pacifist, but considering the Ethiopian crisis and the Spanish Civil War, where budding democracy was weakening in the face of Fascism, she began to believe that democracy and socialism were in peril. Faced with a dilemma of conscience MacInnis wondered if she should oppose the war on moral grounds, which would be against the opinions of her party members, or throw her support in with the government's sanctioning of the war. The answer was not simple for MacInnis nor for the CCF. In the end she decided to support the government. "I realized this thing had no end," she said. "It had got too big to sit and wait. So by the time the decision had to be made, very painfully I had to acknowledge I'd changed my mind. It was a terrible thing to have to do."[18]

As MacInnis' status in the political community grew, she was constantly being encouraged to run for political office herself. She repeatedly declined, feeling it was not morally right for her husband and herself to have two incomes when so many people were unemployed. By the 1940s, however, the value of industrial production had doubled, owing to ship and aircraft construction, and women's contribution to the work force increased. MacInnis knew it was finally time for her to participate in politics. She was free of the family responsibilities that took the time of many women; the MacInnises had chosen not to have children, feeling that children needed two parents on hand, something that was not possible for either of them owing to their heavy political schedules. So in 1941 she accepted the provincial CCF nomination for Vancouver-Kingsway and joined 15 other newly elected CCF MLAs in the British Columbia legislature.

J. S. Woodsworth must have been proud of his daughter but his failing health gave way and he died on March 21, 1942. He gave his life to social advocacy and in so doing left a legacy of integrity, social responsibility and courage. His ashes were committed to the sea which he had loved. MacInnis wrote, "In the immensity of sea and sky the launch rode at anchor while mother carried out his last wish .... We saw that she held in her hand a few leaves of her shamrock plant, a growing slip from the love-token he had given her before they were married. She looked at the living green for a moment and then very slowly she let it drift into the water."[19]

MacInnis joined two other women in the legislature, Laura Jamieson and Dorothy Gretchen Steeves, the triumvirate of the CCF. Although they disagreed significantly over international politics, they each addressed the issues of women's rights, housing, and living conditions. Unfortunately, MacInnis didn't really get the chance to affect any significant legislation concerning poverty and women's issues this time around; Canada was at war and war issues were the major focus of the government.

Four months into MacInnis' term as an MLA, Japan bombed Pearl Harbor. Afraid of coastal sabotage, the federal government passed an order-in-council forcing Japanese nationals and Japanese-Canadians living within a 160-kilometre coastal strip to be removed. Twenty-two thousand Japanese were interned in work camps in the interior of the province or sent to southern Alberta and Manitoba to work in the sugar-beet fields. The MacInnises were incensed at the injustices the Japanese endured at the hands of the government, and they worked hard to reunite families and lessen some of the hardships suffered by individual Japanese. In 1936 Angus and his wife had worked toward getting the vote for Japanese-Canadians; in 1944 the government disenfranchised those who had previously held the vote. The CCF party did little to protest this move, but MacInnis did not stand idly by. She made it known to the members of the CCF that

*Left to right: Laura Jamieson, Dorothy Gretchen Steeves and Grace MacInnis.* (Courtesy BC Archives, E-00046)

this was inappropriate in the extreme. Although neither of the MacInnises was able to change much in the way of policy and procedure with respect to the Japanese, they did help individuals, and importantly, they acted as Canada's social conscience and gatekeepers of social democracy. For all of her assistance, MacInnis was honoured at a testimonial dinner in 1986, sponsored by the Greater Vancouver Japanese Canadian Citizens Association.

With the growing popularity in British Columbia of the socialist movement, the Conservatives and the Liberals came together to create a temporary coalition for the 1945 provincial election; MacInnis lost her seat. Her next foray into the public arena did not take place until her election as a federal MP in 1965. In the interim she worked the campaign trail for Angus, and continued honing her political skills. She wrote a book of memories about her father in 1952 — *J.S. Woodsworth: A Man to Remember* — for which she won an award from the University of British Columbia. Both the MacInnises began to suffer from increasing bouts of ill health. Grace MacInnis was diagnosed with rheumatoid arthritis when she was 55, and required long periods of rest. As Angus' health deteriorated, she acted as his representative at functions that required his presence. In 1957 Angus retired, having served the public for 27 years. After this, they both withdrew somewhat from political life. MacInnis did, however, continue to work for the CCF and in the following year she became the president of the British Columbia CCF. There was a lot of work to be done, for the CCF merged with elements of the Canadia labour movement in 1961 to create a new party at the federal level: the New Democratic Party. T.C. Douglas became the first leader of the NDP, from 1961 to 1971.

At the onset of the 1960s British Columbia still had not addressed social issues in any organized fashion, though population growth was being fueled by the post-war baby boom and by increasing immigration into the province. Universality of education and quality of schooling had yet to be considered; the family allowance scheme had been introduced in 1945 but in general, children's well-being had not been paid significant attention; the drive for equality brought issues of racism and discrimination to light; ambivalence toward the place of women in this new society existed. Social legislation up to this point had been haphazard. There was much to be done to create a blueprint for a just society, and to clear the cobwebs of patriarchy out of the political cupboards.

In the 1960s MacInnis' arthritis began to improve to the point where she could move back into the political arena, but to her distress Angus' health was rapidly deteriorating. When he died on March 2, 1964, Canada lost a well-respected politician and MacInnis lost a loving husband who had been her support for 32 years. They were a good political team who continued to love and respect each other through their years of marriage, and MacInnis would miss their political post-mortems over cups of hot cocoa and coffee. In 1965 she was elected in her husband's old riding  and became the first woman from British Columbia to sit in the Parliament of Canada. It might be tempting to see her position as carrying on from her husband but nothing could be further from the truth. She won the NDP nomination by acclamation. Aware of this possible interpretation she explained, "I never would fall into the category of a wife succeeding her husband. You see I'd been a member of the legislature too and I ran a couple of times for city council and did not do too badly with the result. So I didn't fall into that category. I would have run earlier except for other circumstances."[20] She came to Parliament with 60 years of political experience.

The late 1960s may have been the era of equality but as the only woman in the House of Commons, MacInnis had to endure constant paternalistic bigotry. While she gave as good as she got, she acknowledged that the banter was difficult for her at times; despite the tittering and guffaws whenever she introduced issues concerning women, she never let them sidetrack her. She often said that it was important to keep your priorities in sight but not to overdrive your vision. If you go too far ahead you lose the crowd; you need to bring them along with you. Always looking for the edges of agreement, she was a master of knowing what to leave alone and what to pursue. "I've always been the kind of person that if I don't get the whole loaf, I'd take a half a loaf or a slice or even a few crumbs, because I'd know that each crumb that I got would make me a little stronger to go after some more."[21]

With her election to Parliament MacInnis finally had the chance to parlay her long history of fighting against poverty into legislation. Not one to move slowly, she jumped headlong into the issues and quickly made her presence felt. In her maiden speech MacInnis hit the issue of poverty head on. She emphasized that 23% of the population was living in poverty and that its elimination would require bold action on the part of government.

One of her first recommendations in the House was wages for housewives. MacInnis was of the opinion that women should have equal opportunities for careers and employment but at the same time, she was concerned with the well-being of children. Children needed both parents, she advised, and when both parents were working it was difficult to see to their care. Her arguments never excluded men. In her own life she had seen both her father and her husband domestically involved and she encouraged men to share equally in household responsibilities. Day care was often too expensive, she said, for those women whose skills and education brought them only very modest incomes, and thought it would be less costly to pay those women a modest wage for working at home. The financial burden that wages for housework would place on the population became immediately evident to the political community and the idea was quickly whisked into the background where it has remained ever since. Undeterred, MacInnis lobbied for affordable day care and a pension plan for housewives.

In 1968 MacInnis gave a speech about the need for income-tax exemptions for day-care expenses. A modest breakthrough came three years later when the government allowed a tax break of $500 per child up to a maximum of $2,000 or two-thirds of earned income, whichever was less. By the 1970s 34% of women were working and MacInnis knew that this figure would increase dramatically. She pushed to secure loans under the National Housing Act for the construction of day-care centres but that issue was also quickly sidelined.

MacInnis battled for sex education and the legalization of birth-control information, abortion and family planning. In 1968, as a member of the Health and Welfare Committee, she helped to have the issues of birth control and birth-control information removed from the Criminal Code; up until that time contraceptives had been illegal. She also worked toward legislation that would ensure safer birth-control products, particularly oral contraceptives, in the marketplace. Formal polls showed that 70% of the population wanted abortion to be taken out of the Criminal Code. MacInnis responded by putting forward a private member's bill in 1967, supporting abortion for medical reasons. Abortion, she said, should be legal in cases when serious physical and mental injury would affect the mother, when pregnancy resulted from incest or rape, or when there was a considerable risk of serious disablement of the fetus. Her aim was to get abortion out of the Criminal Code. Unfortunately, this did not happen until 1988, 14 years after her retirement. She never gave up, and year after year, she continued to present her abortion bill. In 1973 she organized a fund for the defence of Dr. Henry Morgentaler who at the time was facing charges for performing abortions.

MacInnis blamed the feminist movement in part for Parliament dragging its heels on decriminalizing abortion. Explaining her impressions she said, "I think the feminist movement to a certain extent contributed to all this, because they always considered abortion as one of the subjects that should be discussed as being only of concern to women, about getting control of their own bodies. I used to say to them, 'Well, look now, look at the House of Commons, it is pretty nearly 100 per cent male — how can you expect, when men don't know anything about this subject, having been precluded from discussions because they're female meetings — to be suddenly confronted with something they know nothing about, but they feel is as dangerous as a live bomb — how do you expect them to be supportive?' "[22]

In 1968 MacInnis introduced a bill to protect women's jobs during maternity leave, which passed. In 1970 the Royal

Commission Report on the Status of Women was tabled and it fell to MacInnis to deal with it. On the whole she was pleased with the report, as it supported her platform issues of poverty and equality. She was critical of the fact that the Royal Commission failed to have a female representative working in the trades, or a low-income housewife and therefore did not represent the very women she had been fighting for. As she said, "It was run by professional women who wanted to liberate women to go and work."[23]

MacInnis was also concerned about television commercials aimed at children. She decried the type of sexist advertising that showed women with their heads stuck in the oven, thanking Mr. Clean for being a good man to wake up to. She was also not impressed with the use of "Restricted" or "Discretion" as the sole means of protecting children from violent films.

MacInnis advocated public housing for the elderly and income-adjusted rental housing for low-income families. In 1973 an amendment to the National Housing Act allowed the Canada Mortgage and Housing Corporation to make loans up to 100%, interest free, to municipalities undertaking rental housing. MacInnis introduced a private member's bill to set up a guaranteed income system and pressed for improvement on seniors' pensions and family allowances, pointing out that France had a system that provided a special allowance for women who stayed at home with small children. MacInnis was extremely frustrated as the government did not appear to be moving significantly in these areas. There had been a marginal increase in social security payments but it still left people below the poverty level. The Guaranteed Income Supplement rose two percent a year but lost a previous cost-of-living adjustment.

As an opposition politician, MacInnis was not always successful but there was no such thing as failure. "I don't believe that because you fail at one stage that that is important. You have another shot at it or somebody else will. I left a lot of unfinished business in Parliament. In fact most of it hasn't been picked up yet. The whole business of family planning and abortion legislation, the idea of a national standard of nutrition and a whole lot of these thing they haven't picked up yet, but they will."[24]

Where MacInnis did experience unmitigated success was as the NDP critic for consumer affairs. She was the first to bring the issue of unit pricing to the fore, attacking the practice of deceptive pack-aging, and weights with confusing size designations such as "jumbo," "giant," and "family." On one occasion, to prove her point she took an ice cream bar into the House of Commons; some ice cream bars were one half-ounce less than the weight printed on the labels. MacInnis also went after fraudulent advertising. At issue were practices like selling two loaves of bread at a cheaper price than one but not letting the consumer know the bread was stale, or giving grocery trading stamps to shoppers according to the total of their check-out bill. The stamps could be traded for items in a special retailer's catalogue; this looked as if the consumer was getting something for free but actually the practice resulted in raising the price of groceries to pay for the scheme. She lobbied for the establishment of a consumer affairs department to look after the interests of consumers, as well as a publicly accountable prices review board for monitoring corporate profits and corporate concentration. She was successful on both counts. In 1967 the government passed a bill to create a Department of Consumer and Corporate Affairs, and a prices review board came into being in 1973, although it failed to keep prices down. MacInnis accused the government of being secretive and saw the board as favouring large corporations.

In the interest of corporate competition, MacInnis took on the pharmaceutical industry. She believed that people needed reliable information regarding drugs, and protection from high prices. MacInnis wanted the government to grant manufacturing rights to non-patent holders as a means of lowering drug costs to consumers. She pushed for a bill allowing for the introduction of generic drugs in Canada, thereby creating competition and a fairer market price for drugs. During her tenure she also worked for legislation to protect the environment and was especially concerned about the growing effects of water pollution. As a member of the Standing Committee on National Resources and Public Works, whose purpose was to study the Canada Water Act, she assisted in passing legislation to have phosphates eliminated from detergents, and worked for content labelling on cleaning agents.

In 1974 MacInnis retired from political office, because her increasing periods of disablement with rheumatoid arthritis made it difficult for her to continue an active political career. However, she remained active in the NDP for many years. In 1977 she established the Lucy L. Woodsworth Fund for low-income children. Working through the schools, the fund enabled low-income children to take advantage of many of the "extras" that might otherwise be denied them, such as music lessons, sports equipment and camping trips. The basis of the fund came from a small inheritance MacInnis had received from her mother. My "mother's role was as the other half. She couldn't play a public role much and she was always concerned about low income children .... I knew right away what I wanted to do with [my inheritance]. I took some of my own savings and put it with the inheritance and started out to make the Lucy L. Woodsworth Fund for children."[25]

Retirement became a time when MacInnis received many accolades for her contributions to Canadian society. In the first year of her retirement she was invested into the Order of Canada, the highest form of recognition that Canada can extend to one of its citizens. She added three honorary LL.D. degrees to her collection of five honorary doctorates. In 1979 she won the Governor General's Persons Award, marking the 50th anniversary of the Persons Case. In 1982 MacInnis received the Canadian Labour Congress Award for Outstanding Service to Humanity; in 1986 she was given the distinguished Pioneers Award from the City of Vancouver; she was honoured at many testimonial dinners and in 1990 she was invested into the Order of British Columbia. MacInnis continued to receive awards and testimonials until she suffered a severe stroke and died in 1991 at the age of 85. Her tenacity in the face of opposition and her work on behalf of women made her an inspiration to the women legislators who came after her.

\*\*\*

The decades from the 1950s to the 1980s were generally referred to as the equality revolution, for the amount and kinds of anti-discriminatory legislation that were enacted throughout Canada. In reality, however, women's gains at the political level in British Columbia from 1950 to 1972 were minimal. During the 22-year period when the Social Credit Party was in power under W.A.C. Bennett, the proportion of female MLA candidates went down, from ten percent to six percent. Despite gains in the past, under Social Credit leadership women had definitely lost ground politically. Only six women were ever elected under Bennett's banner: Tilly Rolston, Lydia Arsens, Isabel Dawson, Pat Jordan, Grace McCarthy and Agnes Kripps. Many women in the province were disheartened at the poor treatment they received at the hands of the Social Credit government, and during the 1972 provincial election their feelings became evident when they united against the government in support of the NDP under Dave Barrett.

The New Democratic Party proved to be the right party at the right time for women, particularly as it operated under a banner of promoting greater parity between men and women. After the 1972 NDP win, the proportion of female MLA candidates steadily increased from the six percent during the Social Credit reign to 20% by the late 1980s. Four women were elected in 1972: Daisy Webster, Karen Sanford, Phyllis Young and Rosemary Brown. Many more women were placed in positions of influence in the government. Kathleen Ruff, who was the past president of the Status of Women Action Group, became the chairperson of the Human Rights Commission; Gene Errington, the Ombudswoman for the Vancouver Status of Women Council, became the co-ordinator on women's rights to the government; and Nancy Morrison, an outspoken feminist lawyer, was appointed a provincial judge.

The NDP called an election only two years into their mandate and lost their position as the ruling party. Nonetheless, the stage had been set for women to enter the political process and no longer would they find themselves excluded from a particular political party.

## Rosemary Brown
### 1930 - present

"Take away Rosemary Brown's race and take away her sex, and what have you got?" asked a potential supporter for Ms. Brown's bid for the federal leadership of the New Democratic Party in 1975.

Her response was: "If you take away my race and my sex, what you've got is a socialist."[26]

Tough and quick witted, Rosemary Brown has exchanged views with the harshest of critics and the glibbest of political pundits. Dubbed by one-time Premier Dave Barrett as "BC's favourite daughter," Brown has been a forceful voice for human rights in British Columbia. She was the NDP MLA for the riding of Vancouver-Burrard and later, as the result of a government gerrymander, Burnaby-Edmonds. Brown served as an MLA from 1972 until her defeat to a Social Credit candidate in 1986. She was a popular politician, working through 14 sessions of the legislature, even outlasting the downturn of the NDP's popularity in 1975.

Rosemary Brown, as a feminist and socialist, has spent her life committed to the removal of all political, social and economic barriers that can make one human dependent upon another. What matters most to her, and to the ideology which she embraces, is integrity and a strong belief in equality for all people. She became a social worker to help people change their lives, and she entered politics in an attempt to improve human rights. Brown has seen first-hand the costs in human damage, both psychological and social, when one group maintains dominance over another. She affirms that the harm done to the fragile bonds of society by paternalism, racism and discrimination is too high a price for any country to pay. To her, a society which incorporates such divisions inevitably becomes insensitive and callous towards the welfare of all its citizens, and that is amoral.

Brown's philosophy and attitude to life go back 300 years to her roots, when her ancestors were enslaved. Born Rosemary Wedderburn on June 17, 1930, in Jamaica, Brown came from a strong family whose political and community work influenced her greatly. Her grandmother, Imogene Wilson-James, was the descendant of indentured workers from India who migrated to Jamaica after the abolition of slavery to work in the sugar-cane fields. As a young child Brown listened to her grandmother talk about universal suffrage, injustice and socialism. Her aunt, Leila James-Tomlinson, was a social worker who developed a comprehensive welfare system for Jamaicans. She was appointed to the Bench as a lay judge where she worked until she died at the age of 81. Aunt Leila was very influential in her niece's life. She taught Brown that poverty persists because the poor do not have control over their lives, and that the result is a loss of motivation and lack of confidence that lead to the continuation of poverty. Brown also learned another valuable lesson from her aunt that would come to govern her approach to politics: that merely tinkering with the system or changing individuals without parallel structural changes in society will never work in the long term. It was because of her aunt that Brown became a voracious reader of politics and history, attempting to understand the world around her.

Although Brown's family was well off, they had never been impressed by wealth or title. The main criteria by which they judged people were integrity and intelligence. Scholarship was important to her family. Her Aunt Leila was the first woman in Jamaica to win a Jamaican scholarship to London University in England and her Uncle Karl Wilson-James studied medicine on a scholarship at Edinburgh University. Uncle Karl became one of Jamaica's leading surgeons. He founded the Cancer Institute of Jamaica and was the driving force behind the creation of the University of the West

Indies. He was honoured by Queen Elizabeth for his contributions to medicine and the improvement of health care for Jamaicans.

When it came time for Brown to attend university she and her family decided that she should follow in their footsteps and study abroad. Brown openly disliked England's treatment of Jamaica and consequently did not want to study there, but the United States was viewed by her family as uncultured and racist, with poor educational standards. Many of Jamaica's outstanding citizens had received their education at McGill University and it had a good, solid reputation. Life in Montreal was painted as both exciting and safe so it was eventually decided that Brown would attend McGill. What no one spoke of, and Brown did not anticipate, was the degree of racism that she would run into in Montreal. Never having experienced discrimination because of her skin colour before, Brown was shocked when she first encountered it. She found Canadian racism particularly invidious, for it was polite, denied and accepted. She could not find a roommate at the residence in Royal Victoria College, for no White woman wanted to share a room with a Black woman. She said that she sometimes felt as if she were invisible; as far as White students were concerned, Blacks did not exist.

Race was a major factor when Brown looked for summer employment and housing. She faced rude and hostile behaviour, often having the door slammed on her or being told that "they did not rent to her kind." For the first time in her life Brown felt powerless; she was vulnerable to the prejudices and actions of racist individuals and she was a foreigner. Her sense of rage, fortunately, did not translate into the feelings of self-deprecation so typical of victims of discrimination. Brown had grown up far from the reaches of intolerance and was not subject to its personal destructiveness. As far as Brown was concerned, she might be labelled and treated as a member of a minority group, but her strong sense of self-worth was already deep in her psyche. She did, however, realize that she needed to develop some survival techniques if she was going to continue to study at McGill. The fact that she had only to stay for the time it took to complete her degree provided her with some reassurance. She also withdrew from White Canadian society and joined the active and vibrant West Indian community in Montreal. However, in one of those twists of fate, Canada would eventually become Brown's permanent home and her intended law degree would be sidetracked to a path of social work and politics.

By the time she completed her degree she had fallen in love with Bill Brown. Bill, originally from Georgia, finished his doctorate in biochemistry a year before Brown graduated. He then moved to British Columbia to began a course of study for a medical degree at the University of BC. This meant that they would be separated for a year but they reasoned that if their love prevailed, Brown would follow Bill to BC and they would marry. Their love flourished, and five days after Brown's arrival in Vancouver on August 7, 1955, they exchanged vows in a simple wedding ceremony. After the wedding Brown began looking for a job and a place to live. One of the many commitments they had made to each other was that Brown would support them through Bill's years of medical school and then he would in turn provide for them while Brown went to graduate school.

The job and housing search exposed them to the ugliness of discrimination once again. Finding a place to live should have presented little difficulty, as there was a glut of rental housing on the market. They had hoped to be close to the university so Bill could walk to classes and be near the library, but the surrounding area was off limits to Blacks. After searching throughout the city and becoming desperate for a place to live, they decided to settle anywhere as long as it was clean and safe. They eventually moved into an old converted house at 6th and Spruce, overlooking a very polluted False Creek. Brown faced the same behaviour when she went looking for a job. It was an economic boom period for British Columbia and there were more jobs than people but the message she received was clear: "No Blacks need apply." Deeply hurt and angered, Brown vowed to leave BC within five minutes of Bill's writing his final exam; this was clearly not a place she wanted to live or raise a family.

Through sheer persistence Brown found a job as a clerical worker for the Registered Nurses Association of BC. Her employer, Alice Wright, the president of the RNABC, had been to Jamaica and had fond memories of her time there. She was distressed at the discrimination Brown had experienced and concerned that she was working below her training, insisting that Brown treat the job as only temporary until she found something that required more of her talents. Brown worked one year for the nurses association and then got a job as a library assistant at the University of British Columbia.

Life was going smoothly and Brown continued working at UBC until the birth of her first child. With a baby on the way the Browns needed to find a more appropriate place to live, a daunting task that neither looked forward to. They not only had to face the usual round of racial discrimination but now, with a child, they were doubly burdened. In the 1950s there was no human rights legislation that forbade discrimination against children in housing; many places would not rent to couples with children. The only people, Brown said, who would look beyond their colour and her pregnancy and rent to them were Margot and Phil Ney.

Brown stayed home with her daughter for the first six months and then went back to work at UBC, this time in the Faculty of Commerce. By 1956 more Black students were studying at UBC so the Browns' circle of friends began to increase. They also joined the West Indian Society as well as the BC Association for the Advancement of Coloured People. They became very active in both organizations and Brown sat for a time on the executive of the BCAACP. It was through the BCAACP that she gained a political voice with which to work for human rights. The association was involved in the struggle against racism in the province and worked hard at getting the government of W.A.C. Bennett to introduce human-rights legislation and a human-rights commission, something that was not achieved until after the NDP win of 1972.

In 1958 the Browns were expecting the birth of their second child. At one time Brown had hoped to go back to Jamaica, to raise her children without the disruptive environment of racism. Bill, however, was from the United States and while he had no desire to go back into the racist atmosphere of Georgia, neither did he feel comfortable with the idea of living in a culture to which he had no ties. Bill had wanted to return to Montreal, but life was leading them on a different route, and time and circumstances determined where they would live. Bill had to complete his residency requirement and internships were difficult to obtain; he was fortunate to be offered a position at the Vancouver General Hospital. He had decided to specialize in psychiatry and was given a position in the UBC residency program.

The Browns accepted that they would be staying in Vancouver for some time. They also felt it was time to make a commitment to Canada and decide about citizenship. Brown never got used to discrimination but she developed what she called the "one person" theory of racism. "No matter how many people in a situation are willing to discriminate against you for racial, religious or other reasons," she wrote, "there is always 'the one person' who will refuse to go along with the pack. So the secret to living with discrimination is to hang on and keep fighting until 'the one person' in any given situation is found — because that person always exists."[27] They took out their Canadian citizenship in 1959 and, come what may, the Browns felt that this was now their home.

The early 1960s was the beginning of a decade of social activism. The tensions of the Communist or "Red" baiting of the Joe McCarthy era in the United States had finally subsided and new avenues for participation opened up, with citizens asking for government access and accountability, and protesting against nuclear weaponry, racism and discrimination. Having small children galvanized the Browns into action, and they began working toward ensuring a better and safer environment for their children to grow up in. Brown joined a small group of women in her neighbourhood under the aegis of the Voice of Women. Their focus was to lobby the government to bring an end to nuclear testing. The relationship between nuclear tests and the health of children was of grave concern to many women. They participated in peace marches, prepared briefs and wrote letters urging their politicians to do something about the presence of strontium-90 in breast milk and cows' milk. This early foray into political protesting was not without its consequences. On two separate occasions the Browns had eggs thrown at their front door but as she said, this time "the attack was not because we were Black but because we were working for peace."[28]

With her children getting older Brown was feeling the pull of graduate school, and Bill reaffirmed his commitment to support the family while Brown went back to university. Casting about for direction she felt that law school was out of the question for her now. She did sign up for some writing courses, thinking she might like to become a writer. In the meantime, however, Brown received an unexpected job offer as a social-work aide at the Children's Aid Society in Vancouver. She was attracted to the idea of social work, having seen as a child how her Aunt Leila had made such a difference in people's lives. Brown decided to take the job and, if she liked social work, she would go back to university for additional training.

Brown spent two years working for the Children's Aid Society and during that time learned much about the suffering of children which would nourish her natural talent for politics. Her caseload included children in foster care and group homes, and unmarried mothers. Because of the child neglect she witnessed daily, Brown came to the conclusion that all babies should be wanted and that to prevent unwanted pregnancies, the government should provide programs to educate young women and girls about the difficulties of single parenthood and the need to take responsibility for their sexual actions. She also thought that for those who did become pregnant, the government should have programs to help young mothers become competent parents. Her experience at the Children's Aid Society gave Brown the direction that she was looking for. She applied to and was accepted at the School of Social Work at UBC.

It was a difficult year for Brown as she was trying to be all things to all people: a good homemaker, parent, wife, social advocate and student. Guilt about not being able to perform all roles perfectly was, and still is, the female disease of the times. It was becoming accepted that women could study or enter the job force as professionals but only insofar as their other female roles did not suffer. Fatigue and ill health were common side effects and Rosemary Brown was no different; she was always tired, overworked and fighting colds. Bill completed his last year at UBC and was offered a residency at the Allan Memorial Hospital in Montreal. The timing was perfect. Brown had just finished her program of study and the family was free to move.

Brown had not been back to Montreal since 1955 but she found that the kind of racism she had experienced as a student was still very much in evidence in 1963. Housing was almost impossible to obtain so they had to settle, once again, for substandard housing in Notre Dame de Grace. Brown took a job at the Montreal Children's Hospital, working primarily with children who were brain-damaged, some as a result of illness but many from car accidents.

This experience led Brown to become, later, a driving force for mandatory seat-belt legislation for children under the age of six. When the Social Credit government in British Columbia introduced seat-belt legislation in 1977 it reasoned that children under six need not be included; the thinking was that their parents knew what was best for them. In 1983, when seat-belt legislation finally became mandatory for all people regardless of age, Brown felt that she had achieved a great accomplishment.

In 1964, after Bill concluded his residency, the family drove back home to British Columbia. Racism had lessened somewhat in BC by then, in part because more Blacks were moving to BC but also because the effects of the Black Power movement in the United States were being felt in Canada. People were becoming conscious of

Canada's history of racism and were beginning to press for change. Back in BC Brown returned to working with the BC Association for the Advancement of Coloured People and the peace movement. She also began to prepare for the arrival of their third child, but sadly, this baby died and Brown went through a terrible grieving period that left her depressed for some time.

As fate would have it, an opportunity that came her way was an immense help to Brown in her bereavement. She was invited to be a panelist on a new CTV television show called *People in Conflict*. The panelists — a lawyer, psychologist, family counsellor and Brown as the representative social worker — were to help the program's guests solve difficult social and personal problems. The panel dealt with serious topics such as rape, family violence, infidelity and impotence. The show proved to be popular and what started out as a British Columbia-only program quickly went national. For years afterwards, Brown was stopped by people who remembered the show and were sorry that it was no longer aired.

By 1965 the family was busy with a healthy baby boy and Brown had completed a Master's degree in social work at the University of British Columbia. She was 35 and entering a new period in her life. As the Browns' income increased they were able to insulate themselves somewhat from discriminatory behaviour. The children suffered some taunting but their parents had worked to instill in them a positive self-image. They taught them about Black history and read them Black literature. The children learned that being Black was something to be proud of. While Brown was thinking about going back to work, she was asked to volunteer at Simon Fraser University's new suicide-prevention centre. She was excited about the prospect of the centre and gladly accepted. While there she was able to develop an outreach program to get students into their community doing volunteer work.

In the late 1960s there was a surge of women's groups engaged in reform activity. In 1966 Laura Sabia, the president of the Canadian Federation of University Women, called together representatives of over 30 national women's organizations to discuss their common concerns. The outcome of their meeting was a new organization of women called the Committee on Equality for Women. It called for a royal commission on the status of women to look into issues of women's health, standing in education and law and participation in the work force. At first, the federal government ignored this request but when Sabia publicly stated that she would set two million women on Ottawa, a commission was called. Needing to increase work-force participation, the government reasoned that the commission would enable them to find ways to mobilize women as workers while at the same time placating them. Thus the government agreed to the women's request and on September 20, 1970, the report of the Royal Commission on the Status of Women was tabled, signalling a second wave of feminism and a new kind of feminist activism.

Beginning in 1971 women's organizations, attempting to implement the findings of the Royal Commission's report, began to appear. These were often voluntary groups made up of young professional women who came together to lobby the provincial and federal cabinets to uphold the recommendations of the Royal Commission. For a Black woman in Canada the women's movement was complex. White, professional women often did not consider the different experiences of women of colour. Minority women, leftists and Native women were excluded from positions of power and influence in the various women's caucuses. Differences in class, race and sexual orientation became serious points of conflict in the 1970s. Black women who spoke for the feminist movement were often perceived as compromising their racial heritage.

Prior to the Royal Commission, sexism had not been an issue to which Brown had given much thought, so she read, listened, and absorbed the information available. She concluded that racism did exist within the feminist movement and agonized over this, but did not see women's liberation as a divided issue. Years later she wrote of this struggle, "I believed that Black women had to take control of their lives, establish their priorities and pursue their goals. I also believed that an independent, secure woman had more to contribute to any struggle than an insecure, dependent one, and that the battle against racism would be fought more effectively by women and men standing side by side as equals, rather than by an unbalanced, lopsided team of unequal partners."[29]

Brown was given the opportunity by her part-time employer, Simon Fraser University, to attend a conference that was being co-sponsored by UBC's Department of Continuing Education and the University Women's Club in 1973. The purpose of the conference was to discuss the recommendations of the Royal Commission on the Status of Women. She was delighted because it also gave her the chance to represent the BC Council of Black Women, of which she was president, and the National Black Coalition, of which she was a member, as the western representative. It was out of this conference that the Vancouver Status of Women Council was born, its initial purpose being to ensure the implementation of the commission's recommendations. The council was very political and was seen by feminist organizations across Canada as blazing bold new paths with energy unseen since the suffragist movement.

The Vancouver Status of Women Council also created the first ombudswoman's service in Canada. For the first time, Vancouver women had a person to whom they could go if they had complaints against the government or the law. Brown was the first Vancouver Ombudswoman, a position which suited her skills and knowledge. Many of the complaints she dealt with concerned unfair labour practices, non-payment of court-ordered divorce maintenance, loss of pensionable income upon the death of a woman's husband, and equal pay for work of equal value. The work she did on behalf of the office was brought to the attention of Dave Barrett, the leader of the provincial NDP. He approached Brown and said that she should seriously consider seeking the NDP nomination in her riding for the next provincial election. Initially, Brown ignored the idea and in fact had a good laugh over the thought of British Columbia electing a Black feminist who was an immigrant.

Meanwhile, the Vancouver Status of Women Council had decided that the energy they spent trying to educate male politicians on the issues facing women would be put to better use finding and supporting women candidates for political office. The New Democratic Party and the Liberal Party recognized the power that the council possessed and gave their support; the Social Credit Party did not. The Socreds viewed the council as a threat to the family and as a promulgator of lesbianism. For the 1972 provincial election the Liberal Party ran one woman supported by the council and the NDP supported two successful candidates — Rosemary Brown in Vancouver-Burrard and Phyllis Young in Vancouver-Little Mountain. Up to this point, there had only ever been 18 women in the British Columbia legislature. The Social Credit Party went down to defeat and Rosemary Brown became the first Black woman elected to political office anywhere in Canada. For BC, Brown and Emery Barnes, who was elected at the same time, were the first Black persons to hold office since Mifflin Wistar Gibbs sat as a councillor in Victoria in 1858.

The media, fresh from the fray of the student movements and street demonstrations of the mid-1960s, had difficulty scripting an image of Rosemary Brown; she didn't fit the image of a socialist or a feminist. She was feminine, charming, and witty and could have won a best-dressed award for her style and élan. She had a private-school education, was married to a doctor, lived in the affluent area of Point Grey, and had property on the Gulf Islands. She was profiled regularly in the British Columbia media, and most news stories gave her positive coverage, focussing on her policies and popularity.

The media liked Brown although she said they seemed to create a myth about what kind of person she really was. She related an incident at a dance. During the evening one of her dancing partners asked her name and when she replied, "I'm Rosemary Brown," he was convulsed with laughter and said, "Don't be silly! You couldn't be that man-hating battle axe — you're wonderful!"[30]

First on Brown's agenda was to develop tough human-rights legislation with affirmative action. The importance of married women's contributions to family income through paid employment increased substantially in the 1970s but women continued to be clustered in lower-paying and less prestigious jobs such as sales clerks, secretaries and waitresses. The progress of women gaining entry into non-traditional occupations was painfully slow. Women in the work force were fighting against historic discrimination and at the same time having to juggle their time around their paid employment and their domestic work. Brown introduced a private member's bill for affirmative action to help women get the jobs, promotions and pay that they were entitled to.

Brown was always loyal to her party but never compromised her beliefs. For her, the New Democratic Party was the party of the working people, one whose purpose was to ensure a system of moral and legal justice. Brown was one of the few MLAs, after Grace MacInnis, to maintain the beliefs of the 1933 Regina Manifesto of the original CCF party, to which the NDP owed its origins. She was an irritant for Premier Dave Barrett. There were occasions when, as a MLA, she would openly confront Barrett: for example, she went head-to-head with him over the NDP's 1972 election promise to create and support a women's ministry. Barrett, after his election, publicly rejected the policy of a women's ministry, stating that he did not believe in special rights for any single group. This enraged the women's caucus of the NDP, as it did women's groups all across the province. The Vancouver Status of Women group presented Barrett with a large plastic pig as the recipient of their first Male Chauvinist Pig Award.

Brown also accused the government of job discrimination within the legislative buildings themselves, stating that women were conspicuously absent from jobs that held power. Another time, Brown scandalized Barrett when she publicly embraced Hortense Allende and apologized on behalf of BC for the haste with which the federal government recognized the junta that had overthrown her husband, Salvador Allende, in Chile. She also criticized her government for not

*Rosemary Brown, MLA, 1973.* (COURTESY BC ARCHIVES, I-32427)

giving Kathleen Ruff, the director of the Human Rights Commission, enough staff with which to operate. It was most likely Brown's advocacy of women's matters that kept her from a cabinet post.

Rosemary Brown initially ran for political office hoping to bring about concrete structural change but over time, she became disappointed with the limits placed on her. She wrote, "It seemed that I spent most of my political years attempting to convince cabinet ministers, and their bureaucrats, and governments, of the need to address women's concerns, and the concerns of the poor and other disadvantaged groups, with at least the same level of seriousness and intent they afforded other issues. The fact that my efforts resulted in failure many more times than they did in success reinforced my sense of powerlessness."[31]

Struggling against the inherent paternalism of the government, Brown often lamented the depth of government ignorance about women's conditions. Her experience showed that many male politicians believed they knew better than women themselves what their needs were and how to meet them. Consequently, she said, they disregarded the demands articulated by women, substituting their solutions based on their particular beliefs of what was best for women. As a female politician, Brown was treated cautiously by her male colleagues, and they isolated her from their camaraderie and the respect they showed for each other. Conversations with other women politicians made Brown realize that this was a shared experience rather than a personal one, something that they all had to contend with at one time or another in their political careers.

While Brown may not have had access to the centre of power, she did have a great deal of influence. She dared her male colleagues to shake off their complacency about women's place in the world. She stepped over the line from private to public life, from what has traditionally been considered the women's sphere into a male domain, and in so doing, highlighted the extent of patriarchy within the government.

Brown became the architect of a better society for women and men, racial and cultural minorities as well as the poor and disposed. She awakened the province to the necessity for tough human-rights legislation and ensured that people, no matter their gender, race, religion, marital status or economic position, would be able to live, work, eat and worship wherever they desired. She fought for a women's ministry, and taught the province much about the advantages of multiculturalism, the need for co-operative housing and the importance of job training for persons who were regularly excluded. Brown pushed for public ownership of natural resources, fought discrimination in housing against people with children and helped provide government funding for rape relief centres, women's health collectives and shelters for battered women. She worked for extended medical benefits for seniors and the elimination of racism and sexism in school textbooks. She also legislated mandatory seatbelts for children in moving vehicles. Perhaps most importantly, she gave a new direction and energy to the century-old fight to eliminate barriers for women and disadvantaged groups. Rosemary Brown was an inspiring politician who struck a blow at the heart of racism, discrimination and inequality.

In 1975 Brown sought the federal NDP leadership. It was not an easy decision for her. Despite her outgoing manner she disliked having to knock on doors and sell herself. However, she was finally persuaded by the fact that the process would be invaluable in providing women with the skills of planning and running a campaign. Up to this time, women's experience in campaigns had been primarily in the realm of carrying out instructions. Brown was the first woman to seek the leadership and she ran on a platform dedicated to reform and socialism. In her campaign speech she specifically addressed the 1,600,000 children who lived in poverty, farmers who were losing their lands due to high costs, First Nations people struggling with land claims issues, and women. She pledged to bring them legal and moral justice in the face of attacks from power and privilege. "I will be unbending in my stand against every form of oppression which deforms and crushes people and prevents them from the fulfillment of their lives," she affirmed.[32] It was a close race right to the end; then Brown came in second, with 658 votes to Ed Broadbent's 984.

Brown was asked by Broadbent to run for a federal seat, but after much thought she declined, citing her obligation to the provincial NDP. She may have lost the nomination but she succeeded in changing the ideological balance in the party which became more understanding and favourable to feminism and opened up the opportunity for political debates on women. Later, in her memoirs, she wrote, "The one aspect of the experience that gave me my greatest joy, however, is knowing that on July 7, 1975, all over this country, Black people, children as well as adults, eyes and ears fixed on TV and radio, waited for the results of that final ballot, and for that short while, dared to dream of the impossible."[33]

Brown continued as an MLA for ten more years during which time she received many honours, including an honorary degree of humane letters from Mount St. Vincent University in Halifax. In the 1986 election Brown was defeated in Burnaby-Edmonds. Shortly thereafter she was appointed to the Ruth Wynn Woodward Chair in Women's Studies at Simon Fraser University. In 1989 she wrote a book about her experiences, *Being Brown: A Very Public Life.* In her retirement she has sat on Ottawa's National Security Review Committee, been a lecturer in the faculty of Human and Social Development at the University of Victoria in 1989 and spent three years as the executive director of MATCH International, a Canadian organization dedicated to eradicating the exploitation and marginalization of women throughout the world. She was also a director of the Canadian Women's Foundation in Toronto, which provides grants for innovative projects that are designed to help women and girls achieve greater self-reliance and economic independence. She was on the Board of the South African Educational Trust Fund and was Chief Commissioner of Human Rights in Ontario from 1993 to 1996. Rosemary Brown received the Order of Canada on July 1, 1996.

* * *

While British and European women were organizing and working toward laws for the betterment of their families, Native women were subject to a different law, one that discriminated against them on the grounds of race, sex and marital status. The Indian Act, originating in 1876, regulated the position of aboriginal people in Canada. Women were doubly disadvantaged by the Act, which was grounded in European paternalism and racism.

For example, women were not allowed to vote in band elections for most of this century, or take part in band business. They could neither own nor inherit property on the reserve. If women did have property prior to 1876, by law they had to dispose of all their holdings. If an aboriginal woman married a non-Indian she ceased to be a status Indian in the eyes of the government and because of her loss of status, her children were not recognized as Indian. This had the effect, among others, of denying them access to the cultural and social fabric of their community. On the other hand, men who married non-Indian women did not lose their status.

While the lives of women may not have been all they wished them to be prior to the Indian Act, the politics and laws imposed by the

Act ruptured cultural traditions and introduced discrimination against them within their own bands. Perhaps the greatest indignity was that in the process of stripping away all of their individual rights and powers, the government forced women to depend on the status of their husbands. This was indeed unfortunate for it rendered aboriginal women powerless to affect the direction of their own lives.

Historically, women played a prominent part in the political and cultural life of their traditional societies, and Native women are strong and resolute in their sense of purpose. Today, women are joining together within their bands and across nations, breaking new ground and opening doors for future generations. Since 1992, 50 women have been elected First Nations chiefs under the federal Indian Act. Women are also achieving success in diverse fields. As entrepreneurs, engineers, filmmakers, writers, doctors, and accountants they serve as examples for young women to follow. Organizations such as the Native Women's Association of Canada and the Institute for the Advancement of Aboriginal Women are working to deal with the issues of family violence, employment and employment equity, economic development, long-term care, health, education and justice.

Marggo Pariseau, the manager of the Women's Emergency Accommodation Centre, perhaps best summed up the growth of women's strength and determination to preserve and promote Native culture, language and heritage when she said, "We need to come together in a way that empowers us and shows us as survivors not victims. Recognition of the strength and role of Aboriginal women in our society is important and valuable."[34]

## Rose Charlie
### 1930 - present

There is a Stó:lo legend that talks about the cleverness and cunning of women. While the legend is old, Elizabeth Rose Charlie is the contemporary embodiment of Stó:lo women's sagacity. Born of the Stó:lo Nation on May 9, 1930, she is a member of the Chehalis Band and served as their chief for two years. The Stó:lo Nation, or River People, are culturally part of the Coast Salish peoples and have resided along the shores and tributaries of the lower Fraser River for over 9,000 years.

Rose Charlie's life is one given to the struggle for social justice for the women of Canada's First Nations. She has also been a tireless champion for the rights of the poor and disenfranchised. Because she has raised six children and has 15 grandchildren, she is able to bring a great deal of experience and knowledge to the issues of child welfare. Charlie is a respected Elder and spiritual leader of her community, as well as a researcher and teacher of traditional Salish culture.

Charlie's work has spanned over 30 years of unstinting community service and advocacy. She is a founding member of the Indian Homemakers Association of British Columbia and of the National Indian Brotherhood, now the Assembly of First Nations. Charlie spearheaded the Union of BC Indian Chiefs and at 64 became the Grand Chief of British Columbia. She started two of the main Native women's groups in Canada: the National Association of Indian Rights for Indian Women and the Native Women's Association of Canada. She was a board member of the Vancouver Police Commission, the BC Human Rights Commission, the Citizens Advisory Committee and the Vancouver Indian Friendship Centre, and president of the Mission Friendship Centre.

Charlie has received numerous awards. For her work on behalf of children and child welfare she was presented with the National Year of the Child Award by the BC government. She also received the federal government's Special ARDA Award for Service, was honoured with the Government of Canada Certificate of Merit in recognition of her contribution to the community, and distinguished by the Gitksan Wet'suwet'en Tribal Council for her work on the elimination of discrimination from the Indian Act.

On December 20, 1989, Dr. David Strangway, president of the University of British Columbia, wrote to Charlie, inviting her to receive an honorary Doctor of Laws on the 75th anniversary of UBC. Dr. Strangway told Charlie that the UBC Senate wanted to pay tribute to her achievements and contributions, and to recognize a career that is a model for their students and the society around them.

In 1994 Senator Pat Carney nominated Charlie for the Governor General's Award in Commemoration of the Persons Case for her active participation in Indian rights, especially for her work on behalf of Native women. This was a particularly proud moment for Charlie; she received letters of congratulations from MPs, MLAs, and the Vancouver University Women's Club, among others. David Anderson, Minister of National Revenue at the time, wrote to her, saying that she was to be commended for her success in challenging the discriminatory provisions of the Indian Act and that this recognition for her contribution to improving social justice for the women of Canada's First Nations was well deserved.

As president of the Indian Homemakers Association for 28 years, Charlie worked to improve the living conditions of First Nations communities. The Indian Homemakers Association began in Chehalis in 1950 and eventually spread to include five local clubs by the 1960s. The original intent was to have a home-cooking and sewing club but many women did not have even the basic essentials of life; hunger was a more immediate problem. Recognizing the need for better education and health services, water and sewage facilities, suitable homes and child welfare, the association began to work for improvement in these areas. In the 1960s Native people had a death rate higher than the national average and while the incidence of tuberculosis had been decreasing nationally, for Native people the rate was going up. Low incomes and lack of job security were a fact of life; 80% fell below the poverty level set by the federal government. Housing had been a major problem for a long time: there was not only a shortage of homes but housing was substandard. When the Indian Homemakers Association began organizing politically to fight for their communities, the Department of Indian and Northern Affairs, which had given the association a yearly grant of $100, perceived it as becoming too vocal and withdrew the small grant. In June 1969 the association became independent, under the Societies Act.

Rose Charlie has been a founding member of many national and provincial aboriginal organizations. In 1969, in order to bring attention to a federal White Paper proposing changes in the Indian Act, Charlie organized two "Moccasin Walks." The first began at Vancouver City Hall and ended at Hope, and the second walk, also starting at Vancouver City Hall, wound its way through Abbotsford and over the bridge to Mission to finish at the Pacific National Exhibition grounds. As a result of these two walks, the first-ever all-chiefs meeting took place in Kamloops, BC, in November 1969 to discuss the White Paper. This meeting served as the foundation of the Union of BC Indian Chiefs. As chance would have it, one of the speakers at the meeting was a non-status Indian who congratulated the chiefs on their newly established organization and lamented the fact that there was no similar body for non-status people like him. Charlie approached the speaker and together they started the BC Association of Non-Status Indians.

Prior to the founding of the National Indian Brotherhood there were no national organizations of First Nations people. The NIB, set up in 1968, had its first meeting in Vancouver on August 21, 1970.

This was of special significance for Charlie as she had helped start it, and also because its founding ushered in a new era of Native strengths. The NIB was set up by and for Natives, with an office in Ottawa from which they could, for the first time, present their issues on a national basis. It included more than 50 First Nations, and cut across cultural lines and historical territories. As the national Indian movement began to take shape, First Nations people saw the NIB as a vehicle for pushing for self-government, land title and the settlement of treaty issues. By 1975, the NIB had become a significant force in Ottawa and had gained access to federal power through a joint federal cabinet-NIB consultative committee to revise the Indian Act. In 1982, the NIB became the Assembly of First Nations, which now represents 633 First Nations communities in Canada.

While Charlie was in Ottawa lobbying for revisions to the Indian Act, she met a number of women who were as concerned as she was about the lack of formal organizations for Native women. The federal government interacted only with the National Indian Brotherhood concerning Native issues, and did not see anything amiss with the fact that the NIB was mainly male in composition. Native women had nowhere to turn for political help, and housing, poverty, education and status were of grave concern to many of them. Charlie thought it important that these women have a political outlet to represent them at the federal level, so she established the National Association of Indian Rights for Indian Women in 1977, comprised of both status and non-status women, and the Native Women's Association of Canada.

The members of the National Association of Indian Rights for Indian Women had their work cut out for them. One of the first issues they tackled was the discriminatory sections of the Indian Act that affected women. This was complicated by the fact that 49% of Native people had never heard of the Indian Act and, of the 51% who had, less than half had ever read the Act; education became a priority. In response, the association engaged a researcher, with the aid of the Advisory Council on the Status of Women, to look into the status of Native women who were married to non-Native men. The result, *Indian Women and the Law in Canada: Citizens Minus*, published in 1978, was a comprehensive book discussing the social and psychological losses faced by disenfranchised women. The association also asked the federal government to allow Indian women's organizations an official voice in the joint cabinet-NIB negotiations to revise the Indian Act. Their request was refused.

The Native Women's Association of Canada has been a beacon of support and strength for First Nations women. During the discussions of the Charter of Rights and Freedoms, for example, the federal government provided $10,000,000 to four national Native associations — the Assembly of First Nations, the Native Council of Canada, the Métis National Council and the Inuit Tapirisat of Canada — and invited them to join in the discussions. These were all male-dominated organizations, and only a very small portion of those funds was earmarked for women's issues; $130,000 was given to the NWAC by both the AFN and the NCC. Shocked by the insignificant sum, the NWAC fought in the courts to have women provided with equal funding and the right to participate, and the government subsequently gave the NWAC another $300,000.

One of Rose Charlie's greatest achievements was helping to restore Indian status to 16,000 women and 46,000 first-generation children of mixed ancestry. Charlie started her campaign to remove discriminatory parts of the Indian Act in the 1960s. For well over a hundred years, Native women in Canada were subject to laws which discriminated against them on the grounds of marital status. The consequences of section 12(1)(b) of the Indian Act meant that upon marriage to a non-Native man, a woman had to leave her parents' home and her reserve. The cultural and social consequences were severe. Her children were not recognized as Indian, and she could be prevented from inheriting property left to her by her parents; she could also be prohibited from returning to live with her family on the reserve even if she was in need. The final injustice was that upon death, her body could not be buried on the reserve with her forebears. For Native women, this kind of treatment amounted to statutory banishment. No such restrictions existed for Native men and in fact, their non-Native spouses and children were granted the full rights and privileges of Native status.

Charlie lobbied the government and wrote position papers on the unfair treatment of Native women. She reminded them that there was a clause in the United Nations Declaration of Human Rights, to which Canada was a signatory, that stipulated that no one should be left without a nation. Native women who fell under section 12(1)(b) were people without nationalities, she said. John Munro, then Minister of Indian Affairs, agreed with Charlie and invited her to Ottawa for a five-hour meeting to discuss amendments to end legally entrenched discrimination against Native women.

Charlie had to fight not only the government on this issue but also Native men themselves. The Assembly of First Nations took a stand against Bill C-31, An Act to Amend the Indian Act, reasoning that they did not have the infrastructure to accommodate large numbers of women in the event that many of them would want to return to live on reserves. They estimated that the cost to Ottawa would be $295,000,000 if only 10% returned and $420,000,000 if 20% returned. Three bands challenged the amendments in the Supreme Court in 1995. In the "Sawridge Band v. Canada" case, the bands claimed they had a "woman follows man" custom which meant that women marrying non-band members left the band. They argued that this custom was protected by section 35 of the Canada Constitution Act of 1982 which guarantees aboriginal and treaty rights equally to both men and women. They maintained that the Indian Act amendments violated this custom by requiring that women be reinstated to the band lists. The court rejected this argument, stating that section 35(4) of the Constitution Act extinguished any discriminatory customs. The court also found that the bands had not really proved that there ever was such a custom.

Bill C-31 passed on June 28, 1985, allowing women who married non-Native men, and their children, to regain their status. Rose Charlie, together with many others, such as Mary Two-Axe Early, a Mohawk, who had worked toward Bill C-31, was able to celebrate a hard-won victory for Native women. Mary Two-Axe Early was the first Native woman to be re-enfranchised after Bill C-31 was passed.

However, the definition of who can be recognized as an Indian under the Act does not rest with First Nations people but is left up to the government. In addition, Bill C-31 gives authority to bands to determine who can become a band member, so those who regained status under Bill C-31 are not automatically given band membership or the rights that go with it. The most recent Royal Commission on Aboriginal Rights acknowledges that as an effect of Bill C-31, women and their children may suffer emotional and material consequences from being excluded by band decisions. What are the excluded women to tell their children? That because of Bill C-31 they are not Native in the eyes of the government? That their heritage, cultural traditions and language are out of reach for them? Unity and strength come from a shared history and give people a strong sense of themselves. For some, participation in their Native heritage may be but a distant hope.

It is essential for the health and well-being of any group, and crucial for its existence, to have control over its own fate, but during much of the history of Native and non-Native interaction, that control rested in the hands of the federal government, which spent a great deal of time questioning the value of Native communities. It is through the efforts of people like Rose Charlie that aboriginal groups have taken the first steps toward controlling their destinies.

A letter to Charlie on her receipt of the Governor General's Award epitomizes her unselfish devotion to humanity: "You have been a light in the dark and a beacon of support for many native women around the world. You gave many the belief in themselves to step out as leaders for their people at home and nationally."[35]

*\*\**

During the 1990s, legislative directives protecting women's rights continue to be passed. The British Columbia Ministry of Women's Equality was formed in 1991 and has since done a great deal to bring about fairness and equity in women's lives. The ministry has helped to make more child-care options available to families, provided services for women who are victims of violence and increased women's access to education and training. It has also begun work to help close the wage gap between women and men. In 1994 the ministry published a report titled *Women Count*, a statistical profile of women's lives and work in BC. It is important data, for it looks at the experiences of women in communities across BC and the barriers that limit women's opportunities and choices.

Many positive changes have occurred since women first voiced anger at their unequal treatment before the law. Madam Justice Bertha Wilson voiced her opinion on the difference women can make when she wrote, "If women lawyers and judges thought their differing perspectives on life can bring a new humanity to bear on the decision-making process, perhaps they will make a difference. Perhaps they will succeed in infusing the law with an understanding of what it means to be fully human."[36]

# Chapter Six

# WOMEN IN SCIENCE

O NE OF THE determining features of humankind is our ability to influence the environment. Science and technology have been part of human progress for as long as human beings have populated the world, and women have accomplished as much as men in researching and asking questions about the natural world. British Columbia has been fortunate in the kinds of people who have probed scientific laws and principles, seeking knowledge for the betterment of its citizens.

The abundance of natural resources in British Columbia set the direction for its development, but the priorities of international trade demanded exploitation of the land and the sea, and little attention was given to the symbiotic network of the flora and fauna. BC was rich in furs, salmon, timber and minerals, which were easily carved up by industrialists and speculators, in many cases with the encouragement of the provincial government. For early politicians to become engaged in the broader vision of what BC might become was waved aside as political suicide.

Some people, however, stepped aside from the get-rich-quick schemes and patiently studied and documented BC's abundant natural wealth, either for their own enjoyment or in the hope of creating an appreciation of the intricacies of natural history. Julia Henshaw was one such person. In the early 1900s, in her efforts to understand the rich botanical resources of the province, she hiked up and down mountains and poked around in alpine meadows, recording and writing about plant life. Her work was important to the annals of botany, for her research and books served as a starting point to which other botanists could refer in their investigations.

Julia Henshaw
1869 - 1937

Julia Henshaw's love of science and the natural world made her one of British Columbia's leading botanists. Having achieved international recognition as a writer, lecturer and botanist, Henshaw is listed in *Who's Who in Western Canada*. A multifaceted person, Henshaw was editor of *The Vancouver Province* in 1902, had the daring to drive the first motorcar across the Rockies, received the Croix de Guerre as an ambulance driver on the Western Front during the First World War and was a Fellow of the Royal Geographical Society.

Julia Willmothe Henderson was the daughter of William Henderson of Durkham and Ashford Court, Shropshire, England. Unfortunately, not much is known of her early life or her arrival in Canada. She is reported to have moved to British Columbia in 1891, and married Charles Grant Henshaw in 1909. As a botanist Henshaw explored and mapped central Vancouver Island, and it was for her detailed descriptions and explorations of the flora of the central coast that she was made a Fellow of the Royal Geographical Society in 1911.

An energetic woman, she founded the Georgian Club, the first women's social club in Vancouver. The Georgian Club, which operates to this day, has been in existence for 87 years. Henshaw wrote numerous articles and books on her botanical discoveries and one of her books on wildflowers proved to be so popular that it went into a second printing. She excelled at writing and as a pioneer newspaperwoman, she had a regular column in *The Vancouver Province*. In addition to her biological interests she wrote on other topics. One of her books, entitled *Hypnotized*, was the Canadian "book of the year" for 1889; she wrote commentaries on George Bernard Shaw and two novels, *Why Not, Sweetheart?* and *Is It Just?* She also wrote the definitive botanical study of British Columbia, her searches for botanical specimens taking her on hikes all over the

*Julia Henshaw.* (COURTESY CITY OF VANCOUVER ARCHIVES, PORT. P. 1073, N. 943)

province. While walking in the Rocky Mountains she discovered the *Cypripedium acule*, or pink lady's slipper, so rare that she considered it the crowning triumph of her botanical work in that region.

Henshaw joined the Vancouver chapter of the Alpine Club of Canada and continued as a member for many years. She knew the veteran mountaineer Phyllis Munday and judged a photo competition which Munday had entered for the Alpine Club's best collection of photographs of pressed wildflowers. In 1920 an Alpine Congress was held in Monaco and Henshaw was sent to represent the Alpine Club of Canada. It was a big event, for there were members from mountaineering clubs from all over the world. Henshaw gave a talk on the flora and fauna of the Rocky Mountains which she illustrated with hand-coloured lantern slides. After the First World War Henshaw presented a series of lectures in France on botany, at the behest of the French Alpine Club. In appreciation they gave her a silver medal, a privileged honour.

Henshaw's dedication to her country kept her extremely busy during the First World War. She spent a great deal of time with her husband, working in the recruiting office in Vancouver, and gave a series of lectures under the auspices of the Canadian War Contingent to raise money for the purpose of providing every Canadian soldier with a Christmas gift. Feeling the need to participate in the war effort more directly, she went to France and served in an ambulance unit. She often worked heroically under heavy shellfire and aerial bombardment, evacuating and nursing wounded soldiers. For her courageous actions, she received the Croix de Guerre and the Gold Star, and the French government honoured her with a portrait of Napoleon the Third.

Upon her return home to British Columbia, Henshaw continued with her research into botany but sadly, she spent the last nine years of her life in ill health, and died in 1937. Her observations and writing provided a profound understanding of one important part of British Columbia's natural heritage.

In the preface to one of her books on wildflowers, Henshaw showed her love of nature. It could just as well be used for an epitaph on her life. "It matters not at what hour one goes to the mountains, whether in the amethyst dawn, when the golden gates of sunrise fall ajar and the first faint rustle of the leaves stirs the dreaming world to consciousness, dispersing mists and dew; in the brilliant noon-tide when life marches on with all her banners unfurled and every plant is budding and blowing as the sap runs freely, and the sun's rays gild hill and vale; or in the amber evening when purple shadows steal with phantom feet from cliff to cliff and down in the dusk of the forest, dewdrops spangle leaf and bloom as god lights the star lamps of his high heaven and puts out the day."[1]

\* \* \*

Living in makeshift tents or camps far from other people and eating only what can be gleaned from the wild or from an ever-dwindling supply of canned foods is not how most people would choose to live their lives. But the efforts of a few brave women who have spent years in isolation investigating animals in their natural habitat have revolutionized the science of animal studies. It is through the patience and persistence of women like Jane Goodall, Dian Fossey and Alexandra Morton that scientists have discovered that human beings are not the only creatures capable of showing emotions. Because of their fascination with and desire to understand animals, scientists are learning that joy, sorrow, and mental and physical suffering are felt by many animals. These women have shown, through their studies of chimpanzees, gorillas, whales and dolphins, that the line dividing humans and non-humans is fuzzy.

Science's expanding knowledge of the true nature of animals means a new respect for all non-humans. This raises serious moral and ethical questions. How are people, for example, to treat animals and the environment in which they live? Jane Goodall, the well-known field researcher on chimpanzees, has grave concern about the kinds of decisions that face us. As she explained, "This knowledge leads into some ethical problems with other non-humans. And then this leads into a whole concern for the way we humans are arro-gantly spoiling the natural world, causing deserts and pollution."[2] It is important to turn attention to appropriate and workable solutions for the benefit of all humankind, Goodall advises.

It is the issue of responsible and ethical behaviour that whale- and dolphin-researcher Alexandra Morton has spent the last 20 years addressing. "I have only begun to learn the story of white-sided dolphins," she writes. "While it pleases me that dolphins can still make a living here in the Broughton, I fear for their future among bottom trawlers, salmon farms, and clearcuts in the watershed. I spend less time now listening to whales or pursuing dolphins and more talking to politicians."[3]

Alexandra Morton
1957 - present

Upcoast some 500 kilometres from Vancouver, in a sleepy back-water just north of Cramer Pass, a small wooden house is perched neatly on a rock bluff. In Echo Bay, on the western shore of Gilford Island, Alexandra Morton has lived for the last 14 years. She is a whale researcher, artist, author, environmentalist and mother. Morton belongs to that special class of women who have spent their lives living with and researching wild animals. Known worldwide as "the Whale Lady," Morton has lived all of her adult life listening to, watching, photographing and living with *orcinus orca*, more commonly known as the killer whale. She and her small daughter, Clio, are often seen bobbing among the marine mammals in her six-metre dory, Morton with camera and hydrophone in hand, recording whale activity and communication patterns.

Even when Morton is at home, sitting by the fireplace playing with her daughter or relaxing with a cup of tea, she is still at work, listening to whales through the hydrophone that she has installed in the bay near her house. The orcas' high-pitched, lilting calls often reach her at night when she is asleep and Morton sometimes incorporates their calls into her dreams, struggling to get to them. At other times, when she manages to wake up, she will record their sounds on her tape recorder. Morton doesn't need to see the whales; she knows who they are, so familiar are their calls to her. Both her daughter and her son have logged many hours with the whales, as Morton is a firm believer in involving her children in her research. Often asked by young women about the possibility of taking their children into the field, she assures them that it can and should be done. She cautions them that organization and planning are important, but maintains that you raise a very happy child. It's not surprising that Clio's small vocabulary consists of the words whale, bird and boat and that she would prefer to be sung to sleep by the sound of whales rather than the latest pop diva.

Morton was born in Lakeville, Connecticut, in 1957 into a family of artists, musicians, painters, weavers and writers. As a young girl she had a passion for art and for animals and at one point early in her life, she had the opportunity to attend a talk given by Jane Goodall. Excited by all that she had heard, Morton went down to the podium to talk to her. Waiting politely for her turn, she suddenly became tongue-tied and couldn't remember the questions that she wanted to ask. Sensing Morton's distress, Goodall gave her a warm smile. Morton was touched by her gentleness and thought that she too would like to study primates when she grew up. She would recount this story years later to Jane Goodall when they met at a private luncheon.

Morton followed in her family's footsteps and her art work took precedence. By the time she was 18, she was earning her living as a graphic artist for ABC Television in Washington, DC. Deciding that Los Angeles was the place to be, she moved to California in 1976 to continue her career.

In the 1970s a new physical anthropology was being embraced by the scientific community. Scientists were beginning to realize that animals studied in the field yielded complex behaviour patterns and communication structures that were previously thought to be much simpler. Morton was intrigued by this new science. In Los Angeles she attended a lecture on dolphin communication presented by Dr. John Lilly, a physician and psychoanalyst. He was interested in inter-species communication and had been doing work with dolphins in the Virgin Islands, trying to teach them to speak English.

The idea that language patterns might exist for non-human mammals was exciting to Morton. She managed to get to know Lilly and he, liking her work, hired her to paint a mural in his house. He wanted Morton to portray dolphins and humans in a conscious connection to each other, so she designed and painted a dolphin head and a human head together, with bubbles coming from them expanding to a multicoloured light, implying that they were sharing a thought. One day while working on the mural, Morton noticed a door cracked open with cool air wafting out. Needing some respite from the summer's heat she went toward the door and peeked in. There she found a room that housed thousands of audio tapes, all recordings of Dr. Lilly's work with dolphins.

Morton went to Lilly to ask if she could listen to his tapes. His first reaction was to say no but then he reconsidered and acknowledged that he did need someone to catalogue them. Morton struck a bargain; she would catalogue his tapes if she could also listen to them. Every Sunday for the next two years Morton worked as a volunteer. She listened to every third tape and discovered that Lilly's experiments in trying to teach dolphins to speak English did not work. Little was known at the time about how dolphins produce sounds but Morton realized that since they do not have the vocal cords needed to produce human language, it was impossible for them to learn to speak English. They could make some consonants but no vowels. What really fascinated her was dolphins speaking to dolphins. She wanted to know what they were saying, how they were communicating and most particularly, what a non-human mind was thinking.

Morton realized that her life path was about to change. She would continue to earn her living as a graphic artist, she decided, but she would explore communication patterns in dolphins. With so many questions unanswered she took the next step and asked the local oceanarium, Marineland of the Pacific, if she could study their bottle-nosed dolphins. Tom Otten, the director, was delighted with Morton's request, particularly because Marineland was being closed for renovations and he was afraid the dolphins might be bored with no one to play with. He asked Morton if she would mind swimming with them. Trying to contain her excitement she burst out, "Would I mind?! No problem!" For the next year Morton recorded the dolphins' language, trying to link sounds to behaviour. She developed a system to graph their sounds but she was finding that language models were hard to establish. Dolphin sound production was so quick that individual sounds were hard to isolate. Also, many of their calls were pitched beyond the range of human hearing. She knew she was outclassed but wasn't quite sure what to do about it.

As it happened, one of the killer whales in Marineland was about to give birth and the curator asked her to drop her hydrophone into the tank and record the events surrounding the birth. It seemed such an honour that Morton did not refuse, even though at the time she thought killer whales were boring. What she witnessed in that tank caused her to change direction in her research.

The baby died. Morton stayed by the side of the tank for three days and nights, taking time out only for the occasional nap. She found that Corky, the mother, made the same high-pitched wailing sound, over and over again for three days. Corky also exhibited bizarre behaviour, staying at the very bottom of her tank and rising only to take a breath of air. Every now and again Orky, her male companion, came next to her and made a call that sounded like "wakow." Corky ignored him entirely but by the third night she answered him, rose off the bottom of the tank and swam alongside Orky while both whales repeated the same sound back and forth for an hour. The next day, Corky was eating and began to look at her trainers. She had come out of this period of grieving healed to some degree. Not only was Morton emotionally struck by the mourning that she had just witnessed but she realized that killer whale behaviour and communication were more within the realm of human speed and hearing. That was when she left the dolphin tank.

Morton stayed with Corky and Orky for the next two years, studying their language. She was hoping Corky would give birth again so she could study the development of language in the baby, believing that what the baby first picked up on would provide a clue to their language structure. Corky did give birth again but that baby also died. By now Morton was so emotionally involved with Corky that she grieved along with her. Morton felt ashamed and deeply saddened and knew her species to be responsible for the baby's death. She could no longer study whales in captivity; she had to leave.

Corky had been taken from British Columbia waters in 1969. Orcas, once thought to be pests, were captured indiscriminately throughout the 1960s for aquariums; by 1970 three dozen orcas had been taken from BC. The Canadian government decided to conduct a census before granting more permits for the capturing of these whales, and Dr. Michael Bigg, who was the head of marine-mammal research on the west coast, carried it out. As a result of his study, the capture of orcas from BC waters was disallowed, except for replacement of those that died in Canadian aquariums. Canada continued to issue permits for replacement purposes until 1983 but aquariums preferred to purchase orcas from Iceland, hoping to avoid any controversy.

With the experience Morton had gained from her two years of learning Corky's family language, she wondered about the possibility of finding her family. Dialects were known to exist and Morton hoped to compare the sounds that she had learned from the whales in a captive environment with Corky's family in the wild. She called Dr. Bigg and found him very welcoming and helpful. Yes, he knew Corky's family and told Morton that if she were to go to Alert Bay in August she would most likely see them. That was the summer of 1979.

Morton sold her Volvo, bought an old Toyota pickup truck and packed it with everything she imagined she would need. Anxious to get to Alert Bay, she drove straight through and arrived there in a record three days; the person who had arranged to meet her was nowhere in sight. Not knowing what else to do she pumped up the inflatable boat that she had purchased in California, packed it to overflowing and looked for a place to tie up. Seine boats were jostling for places and Morton, who had never seen a seine boat before and was bewildered by the sights and sounds of the fishing fleet, finally found a spot under the ramp. Suddenly, whales showed up, right off Alert Bay. Morton had a moment of hanging onto the dock thinking, "Wow! There they are but I don't have a chart, and where's Paul and gosh if they're right there I could probably just go out and come right back."[4] She said she has often had this experience in her life; she was really afraid to do something but just couldn't help herself.

"I felt like I was in a dream," Morton continued. "I remember getting into my boat and puttering off. As soon as I got to the whales, I turned the engine off, put my hydrophone in the water and it was the A5s, Corky's family, making the same calls. The first thing I noticed were these long calls, echoing. I'd always heard them in a tank with the drains going and the sound bouncing off the walls. The other thing that got me was these fat sassy little babies romping and splashing around their mums. They looked so healthy. I felt tears come to my eyes. I remember feeling a real pang of guilt that I shouldn't be here, it should have been those whales from Marineland. Corky's family was all around me and it was wonderful not to be at the edge of that little pool looking at captives. I was in their environment; they were at home and I was the visitor."[5]

After that summer Morton went back to California, intending to enter a Ph.D. program at the University of California at Los Angeles to study communication in animals. Exhilarated and somewhat in a daze from her summer with the whales she signed up for some preliminary courses. She was sitting in one of her classes, concentrating on the topic at hand, when she had one of those completely uninvited thoughts: "Go to Canada and stay for a year." Morton's studies were going well but her Ph.D. supervisor told her that she would never get a doctorate studying whales. There was so little known about them that to embark on such a study would take too long. What she needed to do, he advised, was to study something with a short life cycle. He suggested guppies. Morton balked at the idea of studying guppies. She decided to follow her intuition and move to British Columbia to continue her study of orcas. She completed her classwork, then packed her bags and went back to Alert Bay. She knew that she was finally home.

Morton spent that summer following the whales in her inflatable boat, learning the individual families, tracking their behaviour and recording their language. Around the end of the summer she was out in her boat when a filmmaker, Michael O'Neil, said that he had a film crew down at the rubbing beach at Robson Bight and wanted to film a researcher watching the whales underwater. Having lived in Los Angeles Morton was more than a little suspicious of filmmakers so she gracefully declined, citing her research priorities. Not to be put off, he offered to buy her gasoline for her boat. Always short of money, she agreed. She was about to experience again one of those twists of fate which seemed to govern her life. "I was sitting there on the beach," she explained, "waiting for Michael to set up his equipment when his partner, Robin, walks out of the water and strips off his wet suit. Here is this gorgeous man with a whale tattoo on his shoulder. I thought, 'O.K., who is this guy?' He certainly had my complete attention. We proceeded to fall in love very quickly. We were married the following April, moved aboard a boat and had Jarret in December. I am really glad for all of that. I know now that there is no point in waiting."[6]

In order to finance their research and filmmaking, Morton and her husband chartered their 19-metre boat, *Blue Fjord*. They carried clients in Burrard Inlet, Indian Arm, Port Hardy and on up to the Queen Charlotte Islands but more and more, they found that chartering took them away from their work with the whales. They were chartering their boat as a support vessel for an Imax film in Goletas Channel when Morton decided she had had enough. She was in the galley making sandwiches and noticed whales going by. The next thing she knew "this young blond thing," as Morton referred to her, jumped into their inflatable boat to follow the whales. That was it. She told Robin that she would plan the menus, put the food on board and hire a cook; she was not cooking on the boat any more. Robin admitted to feeling the same and he too wanted to get back to his film work with the whales. Also, Jarret was reaching toddler-hood and the Mortons knew that their young son needed to be around other children. They decided to put their roots down and live as inexpensively as they could. The question was, where?

The answer was not far away. On a cold, crisp day in October 1984, Morton, Robin and Jarret were out in their inflatable boat following a family of whales when Fife Sound opened up and in front of them sat a row of neatly placed floathouses with smoke billowing out of the chimneys. They were aghast. Their image of entering a virgin wilderness was shattered. It was late in the day, and they knew that it wasn't wise to try and find their way back to *Blue Fjord*. They putted over to one of the floathomes, knocked on the door and were greeted by a friendly couple who took them in, fed them and gave them a place to sleep for the night. They thought the Mortons more than a little odd. The Royal Canadian Mounted Police had recently visited the community to warn them about an influx of drug runners but despite the community's initial cautious reaction, they welcomed this young couple, and in Echo Bay the Mortons found a home.

Then Robin died tragically, in a diving accident in 1986. He had met with Jacques Cousteau's crew who had been filming in Johnstone Strait. Cousteau didn't have any underwater film of the whales and wanted to see Robin's film. Excited at the thought of selling film to Cousteau, Robin went to the rubbing beach to capture some more underwater footage. He was using a new rebreather unit that he had been given as payment for some of his film footage; a small valve became clogged and the percentage of oxygen dropped. He simply passed out underwater and drowned when the regulator fell out of his mouth. Morton and four-year-old Jarret were near Robin at the time, waiting for him in their inflatable boat. Morton became suspicious when Robin didn't surface.

"Rob went in the water when he saw the whale known as A9 swimming toward him," she explained. "I was pleased for him because I knew he would get some good footage. Suddenly A9 turned around and just barreled out of there. I knew something was wrong but Rob had told me time and time again, 'Don't come and get me when I'm filming. Don't move the boat.' I waited but finally he was just down too long. I couldn't take it any longer so I moved the boat in and found him lying on the bottom. I didn't know what to do. I had a small child in the Zodiac and was afraid to leave Jarret by himself and the water is so cold that without a drysuit I stood a chance of becoming hypothermic. I don't know how it happened but I found I was in the water. I had tied myself to the boat with a long rope so I was able to go down and pull Robin up."[7]

Morton spent a lot of time struggling with Robin's death. She questioned the notion of fate, she blamed herself, she was angry at Robin and at the people who had given him the rebreather. She was alone and lonely, and lamented the lack of a socially sanctioned mourning ceremony. "I would mention him and conversations would go dead," she remembered. "People didn't know how to deal with me. All I really wanted was to be invited in and given a break from my grieving. Instead, people would come up to me and say 'Have you adjusted?' I wanted to shout back, 'What do you mean have I adjusted? No, I'm really hurting here.' There was no way for me to show people that I was still in mourning. We're missing such cultural trappings in our society. I would have loved to have worn a burlap sack, shaved my head and smeared ashes all over me, except I would have been thought insane."[8]

Morton quit whale watching for a few months, needing time to rest and think, and to confront elements in her character she had never known. She spent the rest of the fall making a home for herself and Jarret. One stormy February day, a lone killer whale swam in front of Morton's house. She sat there all day and watched the bull go back and forth in front of her. She felt as if she were in an oceanarium. She wasn't really sure who the whale was, thinking it might be one of the transients named F1. The scientist in her kicked in and she wanted to know who he was and what he was doing. Upon waking the next morning her first thought was, "Is he still there?" She pushed the idea from her mind because she had never had any killer whale stay around, but he was there, still swimming back and forth as if beckoning to her. The storm had abated so she grabbed her camera and hydrophone, got into her boat with Jarret and followed him down Tribune Channel. That broke the dam, and she went out whale watching again.

As a memorial to her husband, Morton used the money from his life insurance policy to pay for the processing of his film. Money was always difficult to come by, and film developing was expensive, so Robin had stored his undeveloped film in their freezer. CBS, Jacques Cousteau and others all bid for Robin's film. The concern Morton had was that they each wanted to use bits of the film to embellish their own. She refused all offers and instead teamed up

*Alexandra Morton, photographing whales.* (COURTESY CHRIS BENNETT)

with Michael Chechik from Omni Films to make a film for the series *National Geographic Explorer*. It was a beautiful and successful film and in some small way helped Morton with her loss.

Left on her own, Morton had to come to terms with living in the untamed northwest. Her first attempt at splitting firewood left her with a broken axe handle, and she lost her boat in a storm because she had failed to tie it up properly. Many people thought that she would leave her home in Echo Bay. They reasoned that it was simply too difficult for her to homestead on her own, but they were not yet acquainted with Morton's dedication to her research, and her inner strength. She learned to split firewood, use a chainsaw, run a generator, live off the land, roof a house and keep the ever-persistent bears from knocking down the walls of her house.

There was one night, she recounted, when she had been canning salmon and a black bear tried to get into her house. She awoke to pounding on the wall behind her head and through the window saw the large bear glistening in the moonlight. She had no idea how to deal with intrusive bears. She grabbed an air horn and blasted it, she pounded on the walls, anything to make enough noise to scare him off, but the bear was oblivious to all her efforts. Unable to deter him and not knowing what else to do, she sat up all night on her bed with a kitchen knife in her hand. After that, Morton learned to shoot a rifle and now when she hears unusual sounds she turns off all the lights, gets her flashlight and dogs, puts some bullets in her pocket and goes out the front door.

As Morton became more independent, she bought an old derelict floathouse which she rebuilt and moved up on the land. Her neighbours came to help shingle her roof. It was in the middle of January, cold and raining. "It took two days to complete the job. There were six of us on the roof. We were laughing and telling stories. I had never experienced anything like that in my life. I love every one of them. Since then I have helped them with their roofs. That's our currency out here. I'm happy to bring my neighbours a fish because they bring me prawns. I am so happy to put somebody's chainsaw out of the rain because I know they are going to bail my boat. It's a nice way to live your life. If, when I was a little girl, I had been given a glimpse of my life now, at the age of 40, I would have been delighted. That is a sign of a successful life. Life is not about how much money you have in the bank or how many possessions you own but about what you give, about living up to your potential."[9]

*Alexandra Morton rowing her son Jarret to school, with dog Kelsey.*
(COLLECTION OF ALEXANDRA MORTON)

In the ensuing years Morton has built up her garden, continued her study of whales, raised Jarret and written two children's books. *Siwiti — A Whale's Story* won the BC Book Prize for children's books in 1991 and *In the Company of Whales* became a Canadian Children's Book Centre choice. Through her books children have learned that orcas live in families, that each family has its own dialect, that each whale has a distinct personality, and that they play games, are quite inventive and love watching sunsets. Children from all over the world come whale watching in Johnstone Strait armed with Morton's books, hoping to see their favourite whales. Her book about Siwiti was ranked by *BC BookWorld* as one of the 200 most significant BC books of the 20th century.

Morton's research was beginning to expand beyond the field of whale acoustics. She started out trying to decode whale communication and social patterns but slowly realized that their behaviour was responsive to and dependent upon their environment. Travelling more widely in her research, Morton began to study all of the marine activity in the Broughton Archipelago. She had no fixed agenda, no axe to grind; she simply studied and watched and let the animals guide her. What she learned about the marine habitat was distressing.

The minke whales had all but disappeared, there had been a 97% decline in humpback whales, orcas were rarely sighted, seals were gone, along with the harbour porpoise and much of the bird life, chinook salmon stocks had collapsed, life on the ocean floor was suffering and toxic algae blooms were occurring for the first time. The Broughton Archipelago as a marine environment was dying.

At the same time as the decline in the ecosystem was taking place, 20 steel-and-net salmon farms were anchored in bays throughout the archipelago. Morton began to notice that in the water beneath and around the salmon farms, changes were taking place. The fish in the local hatchery were picking up diseases that they had never had before, diseases typical in fish farms. Wild hatchery stocks plummeted from an average loss of 3% a year to 50%. Further, Morton found that when a salmon farm introduced baby salmon infected with a strain of furunculosis, the chinook salmon that passed that farm at the time of the epidemic vanished, and the chinook stocks in adjacent Kingcome Inlet collapsed the following year. Morton also noted that prawn fishers found that when salmon farms were situated on or near prime prawn grounds the number of prawns fell to nearly zero. Predatory animals such as harbour seals, sea gulls, blue herons and diving birds, considered pests by the fish farmers, were often shot.

This quiet, mild-mannered researcher could not stand idly by. If she didn't do something there would be no whales to research or fish to catch. Her days of innocence were over. She wrote to scientists in all the major fish-farming countries — Norway, Scotland, and Chile — to gather information; she read and studied scientific reports about aquaculture and its impact on the environment; she wrote to the Department of Fisheries and Oceans, supplying them with all of the facts she had gathered; and she presented papers at hearings and meetings concerned with aquaculture. Her information was in demand in the scientific community and among environmental groups, and she travelled to Washington, DC, to give a paper at an aquaculture briefing at the Smithsonian Institute.

Morton spent a lot of time trying to inform the public and government officials about the impending ecological disaster in the Broughton Archipelago. She was sought after by the popular press and has given countless interviews to journalists and TV reporters from all over the world. She has talked about the problems of disease transfer to wild stocks, the impact of escaped farm fish on wild stocks, the devastation of the sea bottom, the pollution of the seawater due to a build-up of farm wastes and the use of chemicals, the killing of predator birds and sea animals and the deafening of seals through the use of acoustic harassment devices. Morton's information, however, was ignored by the government.

Fish farming is big business, and most of the aquaculture companies operating in British Columbia waters are owned by large international corporations such as Stolt-Nielsen of Norway. Fish farming, Morton says, is frequently promoted as the simple answer to world food shortages. However, farm fish eat expensively harvested, manufactured, medicated, packaged and delivered feed and require 40,000 to 50,000 times more ocean surface area to survive than equivalent numbers of wild fish.

"Imagine a deer farm," Morton suggests, "where the surrounding lands wallow in wastes and antibiotic-resistant bacteria, where neighbouring wild populations of deer bow under open sores and debilitating loads of parasites. If toxic algae blooms were airborne and diseased farmed deer escaped by the thousands to threaten neighbouring cattle, those farms would be outlawed."[10]

Morton spent years fighting this issue on her own, taking time away from her research as well as using up her financial resources. She recognizes this as part of the price of caring and being involved. While her first priorities are her family and her research, it has become increasingly difficult for Morton to maintain her objectivity when faced daily with the destruction of an ecosystem. As a scientist she knows only too well the fragility of the earth's environment, and to turn her back on what was happening would be to deny what it means to be human.

As the crisis over salmon farming worsened, Morton's quiet, peaceful life was disrupted. "Someone has to be here to measure and watch and report," she says. "That is my role right now. It's not very satisfying because right now things are getting worse. It takes a long time to build a momentum and the archipelago can't wait that long."[11]

Christened by the media the "Conscience of the Coast," she has also been spurned and shunned, and had to endure threats. Morton did not ask to be pushed to the forefront of the environmental movement; she did not want to get caught up in political and economic issues. "You can't always avoid politics," Morton warns. "But you have to be careful because it is all too easy to get swept up in political machinations and the next thing you know you're not doing anything else. I know personally I will lose it if that happens. I will become so angry and so frustrated and so depressed that I will fall apart. I can feel it not too far away."[12] But Morton maintains her sense of humour and has her family to help keep her grounded.

"I have Eric, my partner, and my two children to think about," she says. "If I step over that line I know that I will hurt them. I think that's where Dian Fossey lost out; she didn't have anyone, whereas Jane Goodall had her son. All the same, I feel that if I were in Dian Fossey's shoes I would have lost it too. I'm not finding whales dismembered. I haven't been pushed that far."[13] Eventually, the luminaries of the environmental movement such as the Sierra Legal Defence Fund, the David Suzuki Foundation, the Georgia Strait Alliance and others have stepped in to help. She welcomes this change and is content to play the role of a resource person.

Morton can, however, look back on her work with pride, for her research has been of critical importance in piecing together the intricate puzzle of the Broughton Archipelago's marine ecosystem. She has shown what remarkable creatures the orcas are and she has been the catalyst around whom politicians, concerned citizens and other scientists have been able to gather to discuss ways of dealing with a dying ecosystem. Without her, a very valuable part of British Columbia's environment could die.

Among the questions many media people ask Morton are, "Why does the Broughton Archipelago matter? Why do we want the whales? Who cares, really, when it comes down to a person's day-to-day life?" She answers that our environment is not a luxury item; it is our life-support system. "This is all we have in the universe," she says, "and we are chipping away at it with such abandon. We can't disassemble or manipulate parts of the ecosystem, particularly as we don't know how all of the unique interrelationships fit together."[14] As part of her legacy she would very much like to see the Broughton Archipelago turn the tide; she would like to leave it better than it was when she arrived, nearly 20 years ago.

Morton would also like to decode whale communication or at least lay the groundwork. She is buoyed by the hundreds of letters she receives from children who have read her books. One came from a little boy in Spain who said he loved the whale known as Sharky. That is good for Sharky, Morton believes, because the more people can individualize and personalize certain elements in the environment, the more they may want to protect it. She also remembers a letter from a little girl who said she had two things she wanted to accomplish in life: one was to see orcas and the other was to get Morton to write her back. "That was her third letter to me," she says. "I sat down and wrote to her. I love those moments. I love speaking to children because I remember being a child and I know that one person can change your life. One person can let you know that your dreams are possible."[15]

\*\*\*

Questions of gender and science have recently come into the foreground in educational theory and government human-resource policies. Women make up only 19% of people employed in the natural sciences, engineering and mathematics. Fewer yet are represented in the growing industry of computer science. If one believes that knowledge is power, and science and technology are today's line to that power, then women are indeed far behind.

The various research reports that have come out of years of study reveal that as a course of study and occupation, science is largely closed to women. Girls in grade one and two think that they can do anything but by the time they are in grade six they have made up their minds about what is and is not possible, and science, they have decided, is better left to boys. They are perceptive. Women face barriers to entry and achievement at all stages of the professional scientific ladder.

Fortunately, numerous programs are opening up to help increase the participation of women in science. The British Columbia Science Council has supported a group of women who head up the Women in Science, Technology, Trades and Engineering program. Its goal is to develop curriculum which would increase the numbers of women in science and technology within the province. In 1997 the BC chapter of The Canadian Association for Girls in Science was organized by professional women scientists, to promote science and technology among girls. Among a host of other activities, they hold workshops for parents to help them encourage their daughters to study math and science, host conferences for young women, run summer programs for senior high school students that focus on science and explore career pathways with young girls.

There are also scientists like Hilda Ching, a parasitologist, who initiated the first conference for Canadian Women in Science in 1983. The conference was successful and led to the creation by Ching of a variety of science-related programs for women and girls. For example, she started the "Scientists and Innovators" program in the schools which introduced students to individual scientists. She also made a video, "What Do Scientists Do?" that profiles women scientists in various fields. Dr. Maria Issa, who works at the University of British Columbia's Department of Pathology and Laboratory Medicine, has made enormous contributions to the cause of young women and science. She developed a networking system for young Vancouver women interested in science that was so successful that Science World has adopted it. She has also set up a work-experience program in various fields of science for young people in Vancouver who are thinking about a career in science and technology. With the aid and encouragement of women scientists, young women will find that science becomes a more viable option as a career choice.

SUMMARY

By the early 1990s British Columbia had a Ministry of Women's Equality. More than ever before, the voices of women were being heard. More than half of the students enrolled in post-secondary institutions were women and 58% of the labour force in BC was made up of women. As the participation rates of women in highly skilled jobs improved, more women held senior management positions in corporations; 32% of doctors and dentists were women and half of all full-time students in law, medicine and business administration were women. Women increased their presence in politics; 25% of the Members of the Legislative Assembly and 24% of local government representatives were women and 27 First Nations women, elected under the federal Indian Act, were band chiefs. Pay equity laws made a difference in women's earnings and collective bargaining helped promote gender equality as well as better working conditions. Over $100,000,000 was provided for child-care services and child-care space increased by 48%. Increased minimum wages benefited 80,000 minimum wage earners of which 70% were women.

Much has been done but women's lower wages in the paid work force remain a central fact of their working lives, violence against women and children is still present and one in four women works in a low-paying, non-unionized, service-oriented job without benefits. Women are gaining rights but those rights are fragile because as the economy tightens, women's issues and concerns get sidetracked. Poverty is a central fact of many women's lives: 60% of single mothers, and three out of four women over the age of 65 who live alone, live below the poverty level; family allowance, which began in 1945, was de-indexed in the 1990s and phased out completely in 1992, leaving Canada as the only modern industrial nation without either a tax concession or universal family allowance for children. Issues around abortion, pornography, equal pay for work of equal value and pensions remain unresolved. In 1992, the United Nations ranked Canada first in the world as a place to live but eighth for gender equality.

At present, women are forging new solutions; we are becoming leaders in the environmental movement, in business and in technology. Women are setting precedents as leaders in religions; we are on the forefront in medicine and are changing the quality of life for many people. Judi Tyabji, a mother, politician and broadcaster, is a role model and support for young women; Maria Abbott of Victoria is a leader in working for homemakers' recognition and pensions; Sophie Pierre, First Nations Chief for St. Mary's, has made great strides for her community in the area of land claims. There are also controversial women in business and politics: Peggy Witte, president and chief executive officer of Royal Oak Mines and Kim Campbell, former prime minister and current Canadian consul in Los Angeles. There are a host of women to admire in science and technology: Dr. Pauline van den Driessche, a professor of mathematics at the University of Victoria, is internationally recognized for her research in mathematical biology and for the development of an epidemiological model for HIV/AIDS; Dr. Inna Sharf is a mechanical engineer who works in the area of space robotics.

Women are building new realities and pioneering new relationships, and there will be many more stories yet to tell. All of the women in this book persisted in their own ways of doing things; they set the public agenda on their own terms and in so doing challenged us to shake off our complacency about women's place in the world. Perhaps it is time to put women of the past into stories of the present, and hope for the future.

ENDNOTES

Women in Education

1 Wilson, J. Donald, "Lottie Brown and Rural Women Teachers in British Columbia, 1928-1934," Strong-Boag, *British Columbia Reconsidered: Essays on Women*, 341.

2 *Ibid.*, 340.

3 Gaskell, Jane, "Women and Education," *The Canadian Encyclopedia Plus*, (database on CD-ROM).

4 *The Daily Colonist*, May 14, 1912, 1.

5 Cameron, Agnes Deans, Microfiche files, BC Archives.

6 M.A.P, London, Jan. 22, 1910, Microfiche files, BC Archives.

7 *The Westminster*, Canada, Feb. 1910, Microfiche files, BC Archives.

8 *The Toronto News*, Apr. 22, 1909, Microfiche files, BC Archives.

9 McGeer, Ada, "A Memory," *B.C. Historical News*, Nov. 1974, 16-17.

10 Cameron, Agnes Deans, "Parent and Teacher," *National Council of Women of Canada Report*, 1900. Also in *Educational Journal of Western Canada*, Aug.-Sept., 1900, 454-456.

11 —, "The Idea of True Citizenship-How Shall We Develop It?," *Educational Journal of Western Canada*, 233.

12 *The Victoria Times*, June 1951.

13 "1894 School Design Ahead Of Its Time," *The Daily Colonist*, June 16, 1894.

14 *The Daily Colonist*, Apr. 29, 1909.

15 Cameron, *The New North*, 251-252.

16 "Agnes Deans Cameron Heads the Poll in School Trustee Election," *The Daily Colonist*, Jan 19, 1906, 1.

17 Cameron, *The Daily Colonist*, Jan. 21, 1906, 4.
18 Lampman, P. S., Commissioner, *British Columbia Royal Commission on South Park Drawing Books*, 32.
19 Cameron, *The New North*, 83.
20 —, "The Isle of Dreams," *Canada West Magazine*, 235-239.
21 —, "Edmonton, The World's Greatest Fur-Mart," *The Pacific Monthly*, 215.
22 —, *The New North*, p.15.
23 *Ibid.*, 15.
24 *Ibid.*, 60.
25 *Ibid.*, 78-79.
26 —, "Beyond Athabasca," *Westward Ho!*, 743-750.
27 —, *The New North*, 219.
28 *Ibid.*, 246.
29 *Ibid.*, 272.
30 *The Westminster*, Feb. 1910.
31 *The Toronto Globe*, Feb. 6, 1901.
32 *The Rockford Republic*, Illinois, Mar. 6, 1909, Microfiche files, BC Archives.
33 *Woman*, London, Mar. 9, 1910, Microfiche files, BC Archives.
34 *The Toronto Globe*, Apr. 30, 1909.
35 *The Vancouver Daily World*, Feb. 2, 1916, 12.
36 Kierstead, Evlyn, "Wux Femina Facto," 1894, UBC Special Collections, 1.
37 Adilman, Tami, "Evlyn Farris and the University Women's Club," Latham and Kess, *In Her Own Right*, 158.
38 Ormsby, Margaret, *British Columbia: A History*, 4.
39 The Chilly Collective, *Breaking Anonymity: The Chilly Climate for Women Faculty*.

Women in Community Building

1 MacQueen, Bonnie, "Domesticity and Discipline: The Girl Guides in British Columbia 1910 - 1943," 231, Latham and Pazdro, *Not Just Pin Money*.
2 Munday, Phyllis, Originals, 1907-1968, Government Documents, BC Archives.
3 Munday, "The Birth of the First Vancouver Company Girl Guides," Originals, 1913-1988, Government Documents, BC Archives.
4 *Ibid.*
5 *Ibid.*

6 *Ibid.*
7 Munday, Originals, 1907-1968. Government Documents, BC Archives.
8 *Ibid.*
9 *Old Ways to Waddington*, Jan. 1964, BC Archives.
10 Munday, Phyllis, Originals, 1907-1968, Government Documents, BC Archives.
11 *Ibid.*
12 *Ibid.*
13 *Ibid.*
14 *Ibid.*
15 *Ibid.*
16 *Old Ways to Waddington*, Jan. 1964, BC Archives.
17 *Ibid.*
18 *Ibid.*
19 Cole, Douglas, "The History of the Kwakiutl Potlatch," Jonaitis, *Chiefly Feasts: The Enduring Kwakiutl Potlatch*, 137.
20 *Ibid.*, 136.
21 The term Kwakiutl came from Franz Boas' 1897 inaccurate transcription of Native names. The accepted form today is Kwakwaka'wakw nation which refers to Kwakwala-speaking people. Kwakiutl and Kwagiulth are more properly applied to those who belong to that specific tribe. Over twenty villages make up the traditional Kwakwaka'wakw nation.
22 Sproat, 1879a; DIA files; Sessional Papers; Dawson 1885, 140.
23 Cranmer Webster, Gloria, *Potlatch: A Strict Law Bids Us Dance*, U'mista Cultural Society, 1975.
24 Alfred, Agnes, Speech for the opening of the U'mista Cultural Centre, Nov. 1, 1980.

## Women in Art and Literature

1 *St. Louis & Canadian Photographer*, 1879.
2 "Photography: Hannah Hatherly Maynard," *Canadian Women's Studies*.
3 Mattison, David, "The Multiple Self of Hannah Maynard," 14, *Vanguard*, Oct. 1990.
4 *St. Louis & Canadian Photographer*, 1887.
5 "By A Woman's Hand," *The Colonist*, June, 1898.
6 *St. Louis & Canadian Photographer*, July, 1894.
7 Cridge, Edward, Spiritualism or Modern Necromancy, Sermon, July 5, 1870, 9.

8 *New West Magazine*, Winnipeg, 1888, Maynard Originals, BC Archives 1077(47).

9 Weissman Wilks, Claire, *The Eccentric Genius of Hannah Maynard.*

10 Maynard Originals, BC Archives, 1077(47), file 2C.

11 *Ibid.*

12 *The Colonist*, Sept. 29, 1912, 10, Maynard Originals, BC Archives, 1077(47).

13 Foster, Mrs. W. Garland, *Mohawk Princess*, 155.

14 *Canadian Courier*, Dec. 1913, and in Foster, *Mohawk Princess*, 59.

15 Hales, Horatio, *The Critic*, June 4, 1895.

16 Johnson, Pauline, "The Re-Interment of Red-Jacket," The Buffalo Historical Society and in Foster, *Mohawk Princess,* 34-35.

17 Johnson, Pauline,"Cry from an Indian Wife," Foster, *Mohawk Princess*, 39.

18 Foster, *Mohawk Princess*, 40.

19 Johnson, Pauline, *Flint and Feather*, preface.

20 *The Vancouver Province*, March 7, 1913.

21 Johnson, Pauline, *Legends of Vancouver*, 9.

22 Reaburn, Ronald. "Tekahionwake," *Westworld*, 50.

23 Barman, Jean, *The West Beyond the West: A History of British Columbia*, 317.

24 Livesay, Dorothy, *Right Hand Left Hand.*

25 —, *Journey With My Selves: A Memoir 1909-1963*, 91

26 *Ibid.*, 97.

27 *Ibid.*, 101

28 —, *Right Hand Left Hand*, 31.

29 *Ibid.*, 36.

30 —, *Journey With My Selves*, 74.

31 *Ibid.*, 142.

32 —, *Right Hand Left Hand*, 259-262.

33 —, *Journey With My Selves*, 149.

34 *Ibid.*, 150.

35 *Ibid.*, 154.

36 *Ibid.*, 172.

37 —, *The Self-Completing Tree*, 79.

38 —, *Journey With My Selves*, 196.

39 *Ibid.*, 199.

40 *Ibid.*, 198.

Women in Public Health

1 Barman, Jean, *The West Beyond the West: A History of British Columbia*, 231.
2 Redmond, Sister Frances, Clipping file, Vancouver City Archives.
3 MacKenzie, Norman, Address at presentation of an honorary Doctor of Science to Alice Ravenhill, University of British Columbia, 1948.
4 *The Vancouver Province*, Mar. 5, 1952.
5 BC Ministry of Health and Ministry Responsible for Seniors, Women's Health Conference: Moderator's Report, Sept. 26 - 28, 1993, 8.


Women in Politics and Law

1 MacGill, Helen Gregory, *Social Service in Vancouver*, 54. Also in Michael Cramer, "Public and Political: Documents of the Woman's Suffrage Campaign British Columbia, 1871 - 1917: The View From Victoria," Latham and Kess, *In Her Own Right*, 96.
2 *The Victoria Times*, Feb. 21, 1917, 7.
3 MacGill, Elsie Gregory, *My Mother The Judge*, 219.
4 *Ibid.*, 56.
5 MacGill, Helen Gregory, *The Work of the Juvenile Court and How to Secure Such a Court in a Canadian Community*, 10.
6 MacGill, Elsie Gregory, *My Mother The Judge*, 222.
7 *Ibid.*, 223.
8 *Ibid.*, 226.
9 *Ibid.*, 225.
10 Nobel, Terry, Interview with Grace MacInnis, Dec. 1981, BC Archives.
11 MacInnis, Grace, *J.S. Woodsworth: A Man to Remember 1874-1943*, 1.
12 Farrell, Ann, *Grace MacInnis: A Story of Love and Integrity*, 45.
13 *Ibid.*, 52.
14 *Ibid.*, 69.
15 *Ibid.*, 75.
16 Oglanby, Elva, Grace MacInnis: "The Eternal Politician," Public Radio Station CJOR, Vancouver, Oct. 1974, transcript, 63.
17 Nobel, Terry, Interview with Grace MacInnis, Dec. 1981, BC Archives.
18 *Ibid.*
19 Farrell, Ann, *Grace MacInnis*, 145.
20 Nobel, Terry, Interview with Grace MacInnis, Dec. 1981, BC Archives.

21 *Ibid.*

22 Farrell, Ann, *Grace MacInnis*, 250.

23 Stursberg, Peter, Interview with Grace MacInnis, University of British Columbia Special Collections Division.

24 *Ibid.*

25 *Ibid.*

26 Adams, Neale, "What Have You Got: — A Socialist," *The Vancouver Sun*, Feb. 19, 1975.

27 Brown, Rosemary, *Being Brown: A Very Public Life*, 49.

28 *Ibid.*, 60.

29 *Ibid.*, 83-84.

30 *Ibid.*, 227.

31 *Ibid.*, 226.

32 *Ibid.*, 184.

33 *Ibid.*, 190.

34 *First Nations Drum*, Feb. 1998, 6.

35 Charlie, Rose, Personal correspondance.

36 Ministry of Women's Equality, *Guide to Gender-Inclusion Policy and Program Development*, 1998 (online database).

Women in Science

1 Hamlyn, Ethelyn, "A Life of Colour," *The Vancouver Province*, June 13, 1932.

2 Goodall, Jane, Interview given through the Jane Goodall Institute for Primate Studies 1998 (online database).

3 Morton, Alexandra. "Where the Wild, White-Sided Dolphins Play," *California Wild: Natural Sciences for Thinking Animals*, 35.

4 Morton, personal interview, Aug. 1995.

5 *Ibid.*

6 *Ibid.*

7 *Ibid.*

8 *Ibid.*

9 *Ibid.*

10 Morton, Alexandra, "Salmon Farming's Hidden Harm," Paper presented at the Smithsonian Institute, June 2, 1995.

11 *Ibid.*

12 Morton, personal interview, Aug. 1995.

13 *Ibid.*

14 *Ibid.*

15 *Ibid.*

SELECTED BIBLIOGRAPHY

General

BC Ministry of Health and Ministry Responsible for Seniors. Women's Health Conference: Moderator's Report. Sept. 26-28, 1993.

Gaskell, Jane. Women and Education. *The Canadian Encyclopedia Plus, 1997.* (database on CD-ROM)

Gough, Lyn. *As Wise as Serpents: 1883-1939 Five Women & an Organization that Changed British Columbia.* Victoria: Swan Lake Publishing, 1988.

Szychter, Gwen. "The War Work of Women in Rural B.C. 1914-1919." *B.C. Historical News*: 5-9, Fall 1984.

The Chilly Collective. *Breaking Anonymity: The Chilly Climate for Women Faculty.* Waterloo: Wilfrid Laurier University Press, 1995.

Victoria Status of Women Action Group. *Our Hidden Heritage: Women in British Columbia History.* Victoria: Victoria Status of Women, 1975.


Agnes Deans Cameron

Agnes Deans Cameron. Microfiche files, BC Archives.

"Agnes Deans Cameron." *The Daily Colonist*, Aug. 10, 1906:5.

"Agnes Deans Cameron Heads the Poll in School Trustee Election." *The Daily Colonist*, Jan. 19, 1906:1.

Cameron, Agnes Deans. "Beyond Athabasaca." *Westward Ho! Magazine*, Dec. 1909:743-750.

—. "Buying Buffalo on the Hoof." *The Pacific Monthly*, Dec. 1901:591-602.

—. "Edmonton the World's Greatest Fur-Mart." *The Pacific Monthly*, Feb. 1907:205-215.

—. "Miss Cameron Replies." *The Daily Colonist*, Jan. 21, 1906:4.

—. "Parent and Teacher." *National Council of Women of Canada Report*, 1900.

—. "The Avatar of Jack Pemberton." *The Pacific Monthly*, May 1903:305-310.

—. "The Idea of True Citizenship-How Shall We Develop It?" *Educational Journal of Western Canada* 1(8) Dec. 1899:233.

—. "The Isle of Dreams." *Canada West Magazine*, Jan. 1908:235-237.

—. *The New North: Being Some Account of a Woman's Journey Through Canada to the Arctic*. New York: D. Appleton and Company, 1909.

Donald, Wilson. "Lottie Brown and Rural Women Teachers in British Columbia, 1928-1934." In *British Columbia Reconsidered: Essays on Women*, edited by Gillian Creese and Veronica Strong-Boag. Vancouver: Press Gang Publishers, 1992:340-363.

*Educational Journal of Western Canada* 2(5):454-456, Aug.-Sept., 1900.

Lampman, P.S., Commissioner. *British Columbia Royal Commission on South Park Drawing Books*. Victoria: British Columbia Government, 1905.

McGeer, Ada. "Agnes Deans Cameron, A Memory." *B.C. Historical News*, Nov. 1974, 8(1)1:16-17.

Pazdro, Roberta. "Agnes Deans Cameron: Against the Current." In *In Her Own Right: Selected Essays on Women's History in BC*, edited by Barbara Latham and Cathy Kess. Victoria: Camosun College, 1980.

Evlyn Farris

Adilman, Tami. "Evlyn Farris and the University Women's Club." In *In Her Own Right: Selected Essays on Women's History in BC*, edited by Barbara Latham and Cathy Kess. Victoria: Camosun College, 1980.

Kierstead, Evlyn. Wux Femina Facto. University of British Columbia Special Collections 1, 1894.

McClean, Sylvie. *A Woman of Influence: Evlyn Fenwick Farris*. Victoria: Sono Nis Press, 1997.

*The Vancouver Daily World*, Feb. 2, 1916:2.

*Western Women's Weekly*. Evelyn Farris Scrapbook. University of British Columbia Special Collections, 1918.

Dr. Margaret Ormsby

Barman, Jean. "In Memoriam: Margaret Ormsby: 1909-1996 Doyenne of BC History." *UBC Reports*, Nov. 14, 1966.

Norris, John. "Personality and History in British Columbia: Essays in Honour of Margaret Ormsby." *B.C. Studies* 32, Winter 1976-77.

Ormsby, Margaret. *British Columbia: A History*. Toronto: The Macmillans in Canada, 1958, 1959, 1971 eds.

Ormsby, Margaret, Originals, 1975-1981. Notes, correspondence, minutes and research reports collected by Dr. Ormsby during her tenure as a member of the Provincial Heritage Advisory Board, UBC Archives.


Cecilia Spofford

C. Spofford, Miscellaneous Papers, 1877, 1879, 1880. BC Archives.

Hale, Linda Louise. Appendix: "Votes for Women: Profiles of Prominent British Columbia Suffragists and Social Reformers." In *In Her Own Right: Selected Essays on Women's History in BC*, edited by Barabara Latham and Cathy Kess. Victoria: Camosun College, 1980:300-301.


Helena Gutteridge

Campbell, Marie. "Sexism in British Columbia Trade Unions, 1900-1920." In *In Her Own Right: Selected Essays on Women's History in BC*, edited by Barabara Latham and Cathy Kess. Victoria: Camosun College, 1980:167-186.

Wade, Susan. Helena Gutteridge: "Votes for Women and Trade Unions." In *In Her Own Right: Selected Essays on Women's History in BC*, edited by Barbara Latham and Cathy Kess. Victoria: Camosun College, 1980:187-201.


Phyllis Munday

*Old Ways to Waddington*. Interview with Phyllis Munday, BC Archives, Jan. 1964. (audiotape)

Bower, Dan. Interview with Phyllis Munday. Reynoldston Research and Studies, BC Archives, Nov. 3, 1973. (audiotape)

Herbert, Bill. Interview with Walter (Don) Munday for CBC Radio. The Climbing of Mount Reliance, BC Archives, Mar. 9, 1946. (audiotape)

Leslie, Susan. Interview with Phyllis Munday. Mountaineering Project. British Columbia Provincial Archives, 1978. (audiotape)

MacQueen, Bonnie. "Domesticity and Discipline: The Girl Guides in British Columbia 1910-1943." In *Not Just Pin Money*, edited by Barbara Latham and Roberta Pazdro. Victoria: Camosun College, 1984.

Miller, Naomi. "Phyllis Munday: Achieving Great Heights." *British Columbia Historical News,* 22(3):7-10, Summer 1989.

Munday, Phyllis. Originals, 1907 - 1968. Government Documents, BC Archives.

Munday, Phyllis. Originals, 1913 - 1988. Girl Guides of Canada: British Columbia Council. Government Documents, BC Archives.

Munday, Phyllis. "First Ascent of Mt. Robson by Lady Members." *Canadian Alpine Journal*, 68-74, 1924.

—. "Mystery Mountain." *The Alpine Journal* 40(236):99-101, May 1928.

—. *The Unknown Mountain.* London: Hodder and Stoughton, 1948.

### Gloria Cranmer Webster

Converse, Cathy. Personal interview with Gloria Cranmer Webster. Aug. 1995.

Cranmer Webster, Gloria. "The Contemporary Potlatch." In *Chiefly Feasts: The Enduring Kwakiutl Potlatch*, edited by Aldona Jonaitis. New York: American Museum of Natural History, 1991.

Sproat, Gilbert Malcolm to Macdonald. DIA 3669(1665), Oct.27, 1879. In *Chiefly Feasts: The Enduring Kwakiutl Potlatch*, edited by Aldona Jonaitis. New York: American Museum of Natural History, 1991.

U'mista Cultural Society. Cited 1998. (online database)

—. *Potlatch: A Strict Law Bids Us Dance.* 1975. (videocassette)

—. *Box of Treasures.* 1983. (videocassette)

### Hannah Maynard

"By A Woman's Hand." *The Daily Colonist*, June 1898.

Cridge, Edward, Dean of Christ Church. Spiritualism or Modern Necromancy. Sermon, Victoria, July 5, 1870.

Mattison, David. "The Multiple Self of Hannah Maynard." *Vanguard* 9(14):14-19, Oct. 1990.

—. "Richard Maynard, Photographer of Victoria, B.C." *History of Photography* 9(2):109-129, Apr.-June, 1985.

Maynard Collection, BC Archives 1-18:97.

Maynard, Originals, BC Archives 1077(47).

*St. Louis & Canadian Photographer*, 1879, 1887, and July 1894.

Weissman Wilks, Claire. *The Magic Box: The Eccentric Genius of Hannah Maynard.* Toronto: Exile Editions Ltd., 1980.

—. "The Eccentric Genius of Hannah Maynard." *Saturday Night*, Nov. 1980:35-40.


Pauline Johnson (Tekahionwake)

Clipping File, Pauline Johnson. Vancouver City Archives.

Foster, Mrs. W. Garland. *The Mohawk Princess (Tekahionwake): The Life of E. Pauline Johnson.* Vancouver: Lion's Gate Publishing Co., 1931.

Hales, Horatio. *The Critic.* June 4, 1895.

Hartley, Lucie. *Pauline Johnson: The Story of an American Indian.* Minneapolis: Disson Press, Inc., 1980.

"Johnson, A Poet with a Flair for the Dramatic." *The Vancouver Sun*, July 25, 1991.

Johnson E. Pauline. *The White Wampum.* London: John Lane, 1895 and Boston: Lamson, Wolffe & Co., 1895.

—. *Flint and Feather.* Toronto: Musson Book Co., 1912.

—. *Legends of Vancouver.* Vancouver: Douglas & McIntyre, edition 1977.

Keller, Betty. *Pauline: A Biography of Pauline Johnson.* Vancouver: Douglas & McIntyre, 1981.

"Our Poet Pauline." *The Vancouver Sun*, May 18, 1978.

Reaburn, Ronald. "Emily Pauline Johnson: Tekahionwake." *Westworld*, Mar.-Apr. 1977:26-28, 36, 50.

*The Daily Colonist*, Sept. 29, 1912:10.

*The Vancouver Province*, Mar. 7, 1913.

Weir, Harold. "She Sang, Careless of Fame." *The Vancouver Sun*, Mar. 17, 1961.


Dorothy Livesay

Livesay, Dorothy. *Call My People Home.* Toronto: Ryerson, 1950.

—. *Day and Night.* Toronto: Ryerson, 1944.

—. *Green Pitcher.* Toronto: Macmillan of Canada, 1928.

—. *Journey with My Selves: A Memoir 1909-1963.* Vancouver: Douglas & McIntyre, 1991.

—. *The Documentaries.* Toronto: Ryerson Press, 1968.

—. *The Self-Completing Tree: Selected Poems.* Victoria: Press Porcepic, 1986.

—. *Right Hand Left Hand: A True Life of the Thirties.* Erin: Press Porcepic, 1977.

McInnis, Nadene. *Dorothy Livesay's Poetics of Desire*. Winnipeg: Turnstone Press, 1994.

Stevens, Peter. *Dorothy Livesay: Patterns in a Poetic Life*. Oakville: ECW Press, 1992.

Tiessen, Paul, Lindsay Sorney, and Gerald Noonal, eds. *A Public and Private Voice: Essays on the Life and Work of Dorothy Livesay*. Waterloo, Ontario: University of Waterloo Press, 1986.

### Sister Frances Redmond

Redmond, Sister Frances. Clipping File, Vancouver City Archives.

Sister Frances, "City's 'Florence Nightingale' Dead." *The Vancouver Daily Province*, Apr. 15, 1932.

"St. Luke's Home." *World: Souvenir Edition*, June 1896.

### Alice Ravenhill

Black, Charlotte. Originals, 1942-1952. Director, School of Home Economics, UBC, Letters from Dr. Alice Ravenhill. Government Documents, BC Archives.

Daniels, Christine and Robert Bayliss. "Alice Ravenhill Home Economist 1859-1954." *Westminster Studies in Education* 8, 1985:21-36.

Ravenhill, Alice. *A Corner Stone of Canadian Culture: An Outline of the Arts and Crafts of the Indian Tribes of British Columbia*. Victoria: Kings Printer, 1944.

—. *Alice Ravenhill: The Memoirs of an Educational Pioneer*. Toronto: J.M. Dent and Son, 1951.

—. B.C. Indian Arts and Welfare Society. Microfiche files, BC Archives, 1940-1954.

—. *Folklore of the Far West, With Some Clues to Characteristics and Customs*. Victoria: Morriss Printing, 1953.

—. Society for the Furtherance of B.C. Indian Arts and Crafts, Originals. Government Documents, BC Archives.

### Dr. Ethlyn Trapp

"A Plan to Set Up Radiation Therapy Centres for Cancer Treatment." *The Vancouver Daily Province*, Apr. 10, 1951.

"City Doctors Hear Woman." *The Vancouver Daily Province*, Mar. 5, 1952.

"Dr. Trapp Awarded Order of Canada." *The Vancouver Daily Province*, June 29, 1968.

"Formal Opening of the BC Cancer Institute Building in Vancouver General Hospital." *The Vancouver Daily Province*, Dec. 27, 1952.

McGeer, Ada. "Many Thanks Ethlyn." *The Vancouver Sun*, Aug. 16, 1972.

Mary Ellen Smith

Barman, Jean. *The West Beyond The West: A History of British Columbia.* Toronto: University of Toronto Press, 1996:230-231.

Hale, Linda Louise. Appendix: "Votes for Women: Profiles of Prominent British Columbia Suffragists and Social Reformers." In *In Her Own Right: Selected Essays on Women's History in BC,* edited by Barabara Latham and Cathy Kess. Victoria: Camosun College, 1980:299-300.


Helen Gregory MacGill

Crossley, Diane. "The B.C. Liberal Party and Women's Reforms, 1916-1928." In *In Her Own Right: Selected Essays on Women's History in BC,* edited by Barbara Latham and Cathy Kess. Victoria: Camosun College, 1980:229-253.

MacGill, Elsie Gregory. *My Mother The Judge.* Toronto: Ryerson, 1955.

MacGill, Helen Gregory. *How to Conduct Public Meetings in Canada and Where to Find the Rules.* Thomas Allen Ltd., 1918.

—. *Laws for Women and Children in British Columbia.* Vancouver: H. G. MacGill, 1925, 1928, 1935, 1939.

—. *The Work of the Juvenile Court and How to Secure Such a Court in a Canadian Community.* Vancouver: H. G. MacGill, 1943.

—. *Daughters, Wives and Mothers in British Columbia.* Vancouver: H.G. MacGill, 1912.

University Women's Club of Vancouver. Memorial Service for Helen Gregory MacGill, May 4, 1947.


Grace MacInnis

Coverton, Jane. Personal interview with Winona Grace MacInnis for Reynoldston Research and Studies 190(1-2), 1973. (audiotape)

Farrell, Ann. *Grace MacInnis: A Story of Love and Integrity.* Ontario: Fitzhenry & Whiteside, 1994.

"Grace Admits She's Good at Bugging." *The Vancouver Province,* July 5, 1967:1.

"Grace Trying to Change Law." *The Victoria Times,* May 31, 1967:18.

Lewis, Sunny. *Grace: The Authorized Biography of Grace Woodsworth MacInnis.* Madeira Park: Harbour Publishing, 1993.

MacInnis, Grace. "Changing Role of Women." *The Vancouver Province,* Feb. 7, 1967:22.

—. "Japanese Ordeal." *The Vancouver Sun,* Jan 30, 1967:6.

—. *J. S. Woodsworth: A Man to Remember 1874-1943*. Toronto: The Macmillan Co., 1953.

— and Charles J. Woodsworth. *Canada Through C.C.F. Glasses*. Vancouver: Commonwealth Print and Publishing Co., 1935.

—. Speech on the Royal Commission Report on the Status of Women. Victoria: Aural History Institute of the BC Archives 4191(1), May 1, 1971. (audiotape)

"Make Abortion Legal, MacInnis Bill Asks." *The Vancouver Province*, May 31, 1967:6.

McCarthy, Grace. "Political Graces." *The Vancouver Sun*, May 25, 1967:5.

"MP Praises Association at Opening." *The Vancouver Sun*, Sept. 16, 1967:64.

"MP Urges More Housing." *The Vancouver Sun*, March 31, 1967:13.

"NDP Convention Passes Motion." *The Vancouver Sun*, June 3, 1967:2.

Oglanby, Elva, Liv Kennedy, and Lorraine Harris. "The Eternal Politician, Grace MacInnis." *Once Upon a Time*. Vancouver: Radio Station CJVOR, 1974:61-64.

Nobel, Terry. Personal interview with Grace Winona MacInnis. Victoria: Aural History Institute of the BC Archives 3936(1-2), Dec. 1981. (audiotape)

"Snoopy Social Workers Target of Woman MLA." *The Victoria Colonist*, June 4, 1967:11.

"Status of Nationalization Fades in New Policy of NDP." *The Vancouver Province*, July 5, 1967:1.

Stursberg, Peter. Interview with Grace MacInnis. University of British Columbia Special Collections Division.

Walsh, Susan. "The Peacock and the Guinea Hen: Political Profiles of Dorothy Gretchen Steeves and Grace MacInnis." In *Not Just Pin Money*, edited by Barbara Latham and Roberta Pazdro. Victoria: Camosun College, 1984:365-379.

## Rosemary Brown

Adams, Neals. "What Have You Got: — A Socialist." *The Vancouver Sun*, Feb. 19, 1975.

Brown, Nancy. " 'BC's Favorite Daughter' Too Much for NDP: Radical Views Her Major Handicap." *The Daily Colonist,* March 23, 1975:27.

Brown, Rosemary. *Being Brown: A Very Public Life*. Toronto: Ballantine Books, 1989.